WE RISE FOR OUR LAND

Land Struggles and Repression
in Southern Africa

BOAVENTURA MONJANE
Editor

WE RISE FOR OUR LAND

Land Struggles and Repression
in Southern Africa

Foreword by Issa Shivji
Afterword by Masego Madzwamuse

Daraja Press and the
Sam Moyo African Institute of Agrarian Studies

Published by
Daraja Press
https://darajapress.com

ISBN 9781988832685

Cover design and typesetting: Kate McDonnell
Cover photo: Diogo Cardoso

Library and Archives Canada Cataloguing in Publication

Title: We rise for our land : land struggles and state repression in Southern Africa /
    edited by Boaventura Monjane, Sam Moyo African Institute for Agrarian
    Studies.
Names: Monjane, Boaventura, 1983- edito r.
Description: Includes bibliographical references and index.
Identifiers: Canadiana (print) 20200278843 | Canadiana (ebook) 20200279068 |
    ISBN 9781988832685 (softcover) | ISBN 9781988832692 (EPUB)
Subjects: LCSH: Land use, Rural—South Africa. | LCSH: Land tenure—Africa,
    Southern. | LCSH: Natural resources—Africa, Southern. | LCSH: Political
    persecution—South Africa. | LCSH: Social conflict—Africa, Southern. |
    LCSH: Peasants—Africa, Southern. | LCSH: Africa, Southern—Rural conditions.
Classification: LCC HD990 .W4 2020 | DDC 333.00968—dc23

CONTENTS

PART III
Resistance and Struggles for Land Rights

PART IV
Land Occupations and Alternatives

LISTS OF TABLES, FIGURES, PICTURES AND GRAPHS

ACRONYMS AND ABBREVIATIONS

ADR	Alternative dispute resolution
ANC	African National Congress
ARDA	Agricultural Rural Development Authority
CBRLDP	Community Based Rural Land Development Program
CLB	Communal land board
CLRA	Communal Land Reform Act
CONAPAC	Confédération Nationale des Producteurs Agricoles au Congo, CONAPAC (National Confederation of Agricultural Producers of Congo)
CSO	Civil society organization
CPM	Coalition Paysanne de Madagascar (also known as the Fikambanan'ny Tantsaha eto Madagasikara (FTM) – Madagascar Farmers' Coalition)
DRC	Democratic Republic of Congo
DUAT	Direito de Uso e Aproveitamento da Terra (land use right title)
FAO	(United Nations') Food and Agricultural Organisation
FISP	Farm Input Subsidy Program
FOPAC-NK	Federation des Organizations des Producteurs Agricoles du Congo au North-Kivu (Federation of Organisations of Agricultural Producers of Congo in North Kivu)
FRELIMO	Frente de Libertação de Moçambique (Mozambican Liberation Front)
FTLRP	Track Land Reform Programme
FTM	Fikambanan'ny Tantsaha eto Madagasikara (also known as the Coalition Paysanne de Madagascar (CPM) – Madagascar Farmers' Coalition)
ICESCR	International Covenant on Economic, Social and Cultural Rights
IMF	International Monetary Fund
LSCF	Large-scale commercial farms
LGBTIQ	Lesbian, gay, bisexual, transsexual, intersex and queer
MDC	Movement for Democratic Change (Zimbabwe)
MDC	Mpongwe Development Company Limited (Zambia)
MICT	Ministry of Information, Communications and Technology (Swaziland)
MPLA	Movimento Popular de Libertação de Angola (People's Movement for the Liberation of Angola)
PYCD	Platform for Youth and Community Development
PZ	*Polize Zone*
RCD	Rassemblement Démocratique pour la Démocratie (Congolese Rally for Democracy)
RDC	Rural district council
RSTP	Royal Science and Technology Park

SADC	Southern African Development Community
SDAE	Serviços Distritais de Actividades Económicas (District Economic Activities Service)
SEFAFI	Sehatra Fanaraha-maso ny Fiainam-pirenena (The Observatory of Public Life)
SNL	Swazi Nation Land
STDM	Social tenure domain model
SSCF	Small-scale commercial farming
SWAPO	South West African People's Organisation
TA	Traditional authority
WISCO	Wuhan Iron and Steel Corporation
WSC	White settler capitalism
ZANU-PF	Zimbabwe African National Union – Patriotic Front
ZLA	Zambia Land Alliance

FOREWORD

Towards Reconceptualising the Commons

Issa Shivji[1]

The eleven essays in this book, including the Introduction by Boaventura Monjane, give us a pretty good survey of the agrarian question in eight countries – the Democratic Republic of Congo, Eswatini, Madagascar, Malawi, Mozambique, Namibia, Zimbabwe and Zambia – within the SADC region. The authors, who come from different disciplines – sociology, law, history, economics – would identify themselves as scholar-activists involved in one form or another in the struggles of peasant communities. They do not necessarily share a common theoretical approach but perhaps would not shy away from avowing a form of radical outlook on the agrarian question which, in the context of Africa, translates itself into taking a pro-peasant political position.

Empirically rich, though theoretically somewhat eclectic, the essays provide us with a sound base from which to reflect on bigger political and theoretical questions. This is what I intend to do in this short foreword.

The neoliberal context

All the essays are contextualised in the political economy of neoliberalism. Neoliberalism went through three generations, starting with the structural adjustment programmes (SAPs) of the 1980s which the international financial institutions and erstwhile donors imposed on African countries. Trade liberalisation and withdrawal of the state from the economy were among some of the conditionalities that the IMF and World Bank required the states to abide by. Withdrawal of the state was a misnomer because the state was supposed to play a prominent role in creating an enabling atmosphere for the play of so-called market forces. The second generation involved privatisation of state enterprises and removal of restrictions on private foreign and domestic capital. The third generation of neo-liberal measures required

[1] Professor Emeritus, University of Dar es Salaam, Tanzania.

liberalisation of the financial sector and commodification and privatisation of public goods sectors such as electricity, water, sanitation,
health and education. Trade liberalisation and, in particular, removal of
subsidies from staple foods, and subjecting social services such as education and health to the market, hit the popular classes hardest. Poverty
and inequalities mushroomed, leading to the so-called 'bread riots' in
many countries. The legitimacy of the state was in question. To mitigate potential political backlash, the international financial institutions
threw in political conditionalities such as human rights, good governance (the World Bank's coinage) and multi-party, political systems to
legitimise the authoritarian state.

The authors are well acquainted with the economic and policy
measures of neo-liberalism and empirically demonstrate the adverse
impact of these measures on peasant communities. If there are any
gaps in their analyses, then these exist at the ideological and systemic
level. More than its policy and economic prescription, neoliberalism
was an assault on the ideology of nationalism and national liberation.
During the nationalist phase, imperialism had come under severe attack
in the form of discourses on neo-colonialism, underdevelopment and
capitalist exploitation and plunder. Imperialism had to be economically
vindicated and morally rehabilitated; that task was accomplished by
neoliberalism. The indebted African countries suffering from intense
foreign exchange crisis had no alternative but swallow the bitter pill
administered by the IMF.

Secondly, neoliberalism is not a new socio-economic system
nor an ugly face of capitalism. Neoliberalism is in fact the financial-
ised phase of the capitalist-imperialist system which has pillaged and
plundered the countries of the global South for the last five centuries.
Anti-neoliberalism, therefore, perforce has to be anti-capitalist and
anti-imperialist. If this is not fully appreciated by the progressives of
the working people, there is a danger of being identified with narrow
nationalists and populists. On the surface, demagogic nationalists and
populists may mouth patriotic and anti-neoliberal slogans but they are
not necessarily against capitalism and imperialism.

Thirdly, it is important to characterise correctly the dominant tendency of accumulation under neoliberalism. The dominant tendency, I
would argue, is primitive accumulation. Marx's classical primitive accumulation was conceived as an original condition for the development of
capitalism. Among other things, Marx identified the eviction of peasant

producers from land through land grabbing and the enclosure movement, the slave trade from Africa and robbing of treasures from Asia, Africa and the Americas as processes of primitive accumulation. Various policy measures taken by African regimes after independence, under whatever rubric, were really meant to subordinate the process of primitive accumulation to capitalist accumulation, based theoretically on equal exchange. But they did not quite succeed, and, with neoliberalism, primitive accumulation once again became dominant as during colonialism.

Under neoliberalism, primitive accumulation takes on new forms. In much of Africa today, primitive accumulation in its original form – land grabbing, for example – still continues. Specific to neoliberalism are new forms of accumulation predicated primarily on capital cutting into the necessary consumption of labour – whether this is peasant labour, wage labour or labour in the so-called 'informal sector'. The primary characteristic of this new form of primitive accumulation is that, across the board, working people shoulder their own reproduction while ceding a part of their necessary consumption to capital – in effect subsidising capital. Thus they have to exert super-human labour to live sub-human lives. The commodification and privatisation of public goods is also a form of primitive accumulation – a new form of robbing or looting.

In sum, the whole of the working people are thus not only oppressed but actually exploited by the dominant capital. Thus, objectively, they share a common interest. I will return to this question when we discuss the question of agency below.

It is with these paradigmatic premises in mind that I examine below a few concepts which have been used in these essays and suggest some ways of reconceptualizing them from the standpoint of the working people so as to make a clean epistemic break. The objective is to explore how we can intellectually construct an anti-hegemonic discourse which, in my view, is a necessary precondition for the struggle and eventual emancipation of the working people. Let us not forget the old adage of a 19th century abolitionist Wendell Phillips: 'Insurrection of thought precedes insurrection of arms' (Phillips 1859).

Land tenure, ownership and property

Land tenure refers to the system of relation – ownership, possession, use and so on – between a person and a plot of land. In the main stream bourgeois conception, ownership is a relation between a person and an object, in this case land. For this conception to operate, a specified piece

of land must be converted into an object of possession and ownership –
that is, property. Nature does not give land as property nor does it give
particular people as owners. These are historically created categories
and come about as a result of social struggles. For a piece of land to
become property, an area of land has to be mapped, demarcated, registered and made available to individuals to possess or own. Who does
that if not the state, the prime institution or organ which commands the
monopoly of force?

Ownership is a bundle of rights which the owner – an individual
– possesses over land. It includes the right to use and dispose of land
as well as the right to exclude non-owners from your land. Should the
owner wish to dispose of land by sale, they cannot take it to the market.
What they do take to the market is a piece of paper issued by the state
called a title. The system of individualisation, registration and titling
(ITR) is a device by which land not only becomes property but a commodity which can be bought and sold on the market. ITR is often sold
to peasants as giving the owners security of tenure. But in reality, it is
primarily a system of making land negotiable and transferable.

Summing up, we can see that the concepts of ownership, property,
security of tenure and rights are intertwined. They inhere in the capitalist system. They are not given by nature but are historically and socially
constructed. What is presented and appears as an objective relationship
between human and land is in essence a social relation between people
and people. The primary right of the owner is to exclude others from
their land. Ownership does not make sense to a Robinson Crusoe on
an island, who uses land for subsistence. It is only with the appear-
ance of Friday on the scene that the land he cultivates now becomes
'my garden' to exclude Friday from it or to make Friday work on it for
Crusoe's benefit.

These concepts have not existed since eternity. In many pre-colo-
nial African societies, land was neither a property nor an object of ownership or possession. It was rather a means of subsistence for use by the
community as a whole. The community, through their own accepted
custom, were the collective custodians of land, not exclusive owners.
It is only with the reconstruction of custom by the colonial authorities and its conversion into customary law that the concept of communal ownership (like all ownerships guaranteed by the state) appears.
We freely use the concept of security of tenure and communal ownership as progressive demands by peasant communities. These may

have some conjunctural value but, ultimately, they are cast within the dominant bourgeois discourse. Those of us who think in terms of transforming the system and constructing anti-hegemonic discourses have to work towards transcending the concepts of the dominant system and its hegemonic discourses.

State, class, imperialism and the revolutionary agency

Class as a category of analysis has been so much caricatured as 'reductionist', both by mainstream scholars and even by some progressive writers, that it has almost become a taboo. Increasingly, class analysis and, in particular, class struggle, the central problematic of the method of historical materialism, is disappearing from the research and writings of our young scholars. Many young scholars believe that class is the central category of the Marxist method, which it is not. Class was not invented by Marx. The majority of classical political economists before Marx used the concept of class. The Marxist method is historical materialism, not class or vulgar political economy. And in historical materialism, politics is central. Marxist political writings and analyses are rich in complexity in the way they use the concept of class and class struggle. Marxism is anything but reductionist.

Once class is thrown out of the window or belittled, the state gets presented as some kind of a neutral or benevolent or malevolent institution rather than an organ of the ruling class and a terrain of class struggle. Thus, in the essays in this volume, the state hardly appears or, if it does, no attempt is made to analyse its class character. It is in the absence of such analysis that some conjunctural 'progressive' measures by the state or anti-West populist rhetoric are mistaken for an anti-imperialist radical state. Such eclectic analysis has the danger of ideologically disarming the struggles of the working people.

Another term which has become a taboo in some 'progressive' scholarship, particularly in the literature of the various posts (postmodernist, post-colonial, post-industrial, post-development and so on), is imperialism. Instead, we come across the now fashionable term 'Empire'. Empires existed even before capitalism. Empire is not an overarching theoretical construct. Imperialism, on the other hand, is specific to capitalism and is a theory built on the world-wide accumulation of capital from the inception of capitalism.

We are living in a global system of capitalist imperialism and it is the capitalist logic that drives the political economy of our social formations. And so far, Marxism offers us perhaps the best understanding of this system. This does not mean that Marxism has all the answers or that the real-life situation can simply be derived from an overarching capitalist analysis. That is mechanistic or vulgar Marxism, not historical materialism. We still have to do the empirical and basic research in our countries, as the essays in this volume attempt, and theorise our own situations, thus enriching the understanding and changing of our concrete conditions while at the same time contributing to humankind's knowledge. We must be aware and critically take into account various theoretical strands and practical developments. What I am cautioning against is simply picking and choosing eclectically the so-called 'best' from different theoretical frameworks.

It is applying such perspectives that allowed me to suggest the concept of working people in the neoliberal phase of capitalism as a possible agent for change (Shivji 2017). Only concrete struggles on the ground will ultimately determine the revolutionary agency of the working people. The concept of working people has, in my view, a great potential and has to be developed further through concrete studies as has been done in some of the essays in this volume. I would, however, suggest that the concept of the working people allows us, among other things, to overcome the colonial divide between urban and rural spaces. The colonial and post-colonial divide is constructed as a spatial divide which, in turn, is used subtly to create a social division between the working classes in towns and peasant masses in the countryside. Such dichotomy fragments the unity of the working people against capital by highlighting secondary contradictions among them. Objectively, let me repeat, as I have shown elsewhere, that various sections of rural working people (peasants, agrarian working classes – in most cases seasonal and casual – landless, and so on) and urban (traditional proletariat, unemployed, small craftworkers, street hawkers, men, women and children, the precariat and so on) are all the subject of exploitation by the dominant capital, foreign capital allied with domestic capital and compradorial political classes.

Finally, a word on peasant differentiation, lest I be misunderstood. My formulation in no way is meant to minimise, for instance, peasant differentiation and the rise of a peasant bourgeoisie. In any social formation producing commodities, such differentiation is taking place all the time. It represents what has been called accumulation from below. Nonetheless, in a neoliberal, patriarchal formation, the tendency for accumulation from below is aborted by the dominant tendency of accumulation from above, whose primary character is one of primitive accumulation (Shivji 1987). Barring capitalist farmers, I believe the peasant masses, notwithstanding the differentiation among them, can legitimately be included in the working people. This question, needless to say, is a concrete political question to be determined in the course of struggle and analysis of the 'enemies' and 'friends' of the revolution. It cannot be answered a priori.

Reconceptualising the commons

In light of my discussion above, I want to suggest that the concept of 'the commons' offers us a good point of departure for constructing an anti-hegemonic discourse. There are two components to my concept of the commons: the old commons and what I call the new commons. The well-known old commons are land and forests, rivers and lakes, mountains and wild animals and bio-resources. I would add to these all resources found underground and overground, including minerals, seeds, and genetic resources, modified or otherwise, derived from forests.

The new commons are education, health, water, sanitation, energy, knowledge (traditional and modern), information and all ecological resources.

All commons belong to the people for responsible use and their benefit. People, through their democratically organised institutions – villages, communes, cooperatives, state – hold the commons as custodians and as trustees, not as property or commodities. In fact, Karl Polanyi taught us long ago that land is an artificial commodity, for no human labour has gone into creating it.

This way of reconceptualising the commons offers us, first, a possibility to transcend the dominant concepts of land tenure, ownership, property, rights and commodity. It will be noticed that holding of the commons as custodians has shifted from the language of rights to the language of obligations. The custodians have obligations but no rights. Secondly, it gives us a handle around which to construct an anti-hegemonic discourse. The immediate task is to build a coherent theory of the commons, derive a political agenda from it and creatively crystallise immediate and long-term political demands around which working people can and may be mobilised. I believe that such discourse would have a resonance with the working people. It will sound feasible to them because the idea of the commons is not alien to the African peasantries. It addresses their immediate concerns and needs and explains the devastation, poverty and inequality that has been spawned by neo-liberalism.

Of necessity, the suggested concept of the commons is very much in a skeletal form. I am putting it forward for debate and discussion and development.

Issa Shivji
Dar es Salaam
March 2021

References

Phillips, W. (1859). See https://www.laphamsquarterly.org/quotes/74 accessed 6/03/2021

Shivji, I.G. (2017) 'The Concept of 'Working People'", *Agrarian South: Journal of Political Economy*, 6(1) pp 1-13

Shivji, I.G (1987) 'The Roots of Agrarian Crisis in Tanzania – A Theoretical Perspective" *Eastern African Social Science Research Review*, vol. III, no.1, pp 111-134 (Reprinted in Forster, P. & Maghimbi, S. (eds.) (1992) *The Tanzanian Peasantry: Economy in Crisis* Avebury: Aldershot 124-150pp)

ABOUT THE AUTHORS

Sara Lagardien Abdullah is a final year undergraduate student at the University of Cape Town and a Mellon Mays Undergraduate Fellow, majoring in Sociology and African Studies, working concurrently as a research assistant, film writer and assistant producer. In 2016, they co-founded NAH, a zine publication platform for youth discursive expression and critical engagement. Sara's interests oscillate between food, land, autonomy, history, knowledge (re)production, memory, land justice, restoring and decolonial re-storying praxis.

Wu Jin (PhD, Professor) is associate dean of the College of Humanities and Development Studies at the China Agricultural University. Her main research interests are China's international development cooperation. She's participated in more than ten research projects on both China's domestic transformation and international engagements.

Pablo Gilolmo Lobo holds a bachelor's degree in history from the University of Granada and a master's degree in geography from the University of Namibia. He is currently finalising his PhD dissertation in the Center for Social Studies at the University of Coimbra, with a study on the privatization of communal lands in eastern Namibia. His research interests include the political economy of imperialism, the agrarian question in southern Africa and agroecology. He has participated in many congresses and other academic events, and has published in conference proceedings, specialized journals and book chapters.

Uacitissa Mandamule is a research assistant at Observatório do Meio Rural in Mozambique. Mandamule is also a PhD student in sociology at the University of Aix-Marseille, France. Through a multi-scalar approach to land issues, her research portrays socio-political aspects of access, control, use, conflicts and tenure security of land, focusing on rural areas. Her interests are also related to the impacts of extreme weather events on land tenure security and productivity.

Fatima Mandhu (PhD) works in the field of land and property relations as a result of her postgraduate research on the dual land tenure system and land registration in Zambia. Mandhu has been teaching and researching land law and property relations since 1990. She is one of the editors of the book *Responsible and Smart Land Management*

Interventions: An African Context (2020, Boca Raton: CRC Press). Her interest in mining law was raised under the National Science and Technology Council's joint project as the team leader for Zambia and the author of the Mineral Law in Africa book series. Later, as a postdoctoral research fellow, she contributed a series of five publications on gender and small scale mining in Zambia, which has made her one of a network of experts on the Mineral Law in Africa team. As a lecturer and head of the Department of Private Law, she has developed and taught medical law to the third- and fourth-year undergraduate law programs at the University of Zambia.

Justin Alinafe Mangulama (PhD) has a PhD in rural development and management from China Agricultural University's College of Humanities and Development Studies, obtained in August 2020. He has co-authored eight academic papers in internationally recognized journals. His research interests are in politics of land access and peasant resistance.

Freedom Mazwi (PhD) is a Researcher with the Sam Moyo African Institute for Agrarian Studies (SMAIAS), Harare, Zimbabwe. His research and publications over the last 10 years largely focus on the political economy of land and agrarian transition, tenure systems and agricultural financing. Freedom has contributed articles in a number of journals, international newspapers and books.

Steven Mberi is a Research Fellow with the Sam Moyo African Institute for Agrarian Studies (SMAIAS) and Editorial Assistant of the *Agrarian South: Journal of Political Economy* (sage). His research interests lie in the field of climate change, land tenure systems, natural resources management, environmental policy and planning. His current research work has been focused on capital and climate change politics, with specific reference to smallholder tobacco farmers in Zimbabwe. He holds a Master of Science from the National University of Science and Technology (NUST).

Boaventura Monjane holds a PhD in Postcolonialisms and Global Citizenship (sociology), from the Centre for Social Studies/Faculty of Economics, University of Coimbra. He is a postdoctoral researcher at the Institute for Poverty, Land and Agrarian Studies (PLAAS) at the University of the Western Cape (South Africa) and the Centre for African Studies at Eduardo Mondlane University (Mozambique). He is fellow of the International Research Group on Authoritarianism and

Counter-Strategies of the Rosa Luxemburg Stiftung. He was recently attributed the Open Society Fellowship for 2021/2022. Monjane is a research associate at the Sam Moyo African Institute for Agrarian Studies and a member of the Agrarian South Network.

Blaise Muhire Mwanga (PhD) holds a PhD in political geography. Over the past ten years, he has been focusing his research in the field of peacebuilding and land governance. Specific topics he focuses on include land access and conflict, land tenure management, and peasants' struggles over agrarian reforms. Currently, he is a researcher and consultant for several international organisations in the Democratic Republic of Congo as well as in the African Great Lakes region.

Tsilavo Ralandison (PhD) is a senior lecturer at Kyoto University's Graduate School of Economics. He completed his PhD at Kagoshima University's United Graduate School of Agricultural Science in 2010. His PhD thesis examined the implications of economic liberalization reforms on Madagascar's rice markets. Since then, his research has continued to focus mainly on agricultural and rural issues in Madagascar, using a critical agrarian political economy approach.

Ellah TM Siang'andu (PhD) is a lecturer at the University of Zambia. She teaches criminal law, gender discrimination and international law. Her research interests include penal law, criminal law, international criminal justice, international law and women's rights. Her most recent works include: 'Understanding the meaning, context, role and importance of African criminal justice in Africa' in: Sarkin, J. and Siang'andu, ETM (eds.), *Africa's Role and Contribution to International Criminal Justice*. Cambridge: Intersentia (Intersentia, 2020) and 'The use of international criminal law in African countries' in the same edition.

Ronald Wesso lives in Johannesburg, South Africa. He works as a freelance researcher and trainer and is based at the consultancy Beneficial Technologies (Bentec, www.bentec.co.za). As part of Bentec, Ronald has done research and popular education on extractives, water, land and health equity. As an activist he has been active in community, land and labour movements.

Amnesty International is a global movement of more than 10 million people in over 150 countries and territories who campaign to end abuses of human rights.. Our vision is for every person to enjoy all the rights enshrined in the Universal Declaration of Human Rights and other international human rights standards. In southern Africa we work to prevent human rights abuses and hold governments, corporates and other actors accountable for their actions. We undertake research and action focused on preventing and ending grave rights abuses and work closely with the worldwide Amnesty movement, with local civil society organizations, partners and individual rights holders to promote and protect the human rights and fundamental freedoms of all.

CHAPTER 1

Introduction: Land as a central element in rural organisation and agency in southern Africa

Boaventura Monjane

In recent years, southern Africa has aroused the interest of domestic and foreign investors targeting several sectors. Agrarian and extractive capital has been most penetrating in the countryside, causing land conflicts, displacement of local rural and peasant communities and, in worse cases, deaths. Neoliberally oriented, most SADC states have, by and large, colluded with local and international capital, often to the alienation and disfranchisement of the generality of peasants and citizens. The corollary of this has been the espousal of pieces of legislation and policy frameworks that are hostile to the peasantry while advancing the interests of capital. The irony is that high-level government officials, ministers, presidents, kings and traditional chiefs, who themselves often double up as capital, are perpetuating an ideology they opposed during the colonial period.

The peasantry and rural people in general have not, however, been passive in this process. Alone or in alliance with non-governmental organisations and activists, they have positioned themselves strongly against such developments, questioning the sustainability and ideological grounding of such neoliberal developmentalist policies that deprive them of their primary means of production and violate their rights. In fact, resistance movements to capital are taking place throughout the region, even if the response to this has been repression by the states.

This volume is part of a long-running research and advocacy project in which the editor and the Sam Moyo African Institute for Agrarian Studies (SMAIS) seek to (1) promote reflections, deepen the analysis and theorise around agency of those who 'rise' to defend, protect or fight for 'their land', both in rural and urban spaces, and to (2) produce popular education content and materials to inform social movements and activists' thinking and actions. Consequently, this book is combined with a 50-minute documentary film equally titled 'We Rise for Our Land'[1], co-produced by the editor of this volume and SMAIS and directed by Kurt Orderson and Azania Rising Productions[2]. The film, which was reviewed by Sara Lagardien Abdullah (chapter 9, this volume), was launched in October 2020, in Manzini, Eswatini, in collaboration with the Rural Women's Assembly. The book adopts, to a certain degree, a scholar-activist approach, which does not take away its scientific rigor. Like Participatory Action Research, scholar activism is a rigorous academic research, explicitly and unapologetically connected to political projects or movements; It is objective but not neutral knowledge, produced in a way that it is emotionally sensitive, socially comradely and politically committed to the working people (Borras, 2016; Santos, 2018; Shivji, 2019).

The various contributions to this book show the complexity of the land and agrarian questions in the region, making a small contribution to the already rich literature on issues such as land grabbing, but placing more emphasis on rural struggles by men and women for rights. This book is comprised of contributions from authors who critically study the dynamics of agrarian and extractive capital in southern Africa. In their academic and activist work, they offer theoretical, conceptual and practical contributions useful to the struggles of agrarian and rural movements that represent the 'subalternised' rural and urban working people (Shivji 2017). The chapters come from and/or are about the DRC, Namibia, Zambia, Malawi, Zimbabwe, eSwatini (formerly Swaziland), Mozambique and Madagascar.

The chapters of this book reveal, among others, three important trends: first, that land conflicts exist even in the absence of land grabbing, as the case of Mozambique suggests. However, internal land conflicts between and among villagers are likely to ignite penetration of capital, which seizes the opportunity to instrumentalize community disunity and quarrels; second, in spite of the fact that land grabbing does not always lead to resistance from below (Borras and Franco, 2013) in southern Africa communities that are politically organized (in forms of associations, unions or other forms of collective organization) are more likely to organize resistance, eighter in overt or covert forms. The absence of direct actions does not always imply the absence of resistance; third, that since agrarian authoritarianism (Monjane and Bruna, 2019) has generally

....
1 https://vimeo.com/486386008
2 https://www.azaniarizing.com

been a key characteristic in the promotion of authoritarian agrarian neo-liberalism across the region, repression to resistance and persecution of leaders of popular movements has intensified. As a result of the political calculation made by the villagers, the lack of political reaction in the presence of dispossession does not always equals loss of radicalism.

A weakness in this volume, as rightly appointed by Masego Mad-zwamuse in the afterword (this volume), is the lack of significant gender analysis and the role of women in land struggles in southern Africa. We believe that the documentary film combined with this volume minimizes this weakness, insofar as it is placing the focus on rural and peasants' women struggles in Mozambique, Zambia and eSwatini. Nevertheless, and being this a long running research academic project, women agrarian movements, gender analysis and aspects of social reproduction will have to deserve appropriate dedication in future works.

This book is organised into five parts, each of which delineates, in different ways, rural struggles for land and the nexus between civil society and the state in southern Africa. Using different case studies in the region, the book unpacks and explores local struggles and aspirations for access to and ownership of land and the role of state and non-state actors in the matrix. After this introduction, the first part discusses how governments have responded to demands for rights and freedoms in five countries in the region. In Chapter 2, Ronald Wesso uses Angola, Mozambique, Namibia, South Africa and Zimbabwe to paint a vivid and poignant picture of how governments have unleashed state machinery to muzzle and repress civil society space. His contribution sheds light onto the complex stages that state-citizen relations have gone through, not only demonstrating the existence of state repression and shrinking civic space, but that resistance has been a common feature in southern Africa. The author uses the work of Afrikagrupperna and its partners in those countries to make a compelling argument about how civil society provides support for popular movements, and the extent to which former liberation movements now pursuing neoliberal policies in government have become increasingly hostile to such movements and their backers. Wesso demonstrates how new groups have used tactical mistakes and frustrations as strategic and organisational tools to deal with this shift to authoritarian neoliberalism. The chapter thus sets the stage for the ensuing chapters by foregrounding governments' neoliberal agendas, citizen struggles (such as for land) and state repression as important themes in the book.

Part II of the book explores the nature, form and texture of land conflicts in southern Africa, with a particular focus on the circumstances causing them and the manner in which they have mutated in different countries. In Chapter 3, Fatima Mandhu and Ellah T.M Siang'andu trace and unpack the underlying factors leading to conflicts over land in Zambia. First, they demonstrate the importance of land and other natural resources (especially minerals such as copper) as key to the livelihoods of rural communities and the country more generally. This, they posit, has made land a vital resource coveted by private capital, leading to the transfer of land from the smallholder sector to large scale commercial enterprises in the period after 2000. The inevitable corollary of this has been the rise of social movements, with the support of some civil society groups and NGOs, in opposition to the encroachment of large-scale farmers with the tacit support of the state. More refreshingly, the authors extend their analysis to the role of the judiciary in the matrix, evincing how, by invariably ruling in favour of statutory land tenure over customary land rights, it has taken the side of the state and agrarian capital.

In Chapter 4, Uacitissa Mandamule continues on the theme of land conflicts, using the Nhamatanda district of Mozambique as a case study. She unpacks the different political, economic and social imperatives that lie at the root of land conflict in Mozambique. She adopts Roy's (1991) argument that conflicts are a normal expression of the diversity of interests in society, and here she focuses on the competing interests of the state, capital and ordinary peasants insofar as access to and use of land is concerned. Writing from a sociological viewpoint, Mandamule discusses the different dimensions of land conflict, ranging across family, communal and institutional levels. The author deploys oral interviews and statistical data to show the causes and prevalence of land-based conflicts in the Mozambican district. This chapter advocates for strengthening training programmes on matters of conflict prevention and management for community authorities, as well as the importance of women's participation in the conflict resolution process.

Chapter 5 concludes the second part. It focuses on the land tenure system and policies and forced evictions that occurred in different parts of Eswatini between 2014 and 2018. Penned by the Amnesty International in the form of a report, the chapter dissects the circumstances leading to forced evictions in Nokwane, in September and October 2014, and in the Malkerns in April 2018. The report outlines the 'complex' system of land governance, describing it as an outcome of an attempt to preserve the traditional system where the king holds land on behalf of the people while also accommodating the interests of private capital. The latter, according to the report, forms the basis upon which locals in the aforesaid areas were systematically but unprocedurally evicted from their land between 2014 and 2018. Amnesty Internal particularly emphasizes how Eswatini government has failed to abide by its international, regional and national legal obligations, notably the obligation to guarantee the right to adequate housing. Using a wide array of oral sources and primary documents, and arguing from a human rights perspective, Amnesty International demonstrates how forced evictions have led to homelessness, loss of sources of livelihood, loss of or damage to property and belongings and disruption of children's education. Moreover, they posit that the failure by government to provide basic amenities to evicted families, such as food, clean water, basic shelter and housing, appropriate clothing or means of livelihood, has left evicted families in a tenuous and vulnerable socio-economic position. Finally, they attribute these vices to a land governance system that lacks clarity and certainty regarding land ownership.

Part III of the book shifts the emphasis to resistance movements as peasants and their representatives struggle for access to and ownership of land. Comprised of four chapters, this section of the book uses different case studies in southern Africa to show that, notwithstanding the encroachment of private capital and state repression, peasants and their representatives are not gullible and passive victims, but fight back, overtly and covertly, as they seek to retain what they consider to be their birth right: land. The first chapter in this section, Chapter 6, deals with civil society organisations' struggle for land rights in the Democratic Republic of Congo (DRC), tracing the process of expropriation from the colonial period until the recent past. In this chapter, Blaise Muhire Mwanga first traces and then discusses the institutional and administrative land system in the country, laying bare the colonial legacy on the governance of land as a natural resource, and how this has cascaded down to the post-colonial period. He then outlines the legal and political framework within which peasants continue to be inhibited in their aspirations to access land, and uses the case study of Masisi to demonstrate how peasants have continually lost their rights to land to private players who are, no doubt, using a skewed legal and policy framework. The analysis finally focuses on the resistance and struggles of the Hutu and Hunde communities in Masisi and how numerous civic organisations joined the movement, using a wide array of strategies and approaches. While the author vividly discusses the impact of (sometimes armed) resistance, he convincingly argues that, as long as the legislative system is still pro-elite and the nature of resistance remains uncoordinated, peasants shall continue to lose out as the interests of the elite become more prominent.

In Chapter 7, Pablo Gilolmo Lobo uses the N#a-Jaqna as an analytical prism to examine popular resistance to land alienation from local livestock farmers. He discusses the land enclosures in Namibian communal lands, particularly illegal fencing by elites such as traditional authorities, local entrepreneurs and urban dwellers, and how this has spawned conflicts over land. The chapter explores different dimensions of the conflicts produced by land individuation in N#a-Jaqna, noting that the enclosures are illegal under the Communal Land Reform Act of 2002 and its subsequent amendment in 2013, and they also have the effect of excluding less powerful members of society from access to land. The author argues that, despite internal political divisions, external factors, especially the role of the state in protecting and advancing the interests of elites, are the primary causes of land-related conflicts in the area. Therefore, it is groups' differential access to state power that perpetuates local conflicts, with the state's intervention often aggravating the conflicts. The major argument is that, while some of the enclosures are explained in conservation terms, the vast majority of the San population in N#a-Jaqna has lost control over their land's fencing through a biased and insensitive conservationist model.

More importantly, the chapter explores the quotidian responses of local residents as they seek to carve a niche of their own in a situation that is decidedly tailored to exploit them. The author extensively discusses how villagers invade the enclosures in search of resources such as firewood, plants, herbs and food. These actions, among others, trigger confrontation characterised by violence or threats of it and shooting incidents in some cases. Again, the author tacitly demonstrates that it is the policy framework and the apparently impartial posture of the state and its machinery that offer a breeding ground for conflict in Namibia.

Boaventura Monjane and Tsilavo Ralandison, in the penultimate chapter of this section of the book, use the deal between the government of Madagascar and the Wuhan Iron and Steel Corporation (WISCO), a Chinese state-owned company, to shed light on the opaqueness of the relationship between governments in Africa and international capital. Relying on a battery of written primary sources, particularly reports by civil organisations and international NGOs, the authors offer a refreshing and welcome departure from the popular agrarian capital-peasant dynamic to focus on mining. They offer a panoramic overview of the secretive (and possibly corrupt) nature of the discussions between the two parties, and further outline how a coalition of five civil society organizations in Madagascar, led by the Observatory of Public Life (SEFAFI) led a strong movement that criticized the contracts on account of their opacity. The authors stress that Madagascar is still an attractive destination for high-profile national and transnational consortiums which offer capital-intensive, large-scale projects, but further posit that questions of accountability, transparency, safety and ethics, among other vices, are often met with state resistance and possible harassment. Finally, and as a result of the above point, the chapter recommends that individuals and communities that are directly affected by a project should devise ways of defending their rights and advancing their interests without necessarily jeopardizing their security in light of the possibility of harassment from the state and its apparatus.

In the ninth and final chapter of Part III, Sara Lagardien Abdullah reviews a film documentary, titled *We Rise for Our Land: Land Struggles and Repression in Zambia, eSwatini and Mozambique,* to examine the common themes of land dispossession, indigenous people's resistance and the post-colonial state's heavy-handedness in responding to resistance. First, she discusses the origins of land alienations, which she traces back to colonialism in all countries under discussion. She notes how the colonial system, regardless of the identity of the coloniser, laid the foundation for land-based conflicts throughout the region by alienating indigenous Africans from their land to make way for European settlement and use. Consequently, the author argues, land has continued to be an emotive and politically charged resource whose governance merits radical reform across the African continent. Yet the majority of African states have, instead of seeking to reverse colonial vestiges in land governance, pursued neoliberal agrarian agendas that buttress the colonial antecedent. Thus, in the absence of state willingness to engage in reform, the chapter emphasizes the work of social movements in standing in solidarity with marginalised peasants by actively advocating for the democratisation of land ownership.

Moreover, the author adopts a gender lens with specific reference to Zambia, Eswatini and Mozambique, demonstrating that women have played a vitally important role in spearheading the work of agrarian movements opposed to neoliberal policies. Particular attention is paid to the work of La Via Campesina, an international peasant movement in resistance to the neoliberal globalisation of agriculture, which represents nearly 200 million farmers (the majority of whom are women) across 81 countries. The gender dimension is crucial in the southern African region, which is generally patriarchal in terms of land ownership yet matriarchal in terms of actual agricultural production. Finally, the chapter offers a compelling case for the involvement of women in agrarian movements by outlining some successes that were scored by female-dominated organisations in enabling women to gain rights to land ownership.

Part IV, the last part of this book, considers a range of alternatives available to agrarian movements as they fight for the restoration of their land rights amid the state-supported encroachment of agrarian capital. Authors use case studies from different countries in the region to bring to the fore different mechanisms used by movements, and also to evaluate the effectiveness of such alternatives. Invariably, the chapters end by offering recommendations and ideas on the way forward regarding the disfranchisement of peasants and ways of confronting that phenomenon. In Chapter 10, Freedom Mazwi and Stephen Mberi explore struggles over prime agricultural land in Zimbabwe, using the Chisumbanje sugar and ethanol production plantation as case studies. While Zimbabwe has generally been viewed as a unique case in the region, to the extent that government embarked on a radical land redistribution programme which somewhat redressed colonial land imbalances, the authors show that large agro-industrial estates, conservancies and forest plantations have remained in the hands of private, state-aligned capital. Regarding Chisumbanje, the authors demonstrate that, in fact, the Green Fuel estate has continued to extend its tentacles in southeastern Zimbabwe at the expense of local communities. This state of affairs, they argue, has naturally brought villagers into conflict with capital, but the former have met with limited success because of the government's inclination to support capital. The conflict also emerged as a result of unfulfilled promises after the estate pledged to uplift the socio-economic conditions of local communities but delivered little in that regard. The chapter delineates various forms of resistance by locals, ranging from organised community rural movements to low level illegal land occupations, highlighting the political dimensions associated with individual choices to either resist or support. Finally, the authors note the challenges associated with the country's judiciary in effectively dealing with the dimension of conflict, and suggest that, at the very minimum, the government should devise a mechanism that will compensate affected communities.

The final chapter in this section discusses the origins and anatomy of land occupations in Malawi and assesses the efficacy of such acts of resistance in instigating what the authors call 'land reforms from below'. Paying specific attention to political processes and everyday resistance in Thyolo and Mulanje, Justin Alinafe Mangulama and Wu Jin eschew the often-discussed dimension of the legality of land occupations to extend their analysis to the extent to which these occupations may achieve the intended goals of social movements. This chapter reveals that, although the land occupations in Thyolo and Mulanje have potential to achieve 'land reforms from below', the scale at which this is happening is small, as the majority continue to swim in extreme land poverty. Hence state interventions are needed to solve land woes. The authors give a comprehensive historical and theoretical context within which they ground their empirical study, itself based on selected oral interviews and other primary sources.

They submit that households that occupied land from white-owned tea estates became better-off compared to those who remained on 'traditional lands', leading to rural differentiation. In the main, the chapter argues that although land occupations in Thyolo may have had the capacity to achieve 'land reforms from below,' this potential is limited: the majority of people in the areas under study still do not have access to good farming land and thus remain trapped in poverty. Thus, according to the authors, effective land reform can only be achieved with the active participation of the state. To achieve this, they advocate for the resettling of peasants in other districts and the redistribution of idle estates among land hungry peasants, either on a freehold basis or via lease agreements. Finally, they recommend the adoption of suitable modern technology in order to improve the lot of impoverished peasants in Malawi.

Knitting together all the chapters in this book are the themes of peasant consciousness and resistance to losing land rights to agrarian capital with the post-colonial state in tow. The various chapters

– spanning diverse spatial and temporal horizons – go beyond the discourse of land losses and their impact on indigenous Africans to demonstrate that Africans are not gullible and weak victims of agrarian capital's machinations and state repression, but, using different methods, have mobilised themselves, with the help of civil organisations, to fight back. While their efforts have not always yielded the intended results, the focus and emphasis on resistance and ensuing repression should fillip both policy makers and scholars to imagine new and different ways of confronting the spectre of agrarian neoliberalism. Indeed, some authors in this compilation proffer alternative methods that could be deployed to deal with encroachment of agrarian capital, land poverty and state heavy handed responses to the problem.

The chapters of this book also show how three main forms of oppression, namely capitalism, colonialism and patriarchy, are understood as interconnected and indivisible. The chapters do an interesting job of identifying and enlarging the signs of possible future experiences in land struggles (and future research agendas) and of showing an empowering resource that allows for broader and deeper articulations amongst land struggles, combining the various dimensions or types of domination in different ways (Santos 2016; Santos and Meneses 2014; Monjane 2021)[3].

With this book, we hope, new debates shall emerge on how to confront the land and agrarian issues in southern Africa, which itself has remained an emotive and sensitive question several years after the attainment of political independence and democracy.

References

Borras, S.M., Franco, J.C. (2013) "Global land grabbing and political reactions 'from below'". *Third World Quarterly*, vol. 34, no. 9, pp. 1723–1747.

Borras, S.M. (2016) Land politics, agrarian movements and scholar-activism. Inaugural lecture, The Hague, ISS.

Monjane, B., Bruna, N. (2019) "Confronting Agrarian authoritarianism: dynamics of resistance to PROSAVANA in Mozambique", *Journal of Peasant Studies*, vol. 47, no. 1, pp. 69–94.

Monjane, B. (2021) Rural Struggles and Emancipation in Southern Africa: agrarian neoliberalism, rural politics and agrarian movements in Mozambique, South Africa and Zimbabwe (PhD dissertation), Faculty of Economics, University of Coimbra, Coimbra.

---

3 Boaventura de Sousa Santos develops on this in his work on the *Epistemologies of the South*. The Epistemologies of the South (ES) make a significant contribution in the study of processes of popular struggles and social movements broadly. One of the key contributions of the ES in critical agrarian studies lies in the ways revolutionary subjectivity is perceived. For the ES the cognitive and epistemological richness of societies (or of the processes of struggles) is captured as the struggles – against domination and oppression – occur (Santos, 2021; Monjane 2021, pp 50-51)

Santos, B. S. & Meneses, M. P. (Eds.) (2014) *Epistemologías del Sur*, Madrid, Akal

Shivji, I. G. (2017) 'The concept of 'working people', *Agrarian South: Journal of Political Economy*, vol. 6, no. 1, pp. 1–13

Santos, B. S. (2016) *Epistemologies of the South: justice against epistemicide*, London and New York, Routledge

Santos, B. de S. (2018) *The End of The Cognitive Empire: The Coming of Age of Epistemologies of the South*, Durham, Duke University Press.

Santos, B. de S. (2021) Epistemologies of the South and Marxisms, CES Seminar, https://www.youtube.com/watch?v=rdFOK4KiQ74&t=1679s accessed 19 April 2021.

Roy E. L. (1991) 'État, réforme et monopole foncier', in Le Bris, E. (ed) *L'appropriation de la Terre en Afrique Noire. Manuel d'analyse, de Décision et de Destion Foncières*, Paris, Karthala

PART I

CHAPTER 2

Shrinking or shifting?
The closing of civil society space
in five countries in
southern Africa

Ronald Wesso

Introduction

The shrinkage of space for civil society is a well-known global phenomenon, and a sizable and informative body of literature on this exists.[1]
Right-wing populism has been on the rise throughout the world and
particularly in the global North, its content being a politics of mass
mobilisation of hatred against marginalized groups, often in the name
of exclusionary nationalism. In many places, this has driven the rise
of authoritarian neoliberalism, as states close down democratic space
in order to protect neoliberal policies serving the elites. With regard to
southern Africa, however, most of the literature focuses on the problems
of mainstream international non-government organisations (NGOs)
rather than on the perspective of movement building from below.

This chapter is based on a process of research and discussion of
the shrinking of civil society space in five countries in southern Africa,
namely Angola, Mozambique, Namibia, South Africa and Zimbabwe.
The global context is an important element driving the shrinking of
civil society space in the five countries under discussion. The research
was guided by a focus on the work of Afrikagrupperna and that of its
partners in those countries.

Inevitably, research processes and outcomes are influenced by
the positionality of the researcher. It might therefore be helpful to the
reader to know some of the basics of the position of the researcher: I
am an activist researcher from South Africa with experience in popular
education and movement building.

....

1 The 'Monitor: Tracking Civic Space', published by Civicus, is probably the best known. The latest findings
   published in December 2020 can be found here: https://findings2020.monitor.civicus.org/

Methodological note

The study used a combination of research methods which have to be adapted based on issues that arose during the course of the research. A desktop study drawing on available literature was supplemented by interviews. An online survey and written feedback on an early draft of this paper were also included in the research methods. A presentation of the main argument of the chapter was made to an Afrikagrupperna partners' gathering in Johannesburg in November 2017, which provided further opportunities to correct details and refine arguments.

Conceptual reflections

Two concepts of civil society

I started with the basic question: What do we mean when we say space for civil society is shrinking? The literature includes two concepts of civil society with very different implications for how shrinking space is understood.

The first, and dominant, conception sees civil society as a self-referential entity acting on a mandate drawn from the foundational documents of the modern governance system. In this view, civil society is the self-appointed guardian of people's rights as described in country constitutions, laws, multilateral agreements and United Nations conventions such as the Universal Declaration of Human Rights. Civil society practitioners are seen as professionals who deliver services, practice advocacy and lobby power holders with the aim of ensuring marginalized people enjoy the rights ensconced in these documents.[2]

Civil society groups positioned in this way tend to have a legalistic view of space. Countries are seen as offering space when they have constitutions ensconcing basic human rights and laws enabling professionalized civil society groups to receive funding, deliver services, publish freely and regularly interact with power holders.[3] Conversely, those countries without human-rights-based constitutions and with laws that restrict the funding and activities of civil society organisations (CSOs) are seen as offering less space.

The second conception sees civil society as part of popular movements whose constituent elements are the membership-based organisations of people directly affected by the issues that CSOs are

---

2 Most of these draw on the view of the United Nations that civil society is 'the third sector in addition to government and business'. See UN (n.d.).
3 A typical example of this view is that of Kiai (2016).

trying to address. In this case, CSOs draw their mandates directly from people's organisations through processes that include popular education and mobilization. Human rights documents are often still part of this mandate, but only when they have been adopted as such by popular movements. Civil society practitioners are seen as staff members with particular responsibilities within broader movements whose direction they work under.[4]

CSOs positioned in this way tend to have a political view of space. Countries are seen as offering space when the movements of the poor and popular classes can mobilize freely and use their powers of mobilization to fight for their interests with the support or tolerance of the political authorities. In other words, the measurement of civil society space is not so much tied to the ability of professionalized CSOs to operate, but to the question of whether popular movements are able to operate freely and effectively.

In the literature on civil society space, and in my interviews and interactions with Afrikagrupperna, it is clear that these two conceptions do not exist as neatly separated entities (Afrikagrupperna 2016). There are overlaps, commonalities and blurred boundaries between the two views. However, this should not cloud the differences between the two conceptions, as they ultimately lead to fundamental differences in the practices of CSOs where either of the views predominates. Some CSOs, particularly international NGOs, function quite well in societies where the struggles and movements of people on the ground are severely repressed by states. (Silova 2008). In other cases, such as Bolivia, popular movements are strong but there is not much space for international NGOs (Kiai 2016).

The possibilities for CSOs to contribute to social change are different in these two scenarios. In the first, where CSOs are disconnected from popular movements, the end goals of social change are prescribed by the liberal framework embedded within global governance documents, and the methods through which they can be pursued are determined by what the repressive states would allow. It should be obvious how this restricts both the possible scope and the pace of social change. A true democracy, where the majority rule themselves and social policy serves the people, is only possible where popular movements are at the centre of social change.

....
4   The International Labour Research and Information Group (ILRIG), an Afrikagrupperna partner, is an example
    of an NGO holding such a view. See ILRIG (n.d.).

How civil society is seen

Moral authority is an underappreciated factor of civil society space. The literature talks of civil society space in terms of access to resources, legal protections and political tolerance (WEF 2017, pp. 29-32). The issue of how civil society is seen is discussed only rarely, which is not consistent with its importance to whether CSOs have space or not.

Even when it is raised, it is translated into a question of how the authorities view civil society (Carothers and Brechenmacher 2014, WEF 2017). This is obviously important. States and state officials that have a high regard for civil society will tend to give space for CSOs to do their work. However, this approach to the issue of the moral authority of civil society is tied to a self-referential conception of a civil society drawing mandates from liberalist political documents. This remains true in those cases where the literature discusses the importance of how the public views civil society. Invariably, the 'publics' under discussion turn out to be citizens of richer countries located in the North who make up the funding base of CSOs. How people in poorer countries in the South view civil society, and how their views impact on civil society space, is not really an issue in the literature thus far.[5]

For those who put popular movements at the centre of social change projects, this is a crucial issue, however.[6] It speaks to the question of whether and how civil society organisations can speak for the people they work with. My study is unable to say how positive or negative views of CSOs among people directly affected by poverty and marginalization are impacting on the space available to civil society to do its work. I can only raise this as an important issue that needs to be incorporated into how we understand shrinking space for civil society, and note, as explained below, that repressive governments certainly take this issue seriously and put in a lot of effort to influence people's views on civil society.

A political context of former liberation movements in power

The five countries under discussion are all governed by former movements for liberation from racist colonialism: Namibia by SWAPO (the South West African People's Organisation), Mozambique by FRELIMO (the Mozambican Liberation Front, Frente de Libertação de Moçambique), Angola by the MPLA (People's Movement for the Liberation of Angola, Movimento Popular de Libertação de Angola), Zimbabwe

....

5 See for example Reid, Ampomah, Prera, Rabbani and Zvigadza (2012). While local communities are mentioned, the actual targets for advocacy work are overwhelmingly governments and businesses in the South.
6 Ntando Ndlovu, personal communication.

by ZANU-PF (Zimbabwe African National Union – Patriotic Front) and South Africa by the ANC (African National Congress). This gives a common political context to the five countries, despite important differences and peculiarities. The political repertoires of the five governing parties have so much in common they strike the observer as identical.

The first important commonality in the political repertoires of the former liberation movements is their experience of international solidarity and how it shapes and is shaped by their relationships with civil society. In their phase of being anti-colonial liberation movements, these parties shared a history of working closely with international solidarity movements, including those in Europe and North America. This solidarity carried over into the early years of governance, when there was much collaboration between newly formed post-colonial governments and non-state actors in the global North. As a result, there is, within the political repertoire of these governing parties, a discourse that views international civil society as a partner and source of support and expects it to behave as such (Thörn 2010).

The second important commonality is their experience and discourse of the imperialism and colonialism of the West. The parties have, within their political repertoire, an entire history of anti-Western struggles, which are updated and deployed without much difficulty against the continued domination of the global North (Christiansen 2010). Antagonism to civil society is expressed as a part of the historical struggle against imperialist domination and interference. While this may seemingly be directed against international NGOs, the true targets are mainly local NGOs who depend on solidarity from northern-based citizens and NGOs [for, among other things, funding and organizational support].[7] Ironically, local NGOs receiving direct support from northern governments face less hostility from the governing parties than local movements involved in people-to-people solidarity with activists in the North.[8] This does not mean that northern governments are innocent of using local NGOs as fronts for imperialistic interference. It simply means that the governing parties use anti-imperialist discourses against any local CSOs with northern ties when it opposes the political agendas of these parties.

The third important common element in the political repertoire of the five governing parties in the countries under discussion has to do

7 Ntando Ndlovu, personal communication.
8 Ntando Ndlovu, personal communication.

with their positioning in the Cold War between the Soviet Union and the USA. All of them publicly took the side of the Soviet Union to the extent of identifying with the socio-economic and political system practiced there. Angola and Mozambique, upon independence, established one-party states modelled on the Soviet Union, while Zimbabwe, Namibia and South Africa established electoral democracies where the former liberation movements came to power through winning elections. The crucial common element for all five is the way the relationship between the people and the ruling parties is understood. The party is the embodiment of the people and therefore the will of the people can only be expressed through the will of the party. Civil society groups that deviate from the will of the party are therefore seen as opposing the will of the people and are labelled enemies of the state. In this case, the party sees it as its democratic duty to close down space for civil society.[9]

Neoliberalism goes from triumphant to desperate

The dominant policy frameworks of the states in the five countries can all be described as neoliberal. Despite differences, the common elements contain all the hallmarks of neoliberalism such as privatization, fiscal austerity, weakening of labour and environmental protections, financialization of the economy and a general opening of the economy to global corporations (Permanent People's Tribunal 2017).

Below, I explain how the development of neoliberalism has impacted on the relationship between the five states and civil society. This relationship must be understood against the background of a broad overview of the historical development of neoliberalism globally and in the countries under discussion.

Mozambique, Angola and Zimbabwe became independent in quick succession between 1974 and 1980. At the time, the idea of the welfare state was dominant in global policies and the three new governments followed the dominant practice of strong social welfare spending and protective labour policies. This global consensus collapsed from the late 1980s and was replaced by a new consensus named neoliberalism or the Washington Consensus (Van Driel 2012).

By the time Namibia and South Africa became independent and liberal democracies at the beginning of the 1990s, neoliberalism was triumphant on a global level. The operating idea was called TINA – There Is No Alternative. Power holders took this quite literally, and the

---

9 See for example Ellis (1991, pp. 439-447). There is an abundance of literature, including some produced by the movements themselves, illustrating this point.

end of history as a struggle for new emancipatory social systems was announced (Kramer 2013).

Under pressure from global popular mobilizations, this consensus began to unravel as the first decade of the new millennium came to a close. The symbol of this crisis of credibility became the World Trade Organisation (WTO). This was supposed to be its biggest triumph, as its intention was nothing less than institutionalizing neoliberal inter-government relations in a way that would make it nearly impossible for individual states to deviate. It collapsed under the onslaught of the anti-globalisation movement, and has been unable to recover since then (Graeber 2011). Since then, different institutions and aspects of neoliberalism have suffered similar crises.

The situation has become one of popular mobilization and elite backlash, resulting in what some have called the rise of authoritarian neoliberal regimes. Neoliberal states and political parties have tried to resolve the crisis of credibility by relying on increasing violence, repression and right-wing populism – developments that were seen earlier in many African countries before they attained their current visibility in the global North (Bruff 2014).

How did this history of the development of neoliberalism impact on the relationship between states and CSOs in the five countries?

Changes in the attitudes of African states to civil society

As noted above, the early post-independence period in Angola and Mozambique from 1975 and Zimbabwe from 1980 saw close cooperation between the new governments and civil society groups who continued the international solidarity extended to anti-colonial liberation movements. This began to change from the mid-1980s as neoliberalism became the dominant state policy framework in the form of structural adjustment programmes driven by the International Monetary Fund.

This change did not manifest as an immediate hostility on the part of states to civil society, but what happened instead was a selection process. Civil society organisations which stayed true to the politics of the welfare state became increasingly sidelined in favour of those CSOs which were prepared to overlook or support the turn to neoliberalism.[10] It is important to remember that privatization of essential goods and services was a central part of the overall neoliberal programme. The rollout of neoliberalism took place in societies where governments

....

10   Shereen Essof, interview. Dean van Rooy, interview

have long deployed socialist rhetoric and encouraged hostility to capitalists seeking to make money out of land, minerals, education and health. This was a real obstacle to the legitimation of neoliberalism and privatization in particular. NGOs stepped in and played the role of providing a foothold for undermining the welfare state and public goods. A lot of the initial privatization of essential services was not to private businesses but to NGOs and foundations. The neoliberal turn, therefore, initially led to a rapid growth in the number of CSOs and in the scope of their activities. These were CSOs of a particular kind that did not resist neoliberalism and were content to take over the delivery of services with much fewer resources and far worse-paid workers than the public services (Forte 2014). SWAPO in Namibia and the ANC in South Africa came to power at the height of this moment, and a plethora of CSOs arose to take responsibility for service delivery, often under the progressive guise of 'community empowerment', but in reality, representing nothing but a phase in the neoliberal rollout (Hoehn 2007).

This seamless cooperation between neoliberal states and service delivery CSOs came under pressure from at least three sources. Firstly, at the height of the triumphant period of neoliberalism, most states became ever more aggressive in cutting the resources with which the CSOs were expected to deliver services, leading to situations where service delivery became simply impossible. Secondly, after these CSOs had played their role of justifying privatization, they were often replaced with private businesses. Thirdly, resistance by popular classes directly affected by austerity and privatization began to undermine the power base of the states and the relevance and legitimacy of the CSOs in question. At the same time, those CSOs which put popular movements at the centre of their work gained more confidence and effectiveness. This began to increase tensions between states and civil society as a whole and culminated in the current open hostility and closing down of space.[11]

Mobilizing public opinion against Western imperialism

The specific form of the antagonism the five states directed against civil society is extremely important. The target is not presented as CSOs as such, or very rarely so, but as Western governments accused of using CSOs for the purpose of imperialistic interference. When they attack civil society, political leaders present themselves as victims of imperialism.

---

11 Dean van Rooy, interview.

They draw public attention away from the actual work CSOs do and the people they serve, and suggest that the issue is that local people should choose whether local politicians or those in northern countries should have greater legitimacy to exercise power in African countries.

In this way, public opinion is mobilized against political domination by northern governments in order to justify the closing down of civil society space by African governments (see for example Munusamy 2016).

It is worthwhile to consider the links between this phenomenon and the growing influence of China and Russia on the continent.[12] Both of these countries have authoritarian political systems characterised by repression of human and labour rights. They tend to influence partner governments in the same direction. In the last few years, both China and Russia have targeted Africa for huge investments, and have become very close to some African governments as a result. In 2015, Chinese investment in Africa totalled US$66.4 billion (Yuchen 2019) while that from Russia is set to grow fast (Klomegah 2014). To what extent is this contributing to the rise of repressive states in southern Africa?

An important question arises for Afrikagrupperna and civil society: Is imperialist domination by northern governments a real issue, or is it an invention of African states to justify repression? Based on the answer to this question, civil society's responses to the accusation of being imperialist agents will look different.

If Western imperialism is just an invention, then the lie must be exposed and an explanation must be found as to why this tactic is so effective. Anti-imperialist rhetoric, even if misdirected, certainly seems to connect with the experiences of African publics and do resonate with them.

If it is real, however, then civil society should not only acknowledge it but fight it, as the developmental and emancipatory objectives of civil society cannot be met within relationships of domination by northern states of African ones. This is an issue of principle, but it would also be a good tactic to neutralize the closing down of civil society space under the guise of resisting imperialism.

The literature is ambiguous on this issue. Domination is acknowledged but it is never clear whether we are dealing with the effect of past domination or with a present system of domination. My interviews made it clear that, while there is consensus that the present system of

---

12 Anna Ushamba, personal communication.

international relations is problematic, there are differences in the estimation of the importance of the issue. Some feel strongly that it should be a central focus, while others do not prioritise it. There seems to be a hesitance to confront the issue internally and externally.[13]

Homophobia as the initial issue driving the closing down of space

I have pointed out that the closing down of civil society space is done within a general mobilisation of public opinion against Western imperialism. The literature shows that this is often, in the initial phases, accompanied by a discourse of defending African culture and sexuality against homosexuality in particular. Both state and non-state actors are implicated in this tactic, and it is often religious and traditional leaders who lead the charge (Amnesty International 2013, Nichols 2013).

There is a temptation for CSOs not directly concerned with sexual rights to stay neutral in this battle as it is seen as not their issue. This is in many cases driven by active homophobia, although in most cases it is more of a tactical pose to avoid confrontations with power holders on this issue in order to be allowed to continue to work on other issues without interference. However, experience shows that once some rights and freedoms are established in the public mind as Western impositions, and therefore legitimate targets for repression and the closing down of space, it becomes easy for governments to treat any other rights and civil society organisations in the same way when these become inconvenient to them.[14]

The implication of this is that civil society should take the adage that freedom is indivisible quite seriously. When some rights and CSOs come under threat, it is a threat to civil society as a whole. While the participating organisations might not become leaders of the struggle against homophobia, they should be prepared to be active supporters of such a struggle, both out of principle and in defence of civil society space.

Right-wing populism and authoritarian neoliberalism

The global context is an important element driving the shrinking of civil society space in the five countries under discussion. Right-wing populism has been on the rise throughout the world and particularly in the global North, its content being a politics of mass mobilisation of hatred against marginalized groups, often in the name of exclusionary nationalism. In many places, this has driven the rise of authoritarian

---

13 Anna Ushamba, Agnes Nygren, Dean van Rooy, interviews.
14 Shereen Essof, interview, Samantha Hargreaves, interview.

neoliberalism, as states close down democratic space in order to protect neoliberal policies serving the elites (Bruff 2014).

A close look reveals that right-wing populism and authoritarian neoliberalism had long had footholds in the five countries, the targets being LGBTIQ people, sex workers, marginalized ethnic groups, religious dissidents, women and immigrants respectively. As in the USA, it has been closely tied to the rapid spread of evangelical Christian fundamentalism, with actual cooperation between local and American churches (Win 2013).

Right-wing populism, of both the local and northern varieties, is probably the biggest threat to civil society space in the five countries at the moment. It drives cuts to funding and the setting of more onerous conditions, while creating a mass base for repression by state and non-state actors that includes restrictions on freedom of expression, intimidation, harassment and death threats or assassinations.

Strategic considerations

How civil society space is shrinking and how popular movements are affected

Drawing on literature, interviews and personal observation, I have identified six aspects of the contemporary shrinking of civil society space in the five countries. I list them in the order of importance indicated by the researched organisations:[15]

- Violence and threats against activists
- Weak strategies and capacities of civil society and movements
- Hostility towards civil society from politicians and other authority figures
- Particular challenges and vulnerabilities faced by women
- Increasingly difficult requirements for raising and reporting on funds
- New laws restricting civil society activities and sources of funding.

Before discussing each of these aspects, it is important to understand the historical developments that led to the current situation. Above, I traced the historical changes in the attitudes of African states to civil society. Now I will sketch, in broad outlines, how popular movements were positioned for each of these changes.

....
15 Online survey; Dean van Rooy, Anna Ushamba, Agnes Nygren, interviews.

During the period leading up to independence, there was a rapid growth in popular movements consisting of membership-based organisations of people directly affected by social injustices. In most countries, these movements supported and grew close to the liberation movements and parties, but they never merged with them and maintained an independent existence of some sort in all countries. Trade unions, residents' associations based in townships and village-based peasant associations made up the local formations of these popular movements and provided their mass base. There is a wide consensus among historians that it was the rise of these popular movements that swung the balance of forces against the colonial regimes and led to independence (Saunders 2010).

After independence, the governing parties and popular movements maintained close relationships, to the point where the leaderships of the popular movements were integrated into the parties. This expressed shared ideologies and commitments, but had the effect of co-opting the leaders of the popular movements into the state apparatuses and compromising the capacity for independent action of these movements. At the same time, the integration of the movement leaders into the state led to greater centralization and an erosion of the autonomy and strength of the local formations at the base of these movements (Jauch 2003).

By the time the states turned to neoliberalism and started cutting away the incomes and social protections of the popular classes, the older movements were drained of their strength and unable to lead effective resistance. In many cases, the leaders simply backed their governments against self-organised, often localized rebellions of the poorer classes. In other cases, the older movements mounted some resistance, but found themselves too weakened and alienated from their popular bases to be effective. Resistance tended to be led by new formations which were often weak and localized (Bohmke 2010).

The current situation grew directly out of these developments. As governments became more authoritarian, their targets were not the big older trade unions and associations of residents and peasants, but the newer formations which were often informal networks formed around charismatic individuals. Repressive action often targeted these individuals directly through arrests and, in some cases, even assassinations (Patel 2010, Runciman 2016). While this was going on, cordial relations continued between states and popular movements which have now become bureaucratized to the extent that they can be called former popular movements (Jauch 2003).

The different aspects of the shrinking of civil society space must be understood against this historical background if we want to craft effective responses.

Violence and threats against activists

As suggested above, the violence, arrests and threats we have seen were not necessarily connected to restrictive laws directed at professionalized civil society organisations. The latter are discussed below. Attacks and arrests targeting charismatic activists and their allies in local NGOs around whom the new popular mobilizations are crystallizing have been connected to impunity of local power holders. This is a global phenomenon, where the problem is not so much repressive laws but the tendency of corrupt alliances amongst politicians, traditional leaders, police officers and businesses to go outside the law in defending the get-rich schemes (Lopez 2017). In all the five countries, we have recently seen instances where this type of repressive violence was stepped up to the level of massacres (Allison 2015, Andersson 2011, SAHO 2012).

It is difficult to defend activists against this kind of violence and to put an end to the impunity that facilitates it. A combination of underground methods and public pressure is required, which is sure to have an effect in the longer term. In the short term, exposure to violence and arrests will probably be an unavoidable risk for activists, which must be minimized. International NGOs can play a role in protecting activists by providing training and information, for example.

Here, a frank conversation about moral and political responsibilities becomes necessary. While we all share the political responsibility to end violence and repression, and while being reckless is morally indefensible, it should be clear that people have agency and can knowingly decide to expose themselves to risk. The moral responsibility for violence rests on its enablers and practitioners, and on no one else. Open conversations and sharing risks are ultimately the only antidotes to fears of moral culpability conditioned by inequalities within CSOs and movements. This is easier said than done, but it must be done.

Weak strategies and capacities of civil society and movements

Weak strategies and capacities of civil society and movements, together with threats of violence, were identified as the most important aspect of the shrinking of civil society space.[16] These include internal conflicts in NGOs and movements as well as the lack of unity amongst different organisations and sectors. Another issue that emerged was the lack of capacity to build on small gains made by informal networks.[17] I would also place this right at the top, both for its inherent importance and because this aspect is where the agency of the people directly affected is located. Of all the problems identified, this is the one civil society and popular movements can most directly address. To do so, it once again becomes important to place the issue within its historical development.

The current generation of activists within civil society and popular movements, for the most part, came to social awareness in the immediate pre- and post-independence eras, which was the high mark in the history of the older popular movements. Present day activists have vivid memories of powerful unions, residents' associations and peasant groups, whose leaders could easily call into motion national campaigns and actions, and who sat down with ministers and presidents, who they would often replace.

What the activists of today often lack is an appreciation of the years and sometimes decades of localized, slow building that preceded and prepared the days of popular movements of national scope and powers (Lehulere 2011). In fact, in the years when many of today's activists came to know the big popular movements, the local dynamism and autonomy had already been lost. When activists start out on the road of movement building, they often imitate their idea of the older movements, and try to jump directly into national mobilizations without spending the time building movement strength in localities. Movements therefore take on tasks for which they are not prepared and become exhausted, with their failures at a national level also draining their energy to build painstakingly at a local level.

If you add to this mix that the new activists are operating in completely different political conditions from their predecessors, it becomes clear that weak strategies and capacities are the outcome of history, and cannot be blamed on the new activists. New conditions call for new strategies, and what is needed is a period of deliberate strategy development, where the immediate goals of movements are harmonized with their capacities and conditions. This does not mean

....

16   Online survey.
17   Ntando Ndlovu, personal communication.

an exclusive focus on local mobilisation, but it does mean developing local mobilisations of sufficient strength to lay the basis for movements of broader scope capable of gaining new space for civil society and popular movements.

Hostility towards civil society from politicians and other authority figures

One way to describe hostility towards civil society from politicians is that it is a blunt weapon wielded with sophistication by powerholders in the five southern African countries. Above I have explained that civil society as such is rarely attacked directly; instead, Western imperialism is targeted and all civil society groups working for human rights and social justice are crudely condemned as agents of imperialism.

Closer study reveals the sophistication behind the crudeness. Outbursts of hostility from states and other authority figures against 'imperialist funded NGOs' are usually deployed when a specific CSO or movement has done something that threatens elite interests directly. In other words, we do not see a steady general discourse of hostility against civil society (Bellucci 2002, Presence 2016). Instead, it is deployed very deliberately against specific CSOs to undermine their work at the time. The couching of the attacks in the most general terms is done to make defending against it more difficult.

This means that it is important that the CSOs finding themselves under attack are not isolated. Afrikagrupperna and other CSOs must come to their defence, based on the particularities of the case and assuming the CSOs in question are doing good work, of course. The old union slogan is relevant here: an injury to one is an injury to all, a victory to one is a victory to all. States and power holders close space for civil society by targeting CSOs one by one in classic divide and rule tactics.

Particular challenges and vulnerabilities faced by women

The literature and most respondents in this investigation agree that women are disproportionately affected by the shrinking of space for civil society and face special challenges in overcoming it. This is connected to institutionalized sexism in the five countries, which manifests in many ways, including in a renewal of traditionalist patriarchy and misogynist Christianity (Win 2013).

Respondents in the online survey identified the top three particular challenges for women as:

- Greater hostility from political leaders and other authority figures such as traditional leaders to women's activism
- More vulnerability to violence directed against civil society activists
- Weaker strategies and capacities of women's civil society groups and movements
- The failure of feminist interventions that concentrated on getting women into powerful positions in the state, where these women were unable to effect meaningful change as they were co-opted by patriarchal states and the locus of power shifted to militaries and corporations.

Over the past few years, Afrikagrupperna and its partners have increasingly incorporated feminist politics into their approach. Difficulties arise in those cases where sexist discrimination is practiced inside civil society and popular movements.[18] If anti-sexism is made a precondition, the risks include either the imposition of ideas or exchanging solidarity for hollow declarations. The key is finding strong women activist and feminist groups embedded in local civil society and movements which can lead the processes of creating solutions to these dilemmas.

Increasingly difficult requirements for raising and reporting on funds Difficult requirements for raising and reporting on funds is an overdetermined problem with multiple causes. Rightward shifts in the politics of northern societies have brought into power governments who view civil society with suspicion and social spending as a waste. To the extent that civil society and overseas aid have become established in ways where governments cannot suppress them right now, these governments endeavour to create difficulties for civil society and aid. The bureaucratic processes attending to raising and disbursing funding are made ever more difficult even as the amounts available are being cut (Julie 2009).

Rightward shifts in the politics of the African countries have a similar effect. Governments insist on stricter oversight over funding flowing into their countries and put in place registration and monitoring requirements that also drain the time and resources of civil society (International Center for Not for Profit Law 2011).

Meeting these requirements is less of a problem for the older, more established civil society groups and popular movements, but these are the groups that have largely been co-opted by states and have been distant from current resistance struggles. The newer CSOs and

18   Dean van Rooy, interview. Agnes Nygren, interview.

especially the newer popular movements often lack the organizational infrastructure and skilled personnel to meet the ever-rising bureaucratic requirements attached to receiving funding.[19]

New laws restricting civil society activities and sources of funding It is telling that while the literature has put the aspect of restrictive laws right at the top, participants have put it at the bottom of the list.[20] This does not mean it is not an issue at all; it simply reflects the fact that it is less of a priority for popular movements than for self-mandated, professionalized CSOs. In fact, seeing that the literature practically defines the shrinking of civil society space by this aspect of new restrictive laws, those of us with a wider movement-orientated view of the issue should speak more accurately of a shifting rather than a shrinking of space.[21] As the space in court rooms and lobby halls shrinks, the struggle shifts to township streets, village squares and workplace canteens. For the new movements arising in these marginal spaces where the marginalized are at home and able to mobilise, the legal aspect so important to official civil society can only be a supplementary arena. The main struggle at this point is to learn how to build strong popular mobilizations in the spaces where the people who are directly affected by poverty and inequality live.

Conclusion

The argument of the paper is that the literature reflects two distinct conceptions of civil society. The first sees civil society as a professionalized and self-referential space where institutions draw their mandate from human rights declarations, conventions and laws. The second sees civil society as a support-resource space for popular movements from whose constituencies it draws its mandate. The organisations that participated in this research are broadly located within the second view, while the available literature on the shrinking of civic space is overwhelmingly located within the first view.

With this framing in mind, the study found that the key contextual factors driving the closing down of civic space in the named countries include having former liberation movements as governments who come from a similar pro-Soviet Union alignment during the Cold War and who have all committed to neoliberal policy directions. The shift to neoliberalism has driven an increasingly hostile attitude to popular

19 Anna Ushamba, Agnes Nygren, interviews.
20 Online survey.
21 Dean van Rooy, interview.

movements, while the Stalinist heritage has provided the political repertoire through which this hostility becomes expressed. This repertoire includes mobilising public opinion against NGOs by associating them with Western imperialism, and using homophobia as a beachhead to drive an anti-popular agenda in the name of defending African culture against the West. This has facilitated the growth of a right-wing populism and authoritarian neoliberalism, connected to similar movements in the West intent on closing down the possibilities of progressive change represented by civil society in alliance with popular movements.

The co-option of the older popular movements associated with the pre-independence period has left it to new groups of activists to confront these new conditions. This has led to tactical mistakes and frustrations, as these new groups have not yet developed the strategic and organisational tools to deal with this shift to authoritarian neoliberalism.

Specific challenges facing the new movement building efforts include violence and threats against activists, weak strategies and capacities, hostility from power holders, institutionalised discrimination and violence against women, increasing difficulties with raising and reporting on funds, and new laws restricting CSO funding and activities.

The main struggle for the current generation of movement builders at this point is therefore to learn how to build strong popular mobilizations in the spaces where the people who are directly affected by poverty and inequality live.

References

Afrikagrupperna (2016) 'Terms of reference: shrinking space for civil society organizations' (Unpublished report), Stokholm

Allison, S. (2015) 'Angola: The Mount Sumi massacre – an atrocity that will come to define the new country', *African Arguments*, http://africanarguments. org/2015/05/28/angola-the-mount-sumi-massacre-an-atrocity-that-will-come-to-define-the-new-country-by-simon-allison/, accessed 4 January 2021

Amnesty International (2013) *Making Love a Crime: Criminalization of Same-Sex Conduct in Sub-Saharan Africa*, London

Andersson, H. (2011) 'Soldiers tell of Zimbabwe diamond field massacre', *BBC Panorama*, 8 August, http://www.bbc.co.uk/panorama/hi/front_page/ newsid_9556000/9556242.stm, accessed 4 January 2021

Bellucci, S. (2002) *Governance, Civil Society and NGOs in Mozambique*, Paris, UNESCO

Bohmke, H. (2010) 'Branding of social movements', *Heinrichbohmke.com*, 10 May, http://heinrichbohmke.com/2013/05/branding/, accessed 29 December 2020.

Bruff, I. (2014) 'The rise of authoritarian neoliberalism', *Rethinking Marxism: a Journal of Economics, Culture & Society*, 26(1)

Bull Christiansen, L. (2010) 'Zimbabwe's liberation struggle recycled: remembering the principles of the struggle in political ways', in Saunders, C. (ed) *Documenting Liberation Struggles in Southern Africa*, Uppsala, Nordic Africa Institute

Carothers, T. and Brechenmacher, S. (2014) *Closing Space: Democracy and Human Rights Support Under Fire*, Washington DC, Carnegie Endowment for International Peace

Ellis, S. 'The ANC in exile', *African Affairs*, 90(360)

Forte, M.C. (2014) 'Civil society, NGOs, and saving the needy: imperial neoliberalism' *Zeroanthropolgy.net*, https://zeroanthropology.net/2014/08/28/civil-society-ngos-and-saving-the-needy-imperial-neoliberalism/

Graeber, D. (2011) *Debt: The First 5000 Years*, New York, Melville House

Hoehn, S. (2007) 'NGOs in Namibia – continuing crisis or new beginning?' *The Namibian*, 26 January https://www.namibian.com.na/index.php?id=32474&page=archive-read, accessed 4 January 2021

ILRIG (n.d.) https://www.ilrigsa.org.za/our-work/, accessed 4 January 2021

Jauch, H. *Trade Unions in Southern Africa*,Windkoek, Labour Resource and Research Institute (LaRRI).

Julie, F. (2009) 'The Roots of the Ngo crisis: a look beyond the surface', *NGO Pulse*, February, http://www.ngopulse.org/article/roots-ngo-crisis-look-beyond-surface, accessed 4 January 2021

Kiai, M. (2016) 'Reclaiming space through UN supported litigation', *OpenDemocracy*, https://www.opendemocracy.net/openglobalrights/maina-kiai/reclaiming-space-through-un-supported-litigation, accessed 4 January 2021

Klomegah, K.K. (2014) 'Russia's investment in Africa: new challenges and prospects', *Modern Ghana*, 4 August, https://www.modernghana.com/news/561217/1/russias-investment-in-africa-new-challenges-and-pr.html, accessed 4 January 2021

Kramer, M. (2013) 'There is no alternative!' *The Guardian*, 4 May, https://www.theguardian.com/science/life-and-physics/2013/may/04/no-alternative-bayes-penalties-philosophy-thatcher-merkel, accessed 4 January 2021

Lehulere. O. (2011) 'Document of the movement – August 28, 2011' *Khanya College Journal*, 28, August

Lopez, O. (2017) 'Why Mexico's environmental activists fear for their lives', *Newsweek*, 24 March, http://www.newsweek.com/2017/03/24/why-mexico-environmentalists-fear-murder-isidro-baldenegro-lopez-567814.html, accessed 4 January 2021

Matthews, S. (2017) 'The role of NGOs in Africa: are they a force for good?' *The Conversation*, 25 April, https://theconversation.com/the-role-of-ngos-in-africa-are-they-a-force-for-good-76227, accessed 4 January 2021

Munusamy, R. (2016) 'Chasing butterflies and bogeymen: Mantashe beats 'regime change' drum', *Daily Maverick*, 13 May, https://www.dailymaverick.co.za/article/2016-05-13-chasing-butterflies-and-bogeymen-mantashe-beats-regime-change-drum/#.Wi1Ma0qWaM8, accessed 4 January 2021

Nichols, J. (2013) 'Robert Mugabe, Zimbabwe president, threatens to behead gay citizens', *The Huffington Post*, 26 July, http://www.huffingtonpost.co.za/entry/mugabe-zimbabwe-behead-gays_n_3659454, accessed 4 January 2021

Patel, R. (2010) 'Mozambique's food riots – the true face of global warming', *The Guardian*, 5 September, https://www.theguardian.com/commentisfree/2010/sep/05/mozambique-food-riots-patel, accessed 4 January 2021

Permanent People's Tribunal (2017) *Call to action II*, Southern African Campaign to Dismantle Corporate Power, August

Presence, C. (2016) 'Mahlobo lashes Malema, NGOs', *IOL*, 26 April, https://www.iol.co.za/news/politics/mahlobo-lashes-malema-ngos-2014693

Reid, G.A., Prera, M.I.O., Rabbani, G. and Zvigadza, S. (2012) 'Where is civil society focusing its advocacy efforts?' in *Southern Voices on Climate Policy Choices - Analysis of and Lessons Learned from Civil Society Advocacy on Climate Change, London*, International Institute for Environment and Development (UK)

Runciman, C. (2016) 'South Africa's rebellion of the poor' *Review of African Political Economy*, Roape.net, 16.07.2016, http://roape.net/2016/07/14/south-africas-rebellion-poor/, accessed 4 January 2021

SAHO (n.d.) 'Marikana massacre 16 August 2012', *SAHO*, http://www.sahistory.org.za/article/marikana-massacre-16-august-2012, accessed 4 January 2021

Saunders, C. (ed) (2010) *Documenting Liberation Struggles in Southern Africa*, Uppsala, Nordic Africa Institute

Silova, I. (2008) 'Contested alliances: international NGOs and authoritarian governments in the era of globalization', *Current Issues in Comparative Education*, 10(1/2): 26-3.

The International Centre for Not for Profit Law (2011) 'NGO laws in sub-Saharan Africa', *Global Trends in NGO Law*, 3(3)

Thörn, H. 'Liberation struggles in southern Africa and the emergence of a global civil society' in Saunders, C. (ed) *Documenting Liberation Struggles in Southern Africa*, Uppsala, Nordic Africa Institute

UN (n.d) United Nations http://www.un.org/en/sections/resources-different-audiences/civil-society/index.html, accessed 4 January 2021

Van Driel, M. (2012) 'In this edition', *Khanya: A Journal For Activists*, No. 30, July

WEF (2017) *The Global Risks Report 2017*, Geneva, World Economic Forum

Win, E. (2013) *Between Jesus, the Generals and the Invisibles - Mapping the Terrain for Feminist Movement Building and Organizing for Women's Human Rights*, Cape Town, Just Associates.

Yuchen, T. (2019) 'How Chinese Companies Deal with Labour Strikes and Unions in Kenya', The China Africa Project, 17 August,http://www.chinaafricaproject.com/chinese-companies-deal-labor-strikes-unions-kenya/, accessed 4 January 2021

Zelenova, D. (2017) 'Practices of self-organisation in South Africa: the experience of the 1980s and its implications for contemporary protest', Enough 14, 8.12.2017 https://enoughisenough14.org/2017/12/08/practices-of-self-organisation-in-south-africa-the-experience-of-the-1980s-and-its-implications-for-contemporary-protest/, accessed 4 January 2021

PART II

Understanding Land Conflicts

CHAPTER 3

Harassment and intimidation of social movements involving large scale land alienation for agricultural investment in Zambia

Fatima Mandhu and Ellah TM Siang'andu

Ownership of land for either agriculture or mining is central to economic empowerment since land serves as a base for food production and income generation. In Zambia, ownership of land is based on the dual land tenure system that comprises statutory as well as customary tenure. Statutory tenure is regulated by legislation, while customary rights are governed under local customs. In the absence of a comprehensive national land audit for either form of tenure it is difficult to establish ownership of land, resulting in several land disputes. Conversion of land from customary to statutory land results in the extinction of rights originally held under customary tenure. Most land disputes relate to the interface between statutory rights held over customary land that is converted for purposes of large scale investment and the rights of the rural poor.

There are several non-governmental organisations (NGOs) involved at different levels in promoting and protecting the land rights of rural people. The Zambia Land Alliance (ZLA) is a network of NGOs working for pro-poor land rights and justice in land policies. The network engages in lobbying and advocacy for secured access, control, and ownership over land. ZLA works to coordinate civil society participation and facilitate popular participation and advocacy on land policy reforms. ZLA faces a number of challenges regarding land rights held under customary tenure with the state as the custodian of land in Zambia. In addition, the requirement of registration of NGOs under Section 10 of the NGO Act No. 16 of 2009 has been a contentious issue. The interference in the work of the NGOs by the state as a regulator has created friction. This imposition of regulation by the state on the NGOs can be described as intimidation and results in an antagonistic relationship.

Using a case study approach with reference to two cases decided by the courts of law relating to disputes between large scale alienation of land for agriculture and the rural people's right to customary land, this chapter discusses the harassment and intimidation faced by NGOs such as ZLA in resolving land disputes in Zambia. The major question that is being investigated is how rights to customary land for rural people can be protected under the dual land tenure system in Zambia.

The problems of the dual tenure system

In Africa, land and natural resources are the basic units of livelihood for communities and their members in the rural areas. Women's or men's access to and use and ownership of land for either agriculture or mining is central to economic empowerment, as land can serve as a base for food production and income generation. Zambia has a long history of large-scale farms that have coexisted alongside smallholder communities (Chu 2013). In recent years, the country has experienced a sudden increase in the demand for land to be used for large-scale agricultural purposes. The Land Matrix estimates that 26 deals, covering an area of 389,774 hectares, have been concluded since 2000 (Harding, Chamberlain, Maluleke, Niassy, Anseeuw and Manco 2016). Zambia's dual land tenure system has hindered the promotion of equitable access to and use and ownership of land under statutory, and more prominently under customary, tenure. Two of the main challenges that have been identified include absence of legislation and registration of land rights protecting customary tenure and the lack of a comprehensive national land audit.

At the national level, policy and institutional changes through land reform programs have not been easy to formulate and even more difficult to implement since they have not been supported or recognized as a priority by the state. The adoption of the social tenure domain model (Archer 2016) as an alternate form of tenure is designed to bridge the technical gap by allowing for recordation of all possible types of tenures without making changes to the legislative or institutional frameworks (Lemmen 2010). The choice of STDM over other forms of land tenure reform has been supported since it does not require changes to the policies or legislative and institutional frameworks as an initial stage. This form of tenure is being piloted to protect customary rights.

Other forms of tenure reform are time consuming and require lengthy procedures and government resources which are not available in the case of Zambia. Land reform programmes involving tenure reform are shelved before they can be finalised at policy level owing to the prerequisite of legislative changes. Evidential proof in Zambia is the draft land policy initiated in 2006 which, by 2021, remained to be finalised and launched (Ministry of Lands 2017). STDM, in the continuum of land rights approaches, supports land reforms in a social context by considering the relationship between people and land. The STDM being piloted in Zambia is viewed as a more flexible, fit for the purpose and inclusive approach based on recognition of a diversity of rights, within a context of pro-poor and gender responsive land management and administration. This chapter will consider the role of NGOs in resolving the fight against acquisition of land for large scale agricultural investment and upholding the rights of the rural poor. Using a case study approach, the chapter will examine decisions made by the courts supporting statutory land tenure compared to customary land rights.

Methodology and objectives

This chapter will adopt the case study approach to analyse cases decided by the courts to show the discrepancies between land rights under statutory and customary tenure. The case study, as a method, is essentially an intensive investigation of the particular unit under consideration. In this chapter, the unit will be the two chosen cases. The object of the case study method is to locate the factors that account for the behaviour patterns of the given unit (Kothari 2004). This approach is useful when considering an in-depth understanding of an issue, event or 'phenomenon in a real life context' (Crowe, Cresswell, Robertson, Huby, Avery and Sheikh 2011, p.1). The case study method is a form of qualitative analysis wherein careful and complete observation of an individual or a situation or an institution is done. Efforts are made to study each and every aspect of the unit of interest in minute detail and then, from case data, generalizations and inferences are drawn. The first objective of this chapter is an in-depth study of the decisions in the two cases, outlining the conflict between statutory land and customary land. Secondly, the chapter analyses the harassments and intimidation faced by NGOs such as ZLA in promoting and protecting the land rights of the rural people. Then the chapter examines why customary land rights holders are not able to use alternate forms of action apart from litigation to protect their rights. The chapter concludes by outlining the way forward.

Analysis of two court decisions

In Zambia, the Mpongwe cases[1] are examples of conflicts within the dual land tenure systems of statutory land (that is, registered land) and customary land (that remains unregistered). The conflicts continue in both cases despite several interventions by civil society organisations working with the communities. This chapter will consider the facts, decisions and implementation of the judgement of the supreme court. The supreme court is the highest court at the national level, whose decision is binding on the parties before it. There is no further appeal from the decision made by the supreme court. The question that this chapter addresses is whether the decision of the court has provided a solution to protect the customary land rights of the communities.

The facts of the first case involve a South African company, Dar Farms Limited, which owns about 60,000 hectares of land in Chieftainess Lesa's chiefdom. The initial land allocation to Dar Farms was done during the first republic and then President Kenneth Kaunda did not consult the chiefs in the area when allocating the land to the investor as required by law. Once the allocation was completed, the land was converted from customary to statutory tenure. This allowed for the registration of land and issuing a certificate of title over the property in the name of Dar Farms Limited. As Dar Farms continued to expand its commercial business into the land held by Chieftainess Lesa without her consent, the contention was that this expansion was illegally done. The Chieftainess had clearly stated that the poaching of land from her subjects had been illegal. Several villagers occupying the land under customary tenure since 1998 had been and continue to be displaced from their land. The community had held this land under customary tenure. This conflict between Dar Farms Limited, as a large scale land investment in commercial farming, and the community carrying on subsistence farming on the same piece of land is what led to the court action. The High Court had ruled in favour of the community because it was discovered that the community occupied the said land with the authority of the company. However, this decision was overturned on appeal by the supreme court which ruled against the community, stating that the occupation of the farm by the community was a mistake made mutually by the parties, and the community was ordered to vacate the land. The owner of the land in this case was the registered title holder, being Dar Farms Limited.

1 Mpongwe Development Corporation Limited v Francis Kamanda and 51 Others Appeal No.137 of 2007 and Mpongwe Development Company Limited v Francis Kamanda and Others SCZ Judgement No.14 of 2010.

The second case[2] involved ETC Bio Energy, a South African company which was the former Mpongwe Development Company Limited (MDC), dealing in biofuel plantation, and also a large scale land investor involved in commercial agriculture. In this case the 46,000 hectares of land under contention in the Mimbolo farming area was also part of Chieftainess Lesa's chiefdom.

The facts in this case are different from those stated above in the first case. In this case the president, in 1995, directed MDC to give part of its land to the community so that they could continue their farming activities. The company responded positively but conflict arose regarding boundaries, which led to the community being shifted to a new piece of land from that initially offered to the community. At a meeting held in 2004 where all the stakeholders were present, a resolution was passed that the land in question belonged to the chief and that the community should stay and put up permanent structures. Two weeks later MDC stopped the community, stating that it was the owner of the land in question under a valid certificate of title - in other words, statutory land. The community commenced an action in the high court against MDC, and in 2006, the court ruled in favour of the community, stating that the community occupied the land legitimately. On appeal by MDC, judgement was made against the community which led to the community being displaced from their land. The Supreme Court ruled that the trial judge could not order cancellation of title since there is no evidence that the land was acquired fraudulently and MDC was the beneficial owner of the land.

On the ground, both these cases of displacements have left more than 5,600 members of the community without land, shelter, water or a source of livelihood as the conflict continues between the companies conducting large-scale land investment for agriculture and subsistence farming carried out by the community on land held under customary tenure. The conflict relates to security of tenure under certificate of title issued by the government institutional framework for statutory land and land held under customary tenure that is not registered.

Some of the more specific challenges regarding customary tenure without subjecting it to conversion include lack of clear guidelines on the role and functions of traditional authorities, leaders and local authorities in the administration of customary land. Another challenge is the lack of clear assignment of land rights and responsibilities,

2 Mpongwe Development Company Limited v Francis Kamanda and 51 Others SCZ Judgement No.137of 2007.

especially with regard to gender and social status, since customs and practices vary from one area to another. Also, under statutory tenure, the certificate of title issued by the government serves as collateral for a loan, while the lack of a certificate of title for customary landholding disqualifies it as collateral. The net result is that customary tenure cannot adequately serve as capital in a market economy. This has its basis in the understanding that tenure is held according to local traditions, customs and practices which differ in nature and form across the country, thus causing tenure insecurity. Comparison of the two tenures has created a false sense of security that statutory tenure is superior to customary tenure. Furthermore, the rights of landowners under customary tenure are undefined due to overlapping and sometimes contradictory control and user rights to a parcel of land. Therefore, there is a desire by customary land occupants to legally document their rights to land in order to enjoy legal protection similar to that provided to statutory land rights holders. The only available option, to convert customary land holdings to statutory tenure, is not seen as a desirable option, hence the introduction of the STDM to bridge this gap.

On addressing the current standing of these and several other similar cases, civil society has been faced with the dilemma of what step they should take next, considering that the decision is from the highest national court in Zambia. In both of the Mpongwe cases, civil society organisations have facilitated meetings between the commercial farming companies and the community members regarding their displacements. The battle is to retrieve the land for the communities or to find alternate land on which they can be settled.

The members of the communities are labelled squatters and are being forcefully removed from their land in the name of development and improved status of life promised by the state. The state simply watches and seems disinterested in meeting its basic obligation of protecting its people and denying the community members the right to access and own land, a very basic human right which affects their ability to access food.

Similar cases where litigation has not taken place have also occurred in other areas of Zambia. Lufwanyana is a good example where a hundred households have been displaced (Law Association of Zambia 2016). The data collected by civil society organisations conducting site visits showed that: '...Zambia has not been spared by human induced displacements because of the allocation of land to developers and/or investors at the expense of local people using and occupying the area under customary tenure; an example of vulnerability of the rural poor of Lufwanyana is hereby given' (Law Association of Zambia 2016, p. 32). Such cases concern land rights and the displacement of the rural poor and small scale farmers by large scale land investors without adherence to business and human rights principles or international conventions (United Nations 2007 Article 25). In addition, displacement disrupts community life and, more importantly, the relationship between the land and the local people. Analysis of cases such as these discussed above show that the conflict between statutory land and customary land needs to be balanced to avoid land displacements.

Background to land issues and social movements in Zambia

Land tenure can be described as the relationship, whether legally or customarily defined, among people, as individuals or groups, with respect to land (Amone and Lakwo 2014). In Zambia, land is divided into two tenure categories, statutory and customary tenure, as mentioned already. The dual system of land tenure reflects the country's history of colonial settlement on present-day state land and the initial separation of settlements for the local population in native reserves from the foreign landownership along the rail lines. Customary tenure has been misunderstood as tenure and has been dismissed as being inferior to statutory tenure and an inefficient means of owning land (Hansungule 2001). The legislative framework in Zambia provides for conversion of land from customary tenure to statutory tenure but leaves a gap on whether the rights acquired under customary tenure simply extinguish when the parcel of land is converted or continue to exist. A possible but unsatisfactory answer is that the rights extinguish because, once the parcel of land is converted to statutory land, it can never be reconverted to customary tenure. This answer does not address the issue of the existing rights or the competing rights held by a person under customary tenure for land that is converted. Furthermore, the parcel of land that is converted is subjected to statutory requirements.

Some of the general challenges with respect to statutory tenure are characterised by widespread lack of knowledge of land alienation procedures; over-centralisation of the institutional structures responsible for dealing with land administration and management; and unwillingness by some chiefs to consent to the process of conversion. Additionally, the practical difficulties involved in conversion of customary land to statutory land, scarcity of information on land availability and under-development, including non-utilisation of land, has led to land disputes under customary tenure. The main dispute that continues is the alienation of large tracts of land held by communities under customary tenure to large scale commercial farmers, resulting in the displacement of the communities who carry out subsistence farming on their land. This focal point of dispute is what civil society has to deal with on the ground.

Civil society organisations, or NGOs as they are known in Zambia, work with rural communities to protect their land rights as well as their livelihoods. NGOs as well as civil society organisations (CSOs) are involved at different levels in promoting and protecting the land rights of the rural people. The ZLA[3] is one such network of CSOs working for just land policies and laws that take into account the interests of the poor, which has been very instrumental in advocating for the preservation of customary land. Customary land is important for most of the rural poor who depend on subsistence farming for survival. In most cases, it is the only valuable resource which they possess, and any form of grabbing makes them even more vulnerable and completely disempowered (Hansungule 2001). ZLA has also, for a long time, been advocating for land policy that addresses challenges such as security of tenure (Zambia Land Alliance-FANRPAN 2007).

ZLA aims to advocate for fair land policies and laws that would protect the interests of poor communities and marginalized social groups, especially women. It works to coordinate civil society participation and facilitate popular participation and advocacy on land policy reforms. There are several conflicting issues raised by ZLA regarding land rights, and a major one is the state as the custodian of land in Zambia. Under the current Lands Act (Chapter 184 of the Laws of Zambia), the vestment clause allows the state to acquire land on the basis that all land in Zambia is vested in the president of the republic. Section 3 of the Act provides that, 'notwithstanding anything to the contrary contained in any other law, instrument or document, but subject to this Act, all land in Zambia shall vest absolutely in the President and shall be held by him in perpetuity for and on behalf of the people of Zambia'.

The relationship that vestment clause creates between the president and the people of Zambia is of trust. The obligations placed on

----

3 The ZLA is a network of NGOs working for pro-poor land rights and justice in land policies. The alliance was formed during a process of land reform in the 1990s. The network engages in lobbying and advocacy for secured access, control, and ownership over land. It is a platform for collective action committed to promoting equitable access and secured ownership of land by rural and urban poor, through lobbying and advocacy, networking, research and community partnership (see Zambia Land Alliance 2019).

the president and the government are to ensure that land and natural resources are protected and alienated for the benefit of the people of Zambia. The people of Zambia would no doubt include the rural communities. This relationship of trust is based on the common law fiduciary duties of acting in utmost good faith. There is a clear lacuna in the Constitution and the land laws in Zambia that requires these general duties to be moved from common law into statutory legislation so that, if there is mismanagement of land or natural resources, the individual is able to seek redress. The argument that individuals who lose their land rights should be able to seek redress is supported by the Supreme Court of America in the case of United States v. Mitchel (1983), where an indigenous tribe had sued the United States federal government, arguing that it mismanaged the tribe's land resources contrary to legislative provisions (more particularly the Allotment Act of 1887). The argument presented by the tribe was that the Act imposed a fiduciary duty on the government to manage the resources in a manner that advanced the interests of the tribe. The lower court rejected the argument and the claim for damages on the grounds that the Allotment Act and other similar statutes imposed a trust relationship between the government and the tribe and that the duty was not specific but general.

The government could not be held liable for failure to implement general duties. The matter was subjected to an appeal and the tribes tendered a number of statutes and regulations imposing specific duties on government regarding how to manage the land of indigenous people. The Supreme Court held that these were specific duties and it had been proved that the government had failed to discharge those duties which entitled the tribe to a claim for damages.

Even though this case is only of persuasive value to Zambia, lessons can be drawn from the decision regarding the duty of good faith on the state. It can also serve as guidance to resolve the disputes between the community's customary rights to land and the acquisition of land by the state for large scale agricultural investment in Zambia, the point of discussion in this chapter. Zambia needs to place specific duties, within its legislative provisions, on the authorities responsible for managing land and natural resources to ensure that the fiduciary duty is discharged based on the trust relationship that has been created. It is important to note that there is a lacuna in the Zambian Constitution since it does not provide for social and economic rights.[4] Abuse by the

---

4 Due to a failed referendum, a discussion on the Bill of Rights in the constitution is still in progress.

state can be checked if specific duties of good faith are clearly outlined in the legislative provisions.

The only constitutional guidance under the amended Constitution is the principles of land policy listed under Article 253.[5] Of importance to this chapter are the principles raised under a, b, f and h, which allow the members of rural communities to demand equitable access to their land held under customary tenure through effective and efficient settlement of land disputes, in addition to holding the state accountable where the large scale investments do not benefit them based on the common law doctrine of good faith as elaborated. The point to note is that the Article in the Constitution is not binding or justiciable but merely guidance for the state when drafting the land policy.

On the other hand, in terms of regulations, civil society organisations such as ZLA are regulated under a legislative framework, in particular the The Non-Governmental Organisations Act No. 16 of 2009. Section 10(1) of the Act prohibits the operation of any NGO or CSO without registration. Under the national laws in Zambia, registration of CSOs is mandatory, and without registration, civil society organisations are not able to operate or carry out their objectives. The registration requirement is a clear breach of the guidelines for the freedom of association and assembly at regional level in Africa, which define an association as an organized, independent, not-for-profit body based on the voluntary grouping of persons with a common interest, activity or purpose.[6]

It is clear from the Act that an informal civil society organisation will not be able to operate in Zambia due to the legislative requirement to register. It is for this reason that the relationship between the state and the NGOs has been described by several writers (Elone 2009) as harassment and intimidation of NGOs by the state. Simply put, 'the state has been known to use underhanded methods to reconquer the

5 Article 253 of the Constitution of Zambia (Amendment), Act No. 2 of 2016, provides that:
   (1) Land shall be held, used and managed in accordance with the following principles:
     (a) equitable access to land and associated resources;
     (b) security of tenure for lawful land holders;
     (c) recognition of indigenous cultural rites;
     (d) sustainable use of land;
     (e) transparent, effective and efficient administration of land;
     (f) effective and efficient settlement of land disputes;
     (g) river frontages, islands, lakeshores and ecologically and culturally sensitive areas—
       (i) to be accessible to the public;
       (ii) not to be leased, fenced or sold; and
       (iii) to be maintained and used for conservation and preservation activities;
     (h) investments in land to also benefit local communities and their economy; and
     (i) plans for land use to be done in a consultative and participatory manner
6 The guidelines were adopted at the African Commission on Human and Peoples' Rights' 60th Ordinary Session held in Niamey, Niger, from 8 to 22 May 2017.

political arena and criminalize dissent, as if control of a country's government was a birth right for the ruling elites' (Media Institute of Southern Africa 2014).

The state's requirement to register these organisations has been a contentious issue. The relationship between the state and these organizations can be described as antagonistic. The interplay between the state and civil society can be examined through a legal lens to reveal the contentious relationship between the two parties. The basis of the legal analysis should be the constitutional provision, which is the supreme law of the land providing for fundamental freedoms and rights (including the right to freedom of association and assembly), the guiding principles of land policy in the Constitution (Chapter 1 of the Laws of Zambia and the Constitution of Zambia (Amendment), Act No. 2 of 2016), the Lands Act (Chapter 184 of the Laws of Zambia), the Land Acquisition Act (Chapter 185 of the Laws of Zambia) and the NGO Act (No. 16 of 2009), at the national level. The reflection of the guidelines on freedom of association and assembly in the local legislative framework shows the challenges that social movements encounter with the state in matters concerning land rights of the rural communities.

Analysing the current position under the dual system in Zambia reveals that statutory rights have precedence over customary land rights. However, the law does recognise the existence of customary land rights in Section 7 of the Lands Act (Chapter 184 of the Laws of Zambia). The gap is that there has been no attempt to define recognition and, further, there have been no attempts made to provide appropriate documentation for adequate recognition and protection of individual, community and communal land rights under customary land tenure. While private, individual land rights are well acknowledged within customary tenure, they are not adequately recognised in law.[7] The problem that needs to be addressed is what happens when there is a conflict between the unregistered rights of a person holding land under customary tenure and rights held by a registered proprietor under a certificate of title of statutory tenure over the same piece of land.

Social activism as a tool to resolve conflicts

Zambia is described as a democratic state and has experienced a smooth transition of power from one ruling party to the other. But the adherence to democracy has not allowed for the emergence of a vibrant civil

....
7 See the Draft National Land Policy drawn up by the Ministry of Lands and Natural Resources (2017).

society movement (Mutesa 2009). Civil society remains side-lined and undermined. They do not enjoy the freedom and space to act freely and independently. It has been observed through history that Zambian civil societies have had to constantly negotiate for civic space whenever there has been a change in government.

Under the Zambian Constitution, the Bill of Rights that forms the basis for Zambia's human rights law purports to guarantee certain rights and freedoms, such as Article 16 of the Constitution which guarantees protection from deprivation of property. Individuals have the right to own property which may be take any form, including land, buildings, money or shares. However the protection from deprivation of property provided for in the Constitution becomes meaningless since it is not absolute. The provision contains 27 derogations which allow for the legal acquisition of property. This chapter will not consider these derogations in detail. Suffice to state that the protection guaranteed under Article 16 is more relevant to land under the statutory land system than to customary tenure. Support for this argument is that Article 16 is considered when acquisition is carried out under other statutes, including the Land Acquisitions Act, while under the Urban and Regional Planning Act (No. 3 of 2015), acquisition is provided for under Section 48.

Acquisition of land for large scale investments

Acquisition of property is permitted under the Urban and Regional Planning Act (No. 3 of 2015) by virtue of the powers under Section 3 in the Lands Acquisition Act (Chapter 189 of the Laws of Zambia). Thus, in relation to land under statutory tenure, the state may compulsorily take over property from individuals or companies provided that it adheres to the provisions of the Lands Acquisition Act. The argument that the Act only applies to statutory tenure is somewhat misleading, since tracts of land under customary tenure have been acquired by the state under the Lands Acquisition Act and the vestment clause in the Lands Act. The argument is that acquisition is possible on both statutory as well as customary land since all land in Zambia is vested in the president, irrespective of the tenure it is held under. The question which the NGOs can interrogate is the acquisition of customary land by the president without consulting the community being displaced.

Acquisition of land has one fundamental principle, and that is it must be to achieve a public purpose. However, compensation must be paid to the owner. The owner may challenge the lawfulness of the acquisition or amount of compensation in a court of law, as was illustrated in the decision *Zambia National Holdings Limited and United National Independence Party (UNIP) v The Attorney-General* (1993–1994, ZR 115 SC). The appellants petitioned the high court, challenging a decision by the respondent to compulsorily acquire the appellants' land, known as the UNIP headquarters, being stand No. 10934, Lusaka. The decision about the case challenged the constitutionality and legality of the compulsory acquisition and the refusal of the high court to grant an interlocutory injunction restraining the respondent from taking possession of, occupying or entering the said land. The court went ahead to define *malafides* (bad faith) and held that, although the executive's (meaning the state's in this case) statutory action could be challenged legally if made in bad faith, the circumstances in this case did not disclose any form of *malafides*. The grounds for appeal on this point were deemed insufficient on the basis that the action by the state demonstrated the highest regard for public interest by ensuring that only properties acquired using state funds were compulsorily acquired. In other words, the decision of the state to acquire the land was made in good faith and in the interest of the public, following the requirements of the acquisition laws.

In spite of the constitutional provision to protect individual rights to land or property, compulsory acquisition of land rights is permitted under the Lands Acquisition Act. Section 3 of the Act stipulates: 'Subject to the provisions of this Act, the President may, whenever he is of the opinion that it is desirable or expedient in the interests of the Republic so to do, compulsorily acquire any property of any description.' The section does not specifically set out the instances in which the president may decide that it is 'desirable' or 'expedient' to expropriate property, and thus this remains largely within the president's subjective determination (Taher 2018). It is clear from the legislative point of view that the president may exercise their discretion or opinion that a particular property, including land, is required in the interest of the public to acquire that land, but payment of adequate compensation should follow. The two questions that need to be addressed are what amounts to 'public interest' under the Act and whether public interest litigation is permitted under the Lands Acquisition Act which NGOs such as ZLA can take up on behalf of the communities.

Protecting land rights under customary tenure

The constitutional protection from deprivation of property is under Article 16, while Articles 20 and 21 refer to protection of freedom of expression and freedom of assembly and association respectively. The constitutional provisions in Zambia's national laws can be compared to the guidelines on freedom of association and assembly in Africa. It should be noted that Article 21 of the Constitution needs to be revised for two main reasons. First, the Constitution was enacted before the guidelines were issued, and second, Article 21 makes no reference to civil society since the requirement of registration came into effect in 2015, long after the enactment of the Constitution. Of importance for the amendment to the national constitution is guideline No. 7, which provides that

> National legislation on freedom of association, where necessary, shall be drafted with the aim of facilitating and encouraging the establishment of associations and promoting their ability to pursue their objectives. Such legislation shall be drafted and amended on the basis of broad and inclusive processes including dialogue and meaningful consultation with civil society. (African Commission on Human and Peoples' Rights 2017)

In addition, guideline No. 8, if incorporated into the constitutional provisions, will allow CSOs in Zambia to operate more freely to achieve their objectives in protecting the land rights of rural communities without fear of harassment and intimidation by the state. The voluntary element of participating or choosing not to participate is an important aspect of freedom of assembly and association, and this is the emphasis in guideline No. 8 (See Elgak, Hummeida and Suliman 2014). The choice to exercise the right to freedom of association must always be voluntary; individuals shall not be compelled to join associations, and shall always be free to leave them.8 Those founding and belonging to an association may choose whom to admit as members, subject to the prohibition on discrimination.

Social movements or protest refer, in this context, to popular mobilisation in support of a collective grievance (Alexander, Runciman, Ngwane, Moloto, Mokgele and van Staden 2018). The definition is restricted to gatherings aiming to address issues of land access and use and ownership rights of rural communities and land disputes that arise from the interaction of statutory tenure and customary tenure.

Making reference to equitable access and use and ownership of land, the dual land tenure in Zambia has created several conflicts.

----

8 See the Universal Declaration of Human Rights, Article 20(2) as well as Nkpa v. Nkume, Nigerian Court of Appeal (2000), para. 51.

When comparing one system to the other, customary tenure is dependent on its shared social equilibrium, and its protection of the 'living ancestors' and the sacred groves, its judicial system, its custodianship of the land and protection of the land rights of its villager usufructuaries are unwritten. The rule of law is therefore achieved more easily in a customary system where there are no written rules whatsoever, and where the chief or the traditional authority, if correctly placed in control, is not corrupted, overly dictatorial or weak.

The conflict that CSOs have to deal with in relation to land becomes very clear when the enactment of the substantive land law is being questioned. The question is whether interventions from civil societies can resolve the historic conflicts between registered land and informal and customary land, a feature common to most African countries. In Zambia, such conflicts are common and spread throughout the country. The next part of the chapter addresses challenges to NGOs and their persecution, as well as the cases in which NGOs have intervened.

Challenges to and persecution of NGOs in Zambia

Zambia has a functioning multi-party democracy with regular and free elections. Despite this, there is a trend towards shrinking civic space resulting in a strained relationship between government and civil society (Baldus, Berger-Kern, Hetz, Poppe and Wolff 2019). In order for NGOs to fully carry out their duties as complementary partners to the government (Pompidou Group 2015), there is need for them to be let alone, but this is not what is happening, as described by the former Patriotic Front (PF) government's manifesto criticising the Movement for Multi-Party Democracy (MMD) government:

> Civil society organisations and the state are essentially fraught with suspicion, antagonism and conflict due to lack of appreciation by the MMD government of the role of civil society as a partner in national development. Consequently civil society has found it difficult to play its meaningful role in the area of social justice, good governance and national development. (Government of the Republic of Zambia, Patriotic Front 2011-2016 Manifesto p.48)

However, the Zambian government generally tends to perceive 'NGOs involved in service provision as partners', but 'those involved in advocacy and governance work to be unsettling and provocative' (Baldus, Berger-Kern, Hetz, Poppe, and Wolff 2019, p. 19).

There are a number of challenges and persecutions that NGOs face, which include legal restrictions on freedom of association and assembly, complicated registration procedures and administrative hurdles, attempts at political delegitimization, extra-legal forms of restriction and outright repression. The most prominent strategy for weakening domestic civil society groups is to cut them off from international support, for instance through the adoption of NGO laws that restrict or prohibit foreign funding for (certain types of) civil society organization (Carothers and Brechenmacher 2014). Pertinent to this paper is the freedom of association and assembly.

Civil society and the fundamental right to freedom of association and assembly

Freedom of association is the cornerstone of effective civil society as it allows people to come together to improve their lives, communities, and the world at large (Scott 2018). Freedom of association is not a matter of good will or special concessions from any government; it is a duty. Freedom of association is a fundamental human right embodied in labour movements, freedom of expression, democracy, and among other international instruments ratified by states. It is an obligation of governments to respect freedom of association and avoid threatening civil society organizations or activists (Silen 2010).

At a continental level, the African Charter on Human and People's Rights stipulates under Article 45 (1b) that the African Commission is mandated 'to formulate and lay down principles and rules aimed at solving legal problems relating to human and peoples' rights and fundamental freedoms.' The guidelines provide that the right to freedom of association and assembly is fundamental and should underpin all democratic societies in which individuals can freely express their views on all issues concerning their society. These issues include land rights of the rural communities. The guidelines provide human rights defenders in Africa with a working and advocacy tool to convince states and parties to take them into account when drafting laws that affect rural communities and their rights. Using litigation as a tool to uphold customary tenure in Zambia has not proven to be a positive mechanism in resolving land disputes. Therefore, NGOs dealing with these issues need to think again about alternate methods to succeed in this fight.

Alternatives to litigation to resolve land disputes

The question worthy of interrogating is why customary land rights holders are not using alternates to litigation to protect their rights. Litigation is an action brought in court to enforce a particular right. It is also an act or process of bringing a lawsuit in and of itself – a judicial contest of any dispute (Silwamba, Limyama and Jalasi 2021). From the analysis of the two Mpongwe cases, it suffices to say that litigation favours statutory land rights held by registered large scale farmers at the expense of the rural poor, who end up being displaced from their customary land. Hence, there is a need for NGOs to embrace alternative dispute resolution (ADR) methods to resolve these land disputes.

ADR was developed as an alternative to the traditional dispute resolution mechanism, litigation, which is costly, time consuming, does not give the parties control over the outcome of their disputes and is generally cumbersome (Mwenda 2006). ADR refers to a variety of techniques for resolving disputes without resorting to litigation in the courts (Mwenda 2006). The idea behind the introduction of ADR was to reduce delays and costs associated with litigation, to introduce relatively less formal methods of dispute resolution, to introduce consensual problem solving, to empower individuals by enabling them to control the outcome of their dispute and to develop dispute resolution mechanisms that preserve personal and business relationships. In the case of rural communities, this would be much more appropriate in resolving customary versus statutory land disputes. ADR methods, when used effectively, are intended to produce better outcomes all around. However, to ensure that disputes are resolved speedily and cheaply, the parties have to choose a forum that fits the fuss. In land disputes, the NGOs need to choose an appropriate ADR method that suits the facts of a particular dispute. This is because each ADR mechanism is convenient for some issues and not others.

ADR methods include mediation, arbitration, negotiation, facilitation, med-arb, mini-trials, peer review, conciliation, neutral evaluation, settlement conferences, community dispute resolution programs and adjudication. For the purposes of this chapter, only negotiation, arbitration and mediation will be explained because they are the most suitable ADR methods for resolving land issues.

Negotiation as a method to resolve land disputes

Negotiation is the most basic means of settling differences (Mnookin 1998). It is the back-and-forth communication between the parties to the conflict with the goal of trying to find a solution. This process does not involve an impartial or neutral third party. Hence, the parties work together to come to a compromise. The parties may also choose to be represented by their lawyers during negotiations (Hartje 1984). Civil society organisations such as the ZLA, that work with rural communities in protecting their land rights as well as advocating for the preservation of customary land, should adopt negotiation as a tool to resolve land disputes instead of resorting to litigation. Negotiation enables the parties to sit down and discuss the solution to their problem; thus the parties own the outcome(s) themselves and therefore peace is maintained between the parties. In instances where negotiation fails, parties can always use an alternative ADR method.

Arbitration – the less favourable method for resolving land disputes

Arbitration, unlike negotiation and mediation, is more of a litigation process conducted outside the court of law. It involves the disputants submitting their disputes for a decision to be made by one or more private persons rather than going to a court of law. The person designated is called an arbitrator or arbitrators (McRoberts Solicitors 2015). This type of dispute resolution forum is mostly used in disputes where the question at issue is best suited to be determined by a person or persons with requisite skills or knowledge and where it is hoped that the delays, expense and publicity which are common features in state court systems can be avoided (McRoberts Solicitors 2015).

Looking at land issues involving large scale investments in Zambia, the individuals in displaced communities are usually vulnerable and can be advised by the NGOs to use arbitration to resolve the disputes. Using arbitration as an alternative to litigation will ensure that land disputes are dealt with without delay.

Mediation – the more favourable method for resolving land disputes

Mediation, on the other hand, is an informal process which involves bringing a third party to go between the disputing parties to help them settle a dispute (Staff 2020). The mediator, unlike an arbitrator, does not hear evidence, and the mediation process is not binding on the parties.

There is room for appeal to a court of law (Staff 2020). The mediator meets the parties for discussion and tries to bring them together through discussions and caucusing (separating the parties in a dispute and having discussions with each party privately).

Mediation, as an ADR method, can be used in most non-criminal matters such as those involving verbal harassment. It can also be used in disputes with neighbours over an encroaching bush or the brightness of their outdoor lights, as well as landlords and tenants disputes (Findlaw 2016). This mechanism, if used by NGOs to help resolve customary land issues, can yield positive results. In cases where there is tension between the community representatives and the large scale company, caucusing is the best solution, not allowing parties to see each other until tension is reduced by only communicating through the mediator. The ZLA could have successfully used this method to assist the rural communities in the two Mpongwe cases to protect their customary rights to land.

Way forward

The Mpongwe cases analysed above have attracted a lot of attention both nationally and internationally. However the struggle for the communities that have been adversely affected continues, as they remain homeless and without a livelihood. CSOs can only act as mediators between the large scale commercial farmers and the rural communities in light of the decisions made by the Supreme Court of Zambia, which are binding on both parties. Until the state is able to resolve the issue of tenure security between statutory and customary tenure, land disputes will continue. The possibility of rural communities being protected by enhancing their abilities to access and own land for the purposes of making a livelihood will not be a reality. As long as the state continues its harassment and intimidation of CSOs trying to advocate for the land rights of rural communities, the battle continues. The social movements and their encounters with dominant capital and the state will deepen without resolving land disputes.

References

Alexander, P., Runciman, C., Ngwane, T., Moloto, B., Mokgele, K. and van Staden, N. (2018) 'Frequency and turmoil: South Africa's community protests (2005 – 2017)', *South African Crime Quarterly*, 63

Amone C. and Lakwo C. (2014) 'Customary land ownership and underdevelopment in northern Uganda', *Pertanika Journal of Social Science and Humanities*, 2(3)

Archer T. W., (2016) ' Investigating the Impact of Social Tenure Domain Model (STDM) on Tenure Security – A Case Study of Mission STDM Pilot', Masters' Thesis, University of Twente, The Netherlands

Baldus, J., Berger-Kern, N., Hetz, F., Poppe, A. E., and Wolff, J. (2019) Preventing Civic Space Restrictions: an Exploratory Study of Successful Resistance against NGO Laws, (Peace Research Institute Frankfurt Reports, 1)

Carothers, T. and Brechenmacher, S. (2014) Closing Space. Democracy and Human Rights Support Under Fire, Washington, DC, Carnegie Endowment for International Peace

Chu, J. M. (2013) Creating a Zambian Breadbasket: 'Land grabs' and foreign investments in agriculture in Mkushi District, Zambia, Working Paper 33, Rotterdam, The Land Deal Politics Initiative (LDPI)

Crowe S., Cresswell K., Robertson A., Huby G., Avery A., and Sheikh A. (2011) 'The Case Study Approach', BMC Medical Research Methodology, University of Nottingham

Elone, J. (2009) 'Backlash against democracy: the regulation of civil society in Africa', *Democracy and Society*, 7(2)

FindLaw (2016) 'Mediation Cases: What Cases are Eligible for Mediation?' https://www.findlaw.com/adr/mediation/mediation-cases-what-cases-are-eligible-for-mediation.html accessed 11 February 2021

Government of the Republic of Zambia (GRZ) (2011) Patriotic Front 2011-2016 Manifesto, Lusaka

Hansungule, M. (2001) *1995 Lands Act: An Obstacle or Instrument of Development?* (Report), Lusaka, Zambia Land Alliance

Harding, A., Chamberlain W., Maluleke I., Niassy, S., Anseeuw W., and Manco, G. (2016) 'Large-scale land acquisitions profile, Zambia'

Hartje, J. (1984) 'Lawyer's skills in Negotiations: Justice in Unseen Hands,' *Journal of Dispute Resolution*, University of Missouri, School of Law

Kothari, C. K. (2004) *Research Methodology. Method and Techniques* (1st edition), New Delhi, New Age International Publishers

Law Association of Zambia National Legal Aid Clinic for Women (2016) Report on Zambia's Legal Framework on Land Acquisition and Security of Tenure, December, Lusaka

Lemmen, C. (2010) *The Social Tenure Domain Model: a Pro-Poor Land Tool*, Copenhagen, International Federation of Surveyors

McRoberts Solicitors (2015) *McRoberts on Scottish Construction Contracts* (3rd edition), Wiley Blackwell, Sussex

Media Institute of Southern African (2014) Public sphere under threat in Zambia as press freedom violations mount, Lusaka, Freedom House. https://www.ifex.org/zambia/2014/06/02/public_sphere/, accessed 4 January 2021

Ministry of Lands (2017) The Draft National Land Policy, Lusaka, Ministry of Lands, Natural Resources and Environmental Planning

Mnookin, R. (1998) 'Alternative Dispute Resolution,' Haward Law School, Discussion Paper Series, Paper 232

Mutesa, F. (2009) *State, Civil Society and Donor Relations in Zambia*, Lusaka, University of Zambia Press

Mwenda, W. S. (2006) 'Paradigm of alternative dispute resolution and justice delivery in Zambia', Doctorate of Law, University of South Africa, Pretoria

Odum, H.W. and Jocher, K. (1929) *An Introduction to Social Research*, New York, Henry Holt

Ponce, C. (2012) Limitations to Freedom of Association of Civil Society Organizations in Latin America: Comparative view and special case study of Nicaragua, Bolivia, Ecuador, Cuba and Venezuela, https://www.ohchr.org/Documents/ Issues/FAssociation/Responses2012/other_contributions/World-Report_of_ Sr.Ponce_on_Free_Asociation_in_Latin_Am.pdf, accessed 4 January 2021

Scott, M. (2018) The Guide to Opening Government: An Enabling Environment for Civil Society Organizations, Washington DC, International Centre for Not-for-profit Law Open Government Partnership

Silen, C. E. P. (2010) Limitations to Freedom of Association of Civil Society Organizations in Latin America: Comparative View and Special Case Study of Nicaragua, Bolivia, Ecuador, Cuba and Venezuela, South Carolina, CreateSpace Independent Publishing Platform,

Silwamba E , Linyama L, and Jalasi J. A., (2021) International Comparative Legal Guides, https//iclg.com, accessed 11 February 2021

Staff, P. (2020) 'What are the Three Basic types of Dispute Resolutions? What to know about Mediation, Arbitration and Litigation', Harvard Law School Blog, https://www.pon.harvard.edu/daily/dispute-resolution/what-are-the-three-basic-types-of-dispute-resolution-what-to-know-about-mediation-arbitration-and-litigation/, accessed 11 February 2021

Taher, N. (2018) 'Lands acquisition act and its influence on investor confidence in Zambia; judicial approaches to defining public interest', (unpublished undergraduate research paper), University of Zambia/Zambia Centre for Accountancy Studies University

United Nations (2007) Declaration on the Rights of Indigenous People, New York, UN General Assembly, 13 September

Wilberforce T. (2016) 'Investigating the Impact of Social Tenure Domain Model (STDM) on Tenure Security: A Case Study of Mission STDM Pilot', Netherlands, Master's thesis, University of Twente

Zambia Land Alliance (2019) 'Fact Sheet, Roadmap to the Formulation of the National Land Policy in Zambia', Lusaka, ZLA

Zambia Land Alliance-Food, Agriculture and Natural Resources Policy Analysis Network, (2007), Civil Society Position on Zambia's Draft Land Policy of October 2006, Lusaka

Cases

Mpongwe Development Corporation Limited v Francis Kamanda and 51 Others, Appeal No.137 of 2007

Mpongwe Development Company Limited v Francis Kamanda and Others SCZ Judgement No.14 of 2010

Mpongwe Development Company Limited v Francis Kamanda and 51 Others SCZ Judgement No.137of 2007

United States v. Mitchel [1983] 463 U.S. 206

Zambia National Holdings Limited and United National Independence Party v. The Attorney-General (1993 - 1994) ZR 115 (SC)

Legislation

The Constitution of Zambia 1991 as amended by Act No.18 of 1996 and Act No. 2 of 2016

The Lands Acquisition Act, chapter 189 of the Laws of Zambia

The Lands Act, chapter 184 of the Laws of Zambia

The Non-Governmental Organisations Act No. 16 of 2009

The Urban and Regional Planning Act, No. 3 of 2015

CHAPTER 4

Understanding land conflicts in Mozambique: the case of Nhamatanda district

Uacitissa Mandamule

Introduction

There are various interests around the land, ranging from political and economic to social and even cultural interests. Land conflicts are there-fore a normal expression of this diversity of interests in the relation-ships that exist for access to and use of land (Roy 1991). Land conflicts can be defined as a misuse, restriction or dispute over rights of access to, possession of and use of land (Wehrmann, 2008), and may involve individuals, families or legal persons, including companies, and these in their relationship with the state or public administration institutions.

Conflicts are one of the best indicators of the functioning of a local society, revealing knowledge of its operating standards and codes (Bierschenk and Sardan 1994). Depending on the nature of the rights contested, conflicts can take several forms:

- *Conflicts over boundaries*: these relate to exceeding boundaries and non-compliance with the boundaries of a given plot of land. This situation is more frequent in contexts of strong pressure on land and scarcity of cultivable land.

- *Conflicts over rights*: these are disputes over the rights users have over a given area, and one or more of these rights may be contested. These are the right of access, the right of possession, the right to use, the right to manage and the right to dispose of or sell.

- *Conflict of rules*: this refers to the complexity of the legal framework (the coexistence of customary law, the main reference framework in rural areas, and the statutory, modern law of the state), insofar as different bodies contribute to land management and the granting of rights over the same spaces, resulting in conflicts (Chaveau and Mathieu 1998).

Land conflicts can occur in various dimensions – individual, family, community or institutional. The dimension refers to the scope in which the conflict takes place, depending on the parties involved and the nature of the rights contested (discussed further later in this chapter).

Table 4.1 shows that, from 2005 to 2010, there were about 548 cases of land conflict throughout the country, of which 475 were resolved. From 2013 to 2014, about 107 cases were registered and 61 were resolved. Of these conflicts, more than half occurred in the province of Tete, which has a significant presence of extractive projects. In 2016, 23 cases were registered and 11 cases were resolved. Of these cases, 11 occurred in Maputo province (Salimo 2017).

Table 4.1: Cases of land conflicts registered and resolved (2013 to 2016)

Year	Registered cases	Resolved cases	Pending cases
2005 to 2010	548	475	73
2013 to 2014	107	61	46
2016	23	11	12

Source: Salimo (2017)

Although it is an important avenue for research and an element for understanding the dimensions of the land conflicts currently underway in the country, the data presented above, from the then Ministry of Land, Environment and Rural Development (MITADER), excludes conflicts that are not brought to the attention of the institutions of justice, either because they are resolved at the family level, or because of lack of knowledge about the legal procedures to be followed for this purpose, with rare cases where conflicts of a family nature are referred to the community courts. Previous studies had already indicated that the proportion of cases not reported to formal or informal institutions was quite significant and that most land conflicts were resolved in informal institutions (Baleira 2010).

This chapter presents the agrarian structure and results of land conflict mapping in Nhamatanda district in Sofala province, which has experienced strong pressure on land and other natural resources, partly due to its strategic location along the Beira Corridor, its agro-ecological conditions and its resource potential, which are favourable to the development of agro-livestock activities.

Methodological description

This study was carried out in two phases:

Project design and networking ran from May to December 2018. Exploratory interviews and consultations were carried out with organisations working in the field of natural resources and active in the study site, among which : Centro Terra Viva (CTV), Fundação Iniciativa para Terras Comunitárias (Community Lands Initiative Foundation – iTC-f), Centro de Formação Jurídica e Judiciária (Centre for Legal and Judicial Training - CFJJ), Organização Rural de Ajuda Mútua (Rural Mutual Aid Organisation - ORAM) and União Nacional dos Camponeses (National Peasants Union – UNAC). These consultations helped, on the one hand, to provide preliminary data, important for the identification of places of conflict and main causes. On the other hand these organisations helped in establishing contacts and setting up a network of local informants and enquiries.

The **research and reporting phase** began in January 2019, and consisted of a review of the literature on land conflicts and their resolution in Mozambique and other eastern and sub-Saharan African countries, followed by data collection on the ground. The study focused on land conflicts, specifically mapping places of conflict, number of conflicts, motive, actors involved, type of rights claimed and forms of resolution adopted in each situation.

Data collection in the field consisted of 15 semi-structured interviews with men and women from local communities, five focus groups and 162 questionnaires conducted with individuals. The data collection in the field was followed by capturing the data from the questionnaires, analysis using the statistics programme SPSS, and interpretation. At each site, officials from the Serviços Distritais de Actividades Económicas (District Economic Activities Service – SDAE) were interviewed, including heads of administrative posts, localities and community authorities, members of communities and peasants.

In order to select respondents, fieldwork proceeded by iteration, a methodology that invites a deliberate choice from people to be included in the research, in a continuous process of coming and going of a field researcher (Sardan 2017). According to Sardan (2017), iteration begins with the researcher going to household X, which tells him to go to the household Y on the other side of the village or neighborhood, then back to the household Z, which lives near household X. This is a methodology in which the interlocutors are not chosen by a specific selection method, but deliberately, according to the researcher's plans and research objectives (Cohen and Manion 1994). From each interview new clues emerge and new possible interlocutors, suggested directly or indirectly during the interview (Sardan 2017:50).

Land conflicts in Africa

There is a vast literature on land conflicts in Africa (Lund, Odgaard, and Sjaastad 2006, Meur *et al.* 2006, Moyo 2012).

In a study on access to land in Uganda, Kigula (1993) presents the nature and typology of land conflicts, which the author divides into four categories:

- private vs. private conflict
- intra-family conflict (family member vs. family member)
- 'invaders' vs. government
- corporations vs. privates/groups.

In places where there is land availability, low population density and relatively strong socio-cultural and historical links between communities, the incidence of land conflict tends to be reduced. Where there are more migrants, land conflicts are more prevalent, mainly due to ethnic differences between locals and 'outsiders', and also because of the fear of insecurity of tenure (Kigula 1993). Addressing land policies in Uganda, Gay (2014) notes that in recent years land conflicts in Uganda have increased, in part because of the strong penetration of capital through oil companies, in part because of the increase in formal and informal land transactions (lease and sale) leading to land shortages, and because of the very nature of the legal system, which advocates a plurality of conflict management and resolution systems.

Another survey of land conflicts in Uganda found that a significant proportion (20 per cent) of land conflicts occurring in the country are not reported to any conflict resolution institution, and that this is a potential precursor to social tensions that could erupt into violence. This is indicative, the study indicates, of the fragility of land management and administration institutions and their inefficiency in addressing issues of property conflicts, boundaries, transmission, occupation, transgression, fraudulent transactions and inheritance disputes (Rugadya 2009).

In Kenya, land conflicts result not only from the colonial legacy of expropriation and deprivation of indigenous peoples' access and use rights, but also from political issues and the rampant exploitation of resources that creates pressure on land and generates conflict among communities. Attempts to regain land governance for electoral gain and seizure of power are also at the root of land conflicts in the country (Golaz and Médard 2015, Onguny and Gillies 2019). Informal institutions such as community elders and traditional leaders have, throughout the country's history, played an important role in the management and resolution of land conflicts (Yamano and Deininger 2005).

In Botswana, as well as intensifying in recent years, land conflicts have also increased social inequalities and created new hotbeds of injustice and political instability. Migration from rural to urban and mining areas has intensified informal land transactions in peri-urban areas and led to conflicts between local people and migrants eager to purchase agricultural land and housing in new locations. Conflicts intensify when these migrants resolve to return to their areas of origin and claim rights over a part of their family or clan, part of which may have been transferred to other migrants, or occupied by another family or clan member (Kalabamu 2019).

Mbonde (2015) assesses the causes of conflicts over land use in Tanzania, based on case studies in two villages in the Kongwa and Dodoma regions. The results indicate that the conflicts are mainly caused by invasion of fields by pastoralists' cattle, the lack of demarcation and duplicate land sales. The effects of the conflicts may include violence and deaths (Mbonde 2015).

Another aspect at the root of land conflicts in many African countries has to do with conservation issues. While conservation aims to protect natural resources, it can increase competition and pressure on land and other natural resources. Conflicts arise mainly within the conservation areas where previously established local populations have restricted access to forest resources, which form the basis of their livelihoods, while at the same time running the risk of attacks by wild animals feeding on their crops (Lund, Odgaard, and Sjaastad 2006).

In Mozambique, several studies have mentioned the relationship between the strong penetration of capital and the occurrence of land conflicts, including situations of loss of land use right titles (Direito de Uso e Aproveitamento da Terra – DUAT) by local populations in favour of large companies in the agro-business, extractive industry, infrastructure and tourism sectors (Baleira and Castro 2016, Selemane 2017, UNAC and GRAIN 2015).

This resonates with the findings of Mandamule (2016) in previous work. For this author, land conflicts in Mozambique take place against a backdrop of increased capital penetration in rural areas, with effects on access to land and security of land ownership for communities. Allied to these factors are the delays in the process of allocation of DUATs owing to the lack of effective control and monitoring at the level of state institutions of existing areas and those already under concession, which culminates in double allocations and, therefore, in conflicts with severe impacts on land occupiers, especially women and vulnerable groups. Mention is also made of land conflicts between members of the same family, between two communities, or between companies and communities, focusing on limits, inheritance, or the right to access and enjoy land.

Figure 4.1: Number of small and medium-sized holdings per district – Sofala

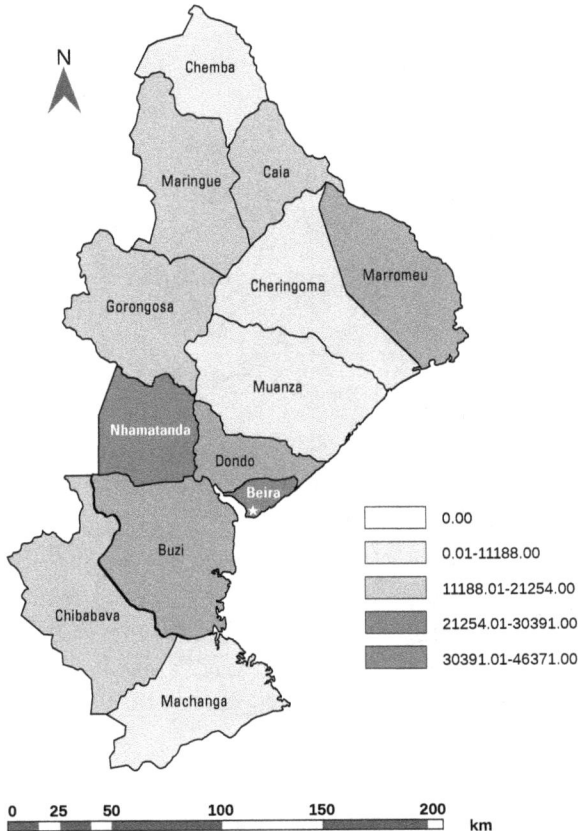

Based on OMR (2019)

The agrarian structure of Nhamatanda district

Located along the Beira Corridor, Nhamatanda district is about 100 km from the provincial capital of Sofala, Beira, and is bordered by the districts of Gorongosa, Búzi, Gondola and Dondo. In addition to some mineral resources, such as gold in Mafufo in the locality of Siluvo and Mecombezi in Matenga, and the production of stones from the Khura, Siluvo, Nharuchonga and Chiro mountains, the district has agricultural and livestock potential, with about 278,567 hectares of arable land, of which only 50 per cent is in use (SDAE 2019).

In Nhamatanda district, as in most other districts of the province of Sofala, small and medium-sized family farms predominate – that is, with less than 10 hectares and below 50 hectares, respectively, a combination of crops is also a common practice. (see Figure 4.1).

Figure 4.2: Number of large exploitations per district – Sofala

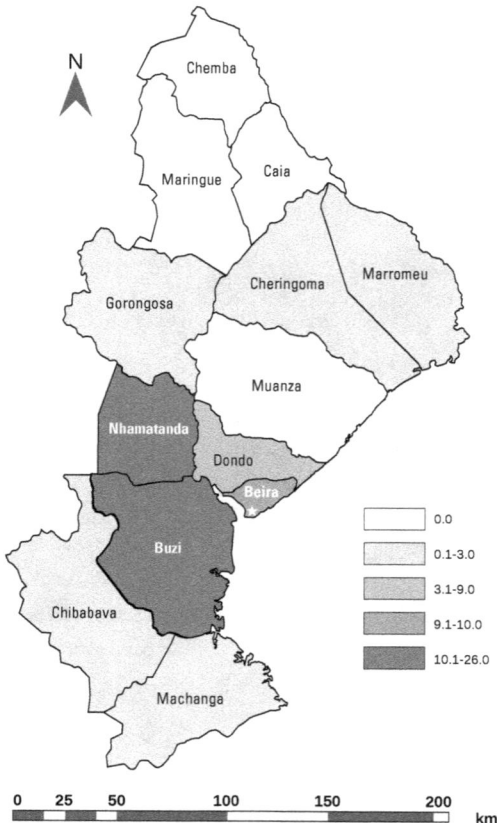

Based on OMR (2019)

Nhamatanda district also has a considerable number of farms larger than 50 hectares (28 in total) compared to the other districts of Sofala province, corresponding to 35.9 per cent of the total number of large farms in the district and 50.1 per cent of the cultivated area, as shown in Figure 4.2.

Most of the plots are not titled and the man in the family is responsible for the plot, although in most cases the land is worked by women working alone or with the help of the children of the family (MAE 2014).

Land conflicts in Nhamatanda district: a descriptive analysis

Understanding the dynamics of land conflict in a given location involves examining the main forms of access to and transmission of rights over land. A recent study of rural land markets in the Beira Corridor indicated inheritance as the main form of accessing and transmitting land rights in Nhamatanda district, followed by purchase and sale without DUAT, at 29.6 per cent and 23.9 per cent respectively, as shown in Graph 4.1:

Graph 4.1: Forms of land access in Nhamatanda

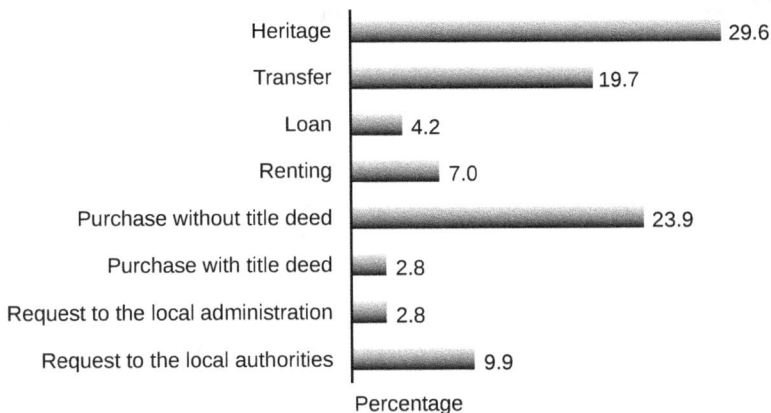

Source: Mandamule and Manhicane Jr 2019

The graph allows us to categorise land conflicts in Nhamatanda district along three dimensions: family, community and institutional. This categorisation takes into account the actors involved, the causes or motivating factors of the conflict and the mechanisms in instances of resolution in which the conflict is addressed. Each dimension corresponds to an arena where conflicts take place and where a set of specific rights are claimed by the parties involved.

The arena is the social space where conflicts and disputes take place. The arena implies that, in a community, not all actors have the same interests or the same representations of reality, and each will tend to maximise their own objectives (Bierschenk and Sardan 1994).

Each of the areas and the type of conflicts arising from them are presented later in the chapter, when the results of the research in Nhamatanda are presented.

Family dimension

The family is still the main institution for the acquisition of rights over land, and the transmission of inheritance of family property and land ownership is also determined by kinship ties. Article 16(1) of the land law (*Lei de Terras no. 19/97 de 1 de Outubro* de 1997) establishes that the right to land use may be transmitted by inheritance, without distinction according to sex, but in practice this has not been observed, giving rise to intra-family disputes (see Table 4.2).

Table 4.2: Dimensions and nature of intra-family conflicts

Dimension	Sub-dimension	Nature of conflicts
Family	Inheritance	• Conflicts between members of the same family (brothers vs. sisters; uncles vs. nephews); • Conflicts over the expulsion of a woman following the death of her spouse
	Exercise of power in the family	• Conflicts of rights (access and control) between men and women; • Conflicts over the expulsion of women after divorce

Source: Mandamule 2017

This first sub-dimension of intra-family conflicts refers to land conflicts resulting from the mechanisms for transmitting inheritance rights, on one hand between male children, who have direct inheritance rights to agricultural land, livestock, housing and property, unlike women (Forum Mulher 2018), in patrilineal societies such as those studied in Nhamatanda district. On the other hand, it is traditionally claimed that women are passing through the land of their parents until they enter into marriage, except that this does not result in the protection of their rights. In fact, when a man dies, his widow is fourth in the hierarchy of inheritance, after his children, father/paternal uncles, and brother/daughter (Gengenbach 1998). With divorce, the woman loses the rights she acquired with the marriage, and in some cases is even forced to leave the couple's land and property, returning to her parents' home (Fórum Mulher 2018, Muteia 1996).

It is said that women's land rights are provisional, as they can easily be extinguished following divorce or death of the spouse, as illustrated by the example below:

> In 2013, there was a conflict between two families because after the man's death, the woman was forced to leave the house and leave the field because she had not had a child with the deceased. The case reached the community court where it was decided that the husband's family should return the *machamba* [piece of farm land] and the house to the deceased's wife.
>
> (Interview with a community leader,
> Bebedo, Mulongoziwa village, 18 May 2019)

Another factor at the origin of disputes over land has to do with the exercise of power within the family. Here a distinction must be made between rights of access (the right to enter a given space and use it safely) and the right of control (the possibility of deciding on forms of land use and the purpose of production). Although women have access to the land of their parents or spouse, and they participate in the entire production process (hoeing, cultivation, irrigation, and so on), they do not have the power to decide what to produce or the destination of produce for cash crops.

Observations in the field also indicated the existence of other conflicts within the family dimension, related to overstepping limits and crossing boundary markers, which occur mainly on family farms.

Community dimension

> The owner of a [piece of] land gave the space to a family in 1992. In 2012 the same lady sold the space to another family, without knowledge of the first [family] to whom she had sold the space. Upon realizing the presence of the new occupants, the family that acquired the land in the first place was to expel them and those remained in the open.
>
> (Survey, Siluvo locality, 16 May 2019)

The community dimension corresponds to conflicts that occur mainly between neighbours or individuals within a given community. Among the causes of the disputes are the different uses of the land (agriculture, pastoralism, mining, extraction of medicinal plants, and so on) within the same space, issues related to limits and boundary markers, and even issues resulting from transactions such as buying and selling space. Limit conflicts often occur in production areas: the more productive the land, the more competition for its access and use. Table 4.2 shows conflicts arising in the community dimension.

The strong population growth and the rapid urbanization that accompany it have expanded the rural land market in the Nhamatanda district. These transactions do not happen without conflict, as indicated in previous studies (Mandamule and Manhicane Jr 2019). The duplicate sale of spaces is an element in the origin of conflicts related to the sale of land, as well as, in cases of temporary lease-type transactions, the refusal to return the leased space after the agreed period for exploration, as can be seen in the example that follows:

> The owner of the *machamba* [plot of farm land] says she is very upset by the fact that, two years ago, she gave up her *machamba* to another lady, for the production of vegetables. The *machamba* was located in a low area, close to a river, and was suitable for the production of vegetables. Last year, when the owner decided to recover her field, the other [person] who produced vegetables did not accept to return the space, claiming to want to buy. To this, the owner of the field simply set limits and started using the area to produce her own crops, much to the displeasure of the lady who rented the field.
>
> (Interview with a woman in Siluvo, Nharuchonga,
> 1° bairro, 15 May 2019)

Currently, to make transactions safer and prevent future conflicts, agreements are made in writing, in the presence of witnesses who may be members of the family, in the case of a *machamba* or family space, or of the association, if the space provided is within an area with an association. The document is signed by the parties involved and the information goes to the community authorities, for a record of the presence of the new occupant and the legitimacy of the agreement.

Table 4.3: Community dimension of conflicts and their nature

Dimension	Sub-dimension	Types of land conflicts
Community	Actors	• Conflicts between farmers and poachers • Conflicts between farmers and artisanal miners • Conflicts between local and nomadic producers • Conflicts between native farmers and collectors of medicinal plants • Conflicts between artisanal miners and collectors of medicinal plants • Conflicts of limits and boundary markers between families • Conflicts between peasants and private companies
	Power over the territory	• Conflicts of power of transmission over the territory between ethnic groups • Conflicts between local community leaders (such as traditional chiefs (Régulos), neighborhood secretaries and land chiefs) • Conflicts of power between chiefs of land and sacred administrators • Conflicts between native and migrant families (nomads) • Challenges to the power of local authorities by local people
	Location of the area	• Land conflicts in irrigated areas • Land conflicts in rain-fed areas • Conflicts in fallow areas • Conflicts over invasion of places of worship • Degradation of family/community cemeteries
	Registration and title deeds	• Conflicts due to lack of registration of individual rights • Conflicts over dual allocation of land rights • Conflicts in non-delimited communities vs conflicts in delimited communities • Conflicts over norms (customary law vs. codified law) • Conflicts over duplicate land sales

Source: Mandamule (2017) and Werhmann (2008)

Table 4.4: Institutional dimension and nature of land conflicts

Dimension	Sub-dimension	Nature of conflicts
Institutional	Social (Conservation)	<ul><li>Conflicts in the buffer zones to national parks and reserves</li><li>Conflicts within conservation areas</li><li>Conflicts between biodiversity conservation and shifting agriculture (deforestation)</li><li>Conflicts between conservation and poaching</li><li>Disputes over converting forests into residential areas</li><li>Human-wildlife conflict</li></ul>
	Economic	<ul><li>Conflicts over expropriation for public benefit purposes without just compensation</li><li>Conflicts in agricultural investment zones</li><li>Conflicts in logging areas</li><li>Conflicts in areas of major infrastructure projects</li><li>Conflicts in mining areas</li><li>Conflicts between population and tour operators</li><li>Conflicts in urbanized areas</li><li>Resettlement or displacement conflicts</li><li>Conflicts over the allocation of 20 per cent or other community benefits reserved for communities result in of the exploitation of forest resources in areas occupied by communities.</li></ul>
	Political	<ul><li>Conflicts between war returnees and new occupants of the areas</li><li>Conflicts between local residents and military over occupation of their land without authorization</li><li>Conflicts due to the allocation, by the state, of refugee lands to private companies</li></ul>

Source: Mandamule (2017); Werhmann (2008) and Forum Mulher (2018)

Institutional dimension of conflicts

The conflict started in 2010 between members of the Associação Agrícola de Bebedo and members of the community. Association members were prevented from obtaining the DUAT due to lack of agreement with those responsible for neighboring areas. The association still continues to function without having a DUAT in its area of less than 20 hectares.

(Survey, Bebedo, 8.º bairro, 14 May 2019).

Another dimension is added to the previous two, the institutional dimension. With this, we refer to those conflicts, elaborated in Table 4.4, that occur between local populations and institutions, be they public or private, having access to and use of the land as a motivating factor.

There are also conflicts over boundaries between companies (forestry and large cattle breeders), as well as between these and local populations. In the latter case, it is the difficulty of cohabitation of different uses that is the source of conflicts, such as the case of agriculture practiced by local families and breeding of cattle.

The boxes below illustrate three cases of institutional conflict.

Box 4.1: Land conflict between cattle breeders and local population

What is at stake now is the exploiters or the owners of cattle. These are what create problems with communities. For example, we have an affair now with Mr. Kennedy, a cattle owner, in the Mosca de Sono area. He has an area he acquired ... at that time after the destabilization war. After the war, people were refugees in other places ... and when the population returned to their areas of origin, he had already occupied those parcels. So, they started living together there and ... they already have very large animals ... and they are already saying that the population that is in that area has to leave. We mediated twice; the (administrative) head of post of Tica was called, the district director of agriculture also intervened. In 2016, the case reached the provincial directorate of agriculture, where someone from the geography and registration services (Serviços Provinciais de Geografia e Cadastro - SPGC) was mandated to mediate the conflict. It was determined that he [Mr. Kennedy] should leave a part of that area to the community ... Some documents were signed, but unfortunately, even now the conflict continues ... he says that the population has to leave.

(Interview with a Chiadeia administrative official, 16 May 2019)

Box 4.2: Conflict over boundaries in the exploitation
         of forest resources

There is a boundary conflict over the exploitation of forest resources (wood) in the village of Impólio, belonging to this locality (Chiadeia), between Mr. Francisco Challe, owner of the Búzi lumber company, and Interbeira company, based in the village of Sovim, Chiadeia, the concessionaire in the exploitation of this resource since 2011, through a memorandum signed in 2010 between the company, the administrative secretariat and the local management committee, with the knowledge of the District Services for Economic Activities (Serviços Distritais de Actividades Económicas – SDAE) of Nhamatanda, using the license of the Kubassira Association of Chiadeia.

The conflict has been going on for more than three years, at the boundary that separates the two localities, being Chiadeia (District of Nhamatanda) and Guara-Guara (District of Buzi).

In 2013, the logger himself, with the support of some technicians from the Provincial Directorate of Wildlife Management, Sofala, in the absence of structures in this location, delimited the area in an illegal way. The irregularity was declared and a district commission headed by the director of the SDAE was created in the presence of the offender and concluded that the delimitation was illegal and was forced to remove the marks that had already been placed. On the 24th of the current month, he seized the Interbeira truck that was carrying wood for the shipyard and paralyzed the felling work, escorted the truck to Tica, and he and the company representative went to the Tica police station, but due to insufficient evidence, all [charges] were dismissed. In the description … referring to infrastructure, he says that there is no infrastructure on the ground, while the injured [party] says that, at the time, there was an attached room.

(Chiadeia Administrative Village 2018)

Results

This section presents the results of the surveys conducted with members of some communities in the Nhamatanda district, specifically in the localities of Bebedo, Chirassicua, Matenga, Metuchira and Siluvo, in the administrative district of Nhamatanda-Sede, and in the localities of Chiadeia, Nhampoca, and Tica headquarters, in the administrative district of Tica. Respondents were asked about the start date of the dispute, in order to understand the evolution of land conflicts over time. As shown in Graph 4.2, conflicts have long existed in the Nhamatanda district. However, it is possible to perceive a trend towards more cases of conflict since 2014, the result of the search for fertile land for agricultural activity, exploitation of forest and mineral resources,

Box 4.3: Land conflict between a tourist complex and families

In 2017, there was a land conflict involving the owner of the Vila Macumbe tourist complex, with some of the families residing in a portion of the village Impólio, estimated to be 24 families, totaling 98 people. The complex occupies an area of 3,000 hectares, part of which (1,493.5 hectares) had already been demarcated in 2004. The dispute started when the owner of the tourist complex decided to demarcate the other part of the area of his complex. The residents did not agree with this second delimitation, claiming that the demarcation of the 3,000 hectares of the area provided by the state had already been made in 2004 and the placement of the relevant markers carried out.

The head of the locality met with the families in conflict to find out about the facts and concluded that the area in dispute was free and had been reserved by the technicians of the geography and registration services (Serviços Provinciais de Geografia e Cadastro - SPGC) as a housing area, with the participation of members of the community, in the process of delimiting and placing the markers.

In view of the impasse, the head of the locality instructed the owner of the tourist complex to bring the requirements for regularization of the area for certification, and concluded that there were some irregularities such as the absence of the administrator's opinion, a lack of signatures of people present at the signing from the community, and a disparity between the outline and the information the National Land Archive (Njonje = Njangombe; the latter name is the area in dispute).

(Chiadeia Administrative Village, 29 November 2017)

resettlements resulting from catastrophes, and the growth of rural and urban land markets (Mandamule and Manhicane Jr 2019).

Some current conflicts result from transactions or agreements made in another time. In fact, whatever the nature of the transaction (loan, lease or sale), when it happens without the knowledge of the members of the nuclear family (usually wife or children), it is likely to result in confrontation, as in the case presented below:

The conflict happened after the war, where a man had an area of 21 hectares. The children fled the war for Buzi and the father stayed in Chiadeia (Nhamatanda). After a few years, the father fell ill and, because he became ill, he sold part of his land five years ago. After the war was over, the children returned and the father had already lost his life and ... they realized that the father had sold part of the land, then the conflict started. The children wanted their father's land ... and the conflict reached

Graph 4.2: Number of conflicts by year when the conflict started

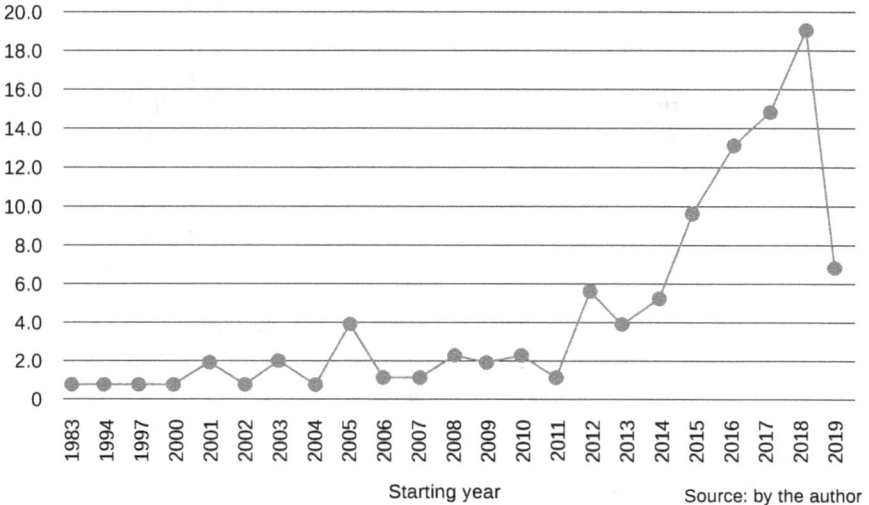

Starting year   Source: by the author

the district. The conclusion was that the children had to keep
the unsold part and had to accept DUAT for the rest of the area.
(Interview with a man in Chiadeia village, 15 May 2019)

Related parties

With regard to the parties involved in the conflict, conflicts between
individuals (37.5 per cent) stand out in Table 4.5, followed by conflicts between private individuals and families (8.1 per cent), families
and private companies (5.6 per cent), associations and private persons
(3.8 per cent), the state and private individuals (3.1 per cent) and private
companies among themselves (1.3 per cent).

Reasons for the conflicts
Regarding the motivation for the conflicts, it appears that more than
half of the land conflicts in the two administrative posts that make up
the district of Nhamatanda – namely Posto Administrativo de Tica and
Vila-Sede de Nhamatanda – result from disputes over limits and invasion beyond boundary markers between neighbours or family members,
at 52.3 per cent and 34.7 per cent of cases in Tica and Nhamatanda-
Sede, respectively. The following is an example:

Someone intruded into someone else's area, but we managed to
intervene and we had an immediate solution. This was in 2018.
That person wanted to produce sesame … and entered another

Table 4.5: Parties in conflict

		Party 1						
		Individuals	Families	Community	Association	Company	State	Traditional authorities
Party 2	Individuals	37.5%	8.1%	1.9%	3.8%	0.6%	3.1%	0.6%
	Families	4.4%	21.3%	1.3%	0.0%	5.6%	0.0%	0.0%
	Community	0.6%	0.0%	0.0%	0.0%	1.3%	1.9%	0.0%
	Association	0.6%	0.0%	0.6%	0.0%	0.0%	0.0%	0.0%
	Company	0.6%	0.0%	0.0%	0.0%	1.3%	0.0%	0.0%
	State	3.1%	0.6%	0.0%	0.0%	0.0%	0.0%	0.0%
	Traditional Authorities	1.3%	0.0%	0.0%	0.0%	0.0%	0.0%	0.0%

Source: By the author based on surveys

person's area, a neighboring machamba, of nearly one hectare. Hence the disagreement began … We mediated the conflict and a consensus was reached. In fact, the person acknowledged that he entered an area without permission. He thought that maybe … I shouldn't ask. He used force. But then a consensus was reached and until today the case has had a positive outcome.

(Interview with Chiadeia village administrative official, 16 May 2019)

The second major cause of conflict is expropriation for investment purposes (agroforestry, tourism, conservation, and so on). In Tica, this represents 8 per cent of the cases and 16.7 per cent in Nhamatanda-Sede (see Graph 4.3). However, illegal occupation, expulsion, overlapping uses for the same area and issues of inheritance and subdivision in the family are some other reasons for land conflicts. To those are added human-animal conflicts and conflicts arising from artisanal mining (gold mining), which represent, respectively, 69 per cent and 19 per cent of the other reasons for referenced conflicts.

Location of the conflict area

A reading of Graph 4.4 allows us to conclude that more than half of the land conflicts, both in the administrative district of Tica (60.2 per cent) and in Nhamatanda (29.2 per cent), take place in areas of common use within communities or family farms. It is also worth noting a significant percentage of conflicts in areas close to roads and railways,

Graph 4.3: Reason for the conflict

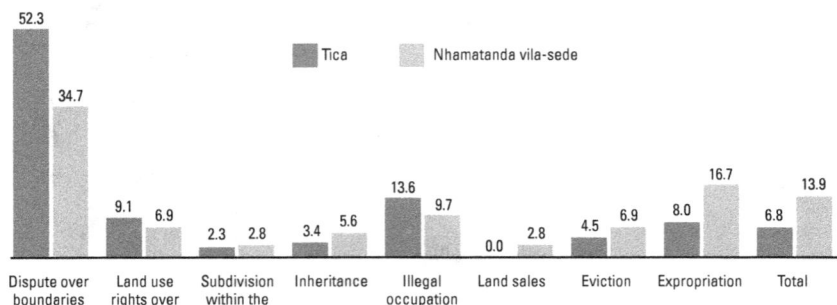

Source: By the author, based on surveys (2019)

due to the easy flow of products, and close to sources of natural water or irrigation, where the demand for areas for production of vegetables is greater.

Graph 4.4: Location of the conflict area

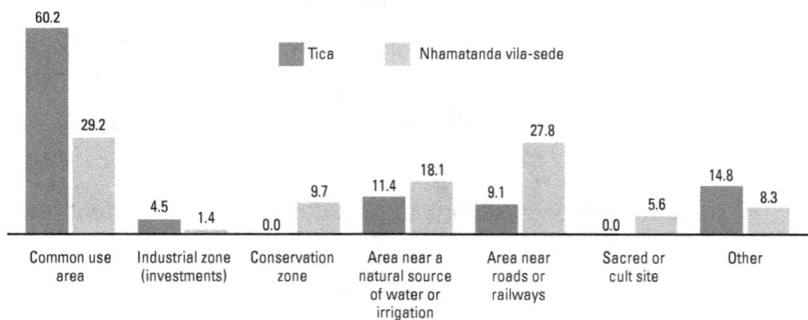

Source: By the author, based on surveys (2019)

Size of the conflict area

The Nhamatanda district has the second largest number of small and medium-sized farms in Sofala province (44,161), corresponding to 48,999 hectares. According to data from the *Census of Agriculture and Livestock 2009-2010*, small farms are classified as those whose cultivated area is less than 10 hectares. Medium farms are those whose cultivated area is between 10 and 50 hectares. Farms whose size is 50 hectares or more are classified as large farms (INE 2011).

It was found that more than 70 per cent of land conflicts registered in this district occur in areas of small farms used for the practice of family farming, as shown in Graph 4.5, on the size of the area in conflict, and Graph 4.6, about the type of use in the conflict area.

Graph 4.5: Size of the conflict area (hectares)

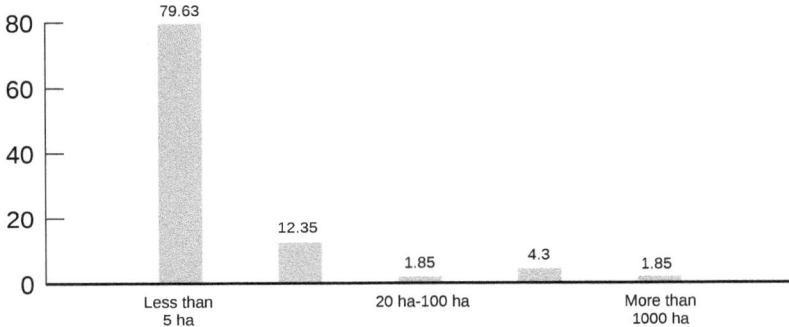

Source: By the author, based on surveys

Graph 4.6: Type of use in the conflict area

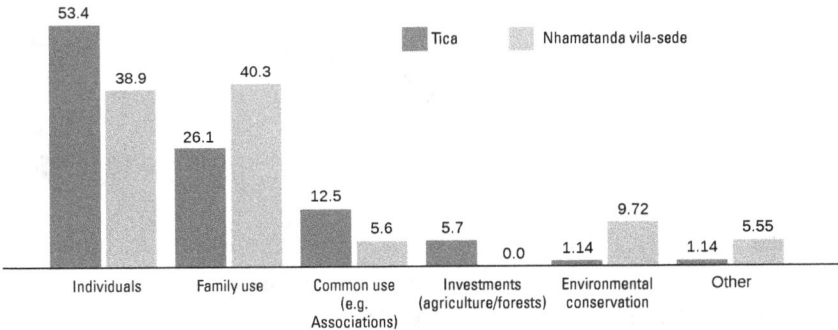

Source: By the author, based on surveys

Violence in conflicts

In 2016, there was a dispute in which there was no agreement on the boundaries between two neighbors, on a *machamba*. When one of the parties involved sowed, the other would go there … There was an exchange of words and even physical aggression, until the case reached the community authorities who decided to meet with the two and … the framework for separating the area from each of them was defined, thus the case was resolved. (Interview with a community leader, Bebedo, Nhamacasa village, 14 May 2019)

Land conflicts can be accompanied by violence. The rights claimed determine the nature of the conflicts and the level of violence associated with them. The violence referred to here is observed in the use of physical force (physical aggression, death), which may also involve verbal violence (threats, insults, intimidation), as well as destruction of property and threats of spells (as illustrated by Graph 4.7).

Graph 4.7: Type of violence in the conflict

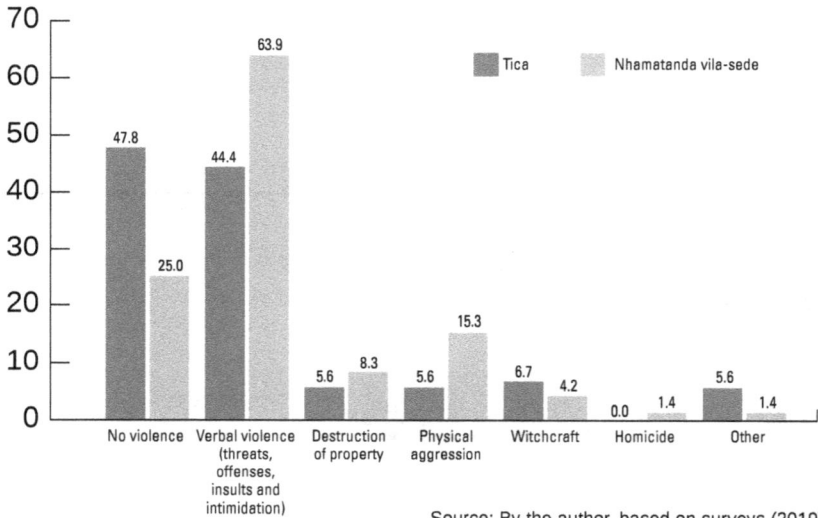

Source: By the author, based on surveys (2019)

There was a record of a death at the administrative post in Nhamatanda-Sede, Bebedo, in the Madangua-vinho community. This locality is in the buffer zone of Gorongosa National Park and the population claims to be constantly attacked by the animals of the park that cross to the residential side to feed on their fields, destroying the corn crops, sorghum, cassava and banana trees:

> In 2018, in an attempt to protect their crops and chase away elephants from PNG [Gorongoza National Park], father and son went to the field in order to protect themselves and elephants mortally attacked the farmer's son ... The case went to the locality, but the resolution did not advance.
>
> (interview at Maguanda-vinho village, 17 May 2019)

There is vandalization of fields of rice, corn, and vegetables, by elephants and buffaloes coming from Gorongosa National

Park, due to the lack of fences ... In Nhamacasa, a community group was created to chase away animals to minimize the situation of attacks on farmland. It puts hives in the areas frequented by the animals.

(Interview with local leader,
Maguanda-vinho village, 14 May 2019)

Regarding the degree of violence, it is at the family level that the most violent and difficult to resolve conflicts occur. Conflicts arising from purchase and sale also have a heavy load of physical violence, even involving death, as described below:

Two individuals are on account with the police of the Republic of Mozambique, accused of murdering a woman and her two children, due to an alleged land dispute in the Nhamatanda district, Sofala province. The victims were surprised at home, after receiving several threats allegedly made by the murderers, who claimed the plot of land where the woman and her children had lived for several years. The alleged ... told the police that the plot in dispute belongs to them, as it was sold to them by the husband of the ill-fated. ... The accused went to [their] house ... and struck against them using an ax. (Redacção 2018)

Forms of resolution

Of the land conflicts mapped in the Nhamatanda district, only 13 per cent were referred to formal bodies, such as community courts (10 per cent) or judicial courts (3 per cent). Most conflicts are handled and dealt with, primarily, at the level of informal institutions such as the family or by community elders, and it is only in the event of their inefficiency that a case can be brought to higher levels, be they community courts or judicial authorities.

Since most conflicts occur in areas of small family farms and common use, one can understand the important role of mediation and informal institutions in resolving land conflicts: about 37 per cent of conflicts which had been settled were resolved by a mediator within the family, and 39 per cent by the community authorities (Graph 4.8).

Other actors who participated in mediation and conflict resolution were also mapped. In this category, the important role of local extension

Graph 4.8: Form of conflict resolution

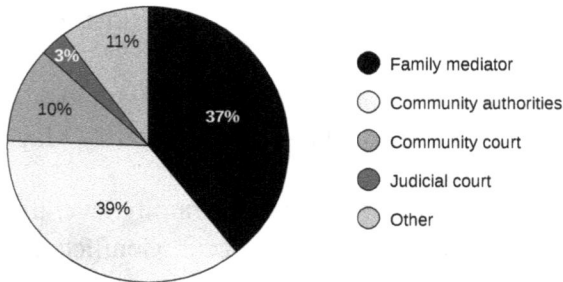

- ● Family mediator
- ○ Community authorities
- ◐ Community court
- ● Judicial court
- ○ Other

Source: By the author, based on surveys

Graph 4.9: Other mediators of land conflicts

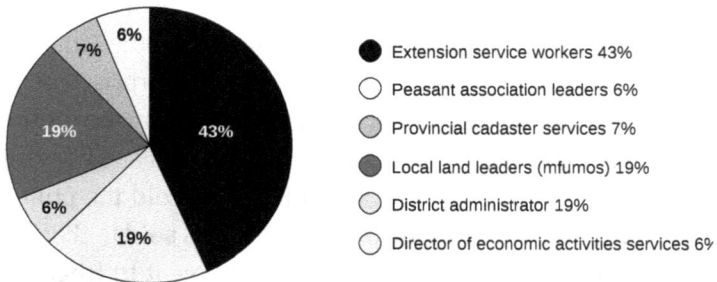

- ● Extension service workers 43%
- ○ Peasant association leaders 6%
- ◐ Provincial cadaster services 7%
- ● Local land leaders (mfumos) 19%
- ○ District administrator 19%
- ○ Director of economic activities services 6%

Source: By the author, based on surveys

workers[1] in conflict resolution stands out (43% in Graph 4.9). In some cases, the district administrator (19 per cent), the land chiefs, *mfumos* (19 per cent), or even the presidents of producer associations (6 per cent) also participated in resolution.

Participation of women in conflict resolution

According to Article 24 of the Land Law, local communities partici-pate in the management of natural resources, in the titling process and in conflict resolution. Equal rights between men and women, both in access to and inheritance of land, are also a right provided for by law.

In this research, we sought to assess the participation of women in conflict resolution, and about 37 per cent of respondents, both men

1 Extensionists are agents (public or private) responsible for facilitating dialogue and exchanging information with local farmers and producers, as well as the formation and dissemination of new agricultural technologies (Maduele 2014). In addition to these functions, rural extension workers are important actors in resolving land conflicts in rural areas, a role that is conferred on them by the prestige they have with peasants and within the community.

Graph 4.10: Women in resolution of conflict

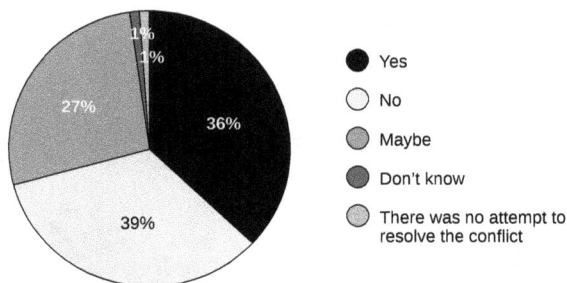

Source: By the author, based on surveys

and women, said that there was no participation of women, against 34 per cent who answered that there was participation of women in conflict resolution (Graph 4.10). These statistics reinforce the idea that women's access to land remains reduced, which is also explained by poor access to information and ignorance of rights.

A report produced recently by Forum Mulher indicates that, in general, conflict resolution bodies are mainly made up of men and, when present, women have no voice, do not have access to information and fear to contradict the decisions of men (Forum Mulher 2018)

Stage of resolution

As for the resolution stage, some land conflicts have been resolved, others are in the process of resolution, and in others there was no attempt at resolution. Traditions and practices can influence the time taken to deal with conflicts, as shown in the example below, where it was necessary to wait 40 days:

> The conflict took place this year [2019] at the home of a prophet of a local Pentecostal church, who was to lose his life. Three days before the funeral, the family argued about the goods that remained such as the house, clothes, land, corn and others. The case is pending, waiting 40 days after its resolution, according to local tradition.

> (Survey, Siluvo, Nharuchonga, 1° bairro, 15 May 2019)

Overall, more than half of the land conflicts presented to informal institutions, both at the administrative post in Tica and in Nhama-tanda-Sede, have already been resolved. Unresolved conflicts represent about 13.3 per cent of conflicts in Tica and 38.9 per cent in

Graph 4.11: Stage of resolution

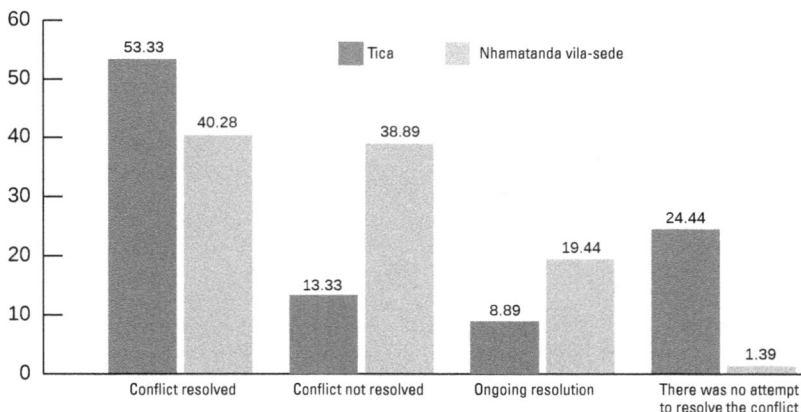

Nhamatanda-Sede (Graph 4.11). The unresolved cases are related to the most recent years – that is, 2018 and 2019 – while the oldest ones already have an outcome.

Conclusion

Studies on land conflicts are a way of understanding the social, economic and political dynamics of a given rural society. In the district of Nhamatanda, data indicate that conflicts are on the rise, as a result of population growth, increasing urbanization, the growth of land markets, inheritance disputes and limits on the delimitation of spaces. The greatest pressure on land is on areas close to access roads or railways, as well as in places close to natural water sources, such as rivers.

This research presents the results of mapping conflicts over land occupation in the Beira Corridor, based on a case study in the district of Nhamatanda, Sofala province. It aims to contribute to understanding the causes of conflicts, the actors, the types of rights claimed, ways of resolving conflicts and mechanisms mobilized to prevent conflict. The results suggest the need to strengthen the training of community authorities in matters of conflict prevention and management, given their role in mediating cases of land conflicts at family and community levels, which tend to increase in the face of greater demand for land and new dynamics marked by the resettlement of populations as a result of extreme weather events.

Empirical data indicated that conflicts occur both in the family and the community as well as the institutional dimensions, and can sometimes be accompanied by some form of violence, whether physical or symbolic. Crossing boundaries and overlapping rights are among the main causes of land conflict.

Although there is a tendency to resolve land conflicts with the involvement of community authorities and family mediators, it is also worth noting the participation of women in the conflict resolution process.

Despite these encouraging factors, it can be said that the existence of a considerable number of still-pending conflicts indicates the complexity and difficulty of dealing with issues related to land conflicts, but it is nevertheless important to recognize the role of informal institutions, such as the family, in the mediation and resolution of land conflicts. Thus, it is worth considering consolidating the training of local authorities and influential members of the community in the process of conflict management and resolution, always ensuring the integration of women in the process.

In addition to expanding the mapping of conflicts to other locations, with a view to know them and their prevention and resolution, it would be important to understand the factors determining the absence of conflicts in other locations in the district and the strategies used by local populations to ensure access to and possession of land.

References

Baleira, S. (28 a 30 de Abril de 2010). A "plena legalidade" na resolução de conflitos como garantia do pluralismo jurídico - o caso dos conflitos de acesso e uso da terra e outros recursos naturais em Moçambique. *Mecanismos Estatais e não-Estatais de justiça e segurança pública. A dinâmica do pluralismo jurídico em Moçambique*, (p. 28). Maputo.

Baleira, S., & Castro, E. (2016). *Estudo sobre a segurança da posse da terra dos pequenos agricultores no norte de Moçambique*. Maputo: Prospectus Consultoria & Serviços, Lda.

Bierschenk, T., & Sardan, J.-P. O. (1994). Enquête Collective Rapide d'Identification des conflits et des groupes Stratégiques... *Bulletin de l'APAD [en ligne], 7*. Obtido em 21 de Janeiro de 2015, de http://apad.revues.org/2173

Chaveau, J.-P., & Mathieu, P. (1998). Dynamiques et enjeux des conflits fonciers. Em P. L.-D. (cood), *Quelles politiques foncières pour l'Afrique rurale? Réconcilier pratiques, légitimité et légalité* (pp. 243-258). Paris: Karthala.

Cohen, L., & Manion, L. (1994). *Research Methods in Education*. Londres: Routledge Publishers.

Geffray, C. (1989). Les hommes au travail, les femmes au grenier. La société makhuwa (Erati) des années trente à 1956. *Cahier des Sciences Humaines, 25*, pp. 313-324. Obtido em 08 de 07 de 2019, de http://horizon.documentation.ird.fr/exl-doc/pleins_textes/pleins_textes_4/sci_hum/30812.pdf

Gengenbach, H. (March 1998). I'll bury you in the border!: women's land struggles in post-war Facazisse (Magude District), Mozambique. *Journal of Southern African Studies, 32.*

INE. (2011). *Censo Agro-Pecuário 2009-2010: Resultados definitivos-Moçambique.* Maputo: INE/Ministério da Agricultura.

Kalabamu, F. T. (2019). Land tenure reforms and persistence of land conflicts in Sub-Saharan Africa - The case of Botswana. *ELSEVIER - Land Use Policy,* 337-345. doi:https://doi.org/10.1016/j.landusepol.2018.11.002

Kigula, J. (Março de 1993). Land disputes in Uganda: an overview of the types of land disputes and the dispute settlement Fora. Ace. *Acess to land and other natural resources in Uganda: research and policy development project.,* pp. 1-54.

Lund, C., Odgaard, R., & Sjaastad, E. (2006). *Land rights and land conflicts in Africa: a review of issues and experiences.* Denmark: Danish Institute for International Studies. Obtido em 03 de 06 de 2019, de http://pure.diis.dk/ws/files/68278/Land_rights_and_land_conflicts_in_Africa_a_review_of_issues_and_experiences.pdf

MAE. (2014). *Perfil do distrito de Nhamatanda, província de Sofala.* Ministério da Administração Estatal - DNAL.

Mandamule, U. (2017). Tipologia dos conflitos sobre a ocupação da terra em Moçambique. Em U. Mandamule, *Terra, poder e desenvolvimento em Moçambique* (pp. 201-238). Maputo: Escolar Editores.

Mandamule, U., & Manhicane Jr, T. (Março de 2019). Os mercados de terras rurais no corredor da Beira. Tipos, dinâmicas e conflitos. (OMR, Ed.) *Observador Rural nr. 72.*

Mbonde, F. J. (2015). Assessment of land use conflicts in Tanzania: A case study of Songambele and Mkoka villages in Kongwa District, Dodoma region. *A dissertation submitted in partial fulfilment of the requirement for the Award of Master of Science (Development policy) Degree of Mzumbe University,* (p. 87).

Meur, P.-Y. L., & al., e. (2006). *Conflicts over access to land and water resources within sub-saharan dry lands. Underlying factors, conflict dynamics and settlement processes.* Paris: GRET-FAO LEAD final report.

Moçambique, G. d. (1997). *Lei de Terras n° 19/97 de 1 de Outubro.* Maputo.

Moyo, S. (2012). The land question in Africa: research perspectives and questions. *Codesria Conferences on Land reform, the agrarian question and nationalism in Gaborone, Botswana (18-19 Octoer 2003) and Dakar, Senegal (8-11 December 2003)* (p. 36). Botswana: African Institute for Agrarian Studies.

Mulher, F. (2018). *Direitos das Mulheres à terra no contexto da pluralidade de direitos: o caso de Moçambique.* Maputo: Fórum Mulher - Coordenação para a Mulher no desenvolvimento.

Muteia, H. (1996). *A problemática de terras em Moçambique. Subsídios para a revisão da legislação.* Maputo: MULEIDE.

Redacção. (30 de Outubro de 2018). *Conflito de terra termina em morte de mãe e filhos em Nhamatanda.* Obtido em 10 de 07 de 2019, de Jornal @ verdade: http://www.verdade.co.mz/newsflash/67219-conflito-de-terra-termina-em-morte-de-mae-e-filhos-em-nhamatanda-

Roy, E. L. (1991). État, réforme et monopole foncier. Em É. L. Émile Le Bris, *L'appropriation de la terre en Afrique noire. Manuel d'analyse, de décision et de gestion foncières* (pp. 159-190). Paris: Karthala.

Rugadya, M. A. (2009). *Escalating land conflicts in Uganda. A review of evidence from recent studies and surveys.* Maastricht: IRI and Uganda Round Table Foundation.

Salimo, P. (2017). *Perfil de Terras em Moçambique.* Maputo: ASCUT.

Sardan, J.-P. O. (2017). *A política do trabalho de campo. Sobre a produção de dados em sócio-antropologia.* Maputo: Alcance Editores.

SDAE. (2019). *Contexto económico e social do distrito de Nhamatanda. Balanço anual.* Nhamatanda - Sofala: SDAE Nhamatanda.

Selemane, T. (2017). *A economia política do Corredor de Nacala: consolidação do padrão de economia extrovertida em Moçambique.* Maputo: OMR.

UNAC, & GRAIN. (2015). *Os usurpadores de terras do Corredor de Nacala.* Maputo: UNAC e Grain.

Wehrmann, B. (2008). *Land conflicts. A practical guide to dealing with land disputes.* München, Germany: Deutche Gesellschaft für.

Yamano, T., & Deininger, K. (2005). *Land conflicts in Kenya: causes, impacts and resolutions.* FASID/National Graduate Institute for Policy Studies and The World Bank. Obtido em 03 de Junho de 2019, de http://www3.grips.ac.jp/~yamanota/Land%20Conflicts%20in%20Kenya%20(FASID%20DP).pdf

CHAPTER 5

Security of tenure and forced evictions in Eswatini

Amnesty International

Introduction

This chapter presents the key findings from Amnesty International's research and recent report on two emblematic cases of forced evictions in Eswatini, in Nokwane in September and October 2014, and in the Malkerns in April 2018. At least 61 people in the Malkerns and at least 180 people in Nokwane were rendered homeless as a result of the demolition of their homes. Amnesty International's research found that the existing domestic legal framework in Eswatini provides fertile ground for forced evictions to take place. The report reveals how the human rights violation of forced evictions is rooted in Eswatini's land governance system, which fails to provide at least hundreds of people with a minimum degree of security of tenure. The report also highlights the failure of the Eswatini government to abide by its international, regional and national legal obligations, especially the obligation to guarantee the right to adequate housing. Amnesty International conducted research in Eswatini in March 2017, November 2017 and April 2018. The latter visit was a week after demolitions had taken place in the Malkerns. Amnesty International first published its full findings from the investigation in August 2018, in the report *'They Don't See Us as People'- Security of Tenure and Forced Evictions in Eswatini* (Amnesty 2018).

Methodological note

Amnesty International interviewed a diverse range of stakeholders including 80 people who had either been forcibly evicted or were living under threat of eviction In Nokwane. Amnesty International interviewed 15 people from at least 19 homesteads who had been forcibly evicted from their homes in 2014, following a government initiative to develop a Royal Science and Technology Park. A further 15 people were interviewed in the Malkerns following their forced eviction on

9 April 2018. Amnesty International also interviewed two communities facing imminent eviction in Madonsa in the Manzini region and Mbondzela near Gege in the Shiselweni region. In addition, Amnesty International interviewed civil society activists, human rights lawyers, church groups, journalists, a member of the judiciary, a professor of political science at the University of Swaziland, and the chairperson and members of the Commission on Human Rights and Public Administration/Integrity. Amnesty International met with government representatives from the Ministry of Economic Planning and Development and the Ministry of Natural Resources and Energy, as well as the deeds registrar, the surveyor general, the attorney general, a member of parliament, representatives from the Regional Farm Dwellers' Tribunal, the Swazi National Provident Fund, the Swaziland Water and Agricultural Development Enterprise, the Swazi Sugarcane Association, the Royal Swaziland Sugarcane Corporation and the Law Society, and a member of the royal family who was leading the development of the constitution. Amnesty International also met with the United Nations Food and Agricultural Organisation (FAO), and members of the diplomatic community, including the European Union delegation and the US embassy.

A complex land governance and policy

Eswatini has a complex land governance system, inextricably tied to the history and political economy of the country. Towards the end of the 19th century, Eswatini's fertile land and mineral wealth made it an attractive and lucrative destination for investors. An influx of European and South African migrants meant there was a high demand for land. As a result, then-King Mbandzeni granted concessions – initially understood by Swazis as temporary land grants – to migrants. In exchange, the holders of what is described as 'concession land' paid rent, which eventually became the country's primary source of revenue between 1886 and 1894. The high influx of migrants into Eswatini, and the granting of concessions to them, was a source of tension between the migrants and the local population. The legacy of this conflict persists in Eswatini today with protracted disputes over ownership of land throughout the country. The constitution of 2006 formally recognizes a dual land tenure system. The king holds more than half of the land, called Swazi Nation Land (SNL), 'in trust' for the Swazi people. The remainder is privately owned title-deed land (TDL).

The system of trust with regard to SNL operates as a patronage relationship, whereby the king allocates SNL to the Swazi people indirectly through local chiefs. Residents may access SNL through a process known as *kukhonta*[1] in Siswati, the national language, which then leads to a tributary relationship between the person to whom the land is allotted and the chief. In exchange for access to the SNL, the resident pays customary fees in the form of livestock, and must pledge allegiance to the chief; this may require tribute labour, or other communal activities. There are no official written records of this land allocation, such as size and to whom it is allocated, and nor is there any other form of formal security of tenure in this arrangement. Under customary law, chiefs have the power to allocate as well as to banish people from land. Title-deed land is privately held land that was previously given to private parties by concession. While TDL holders have security of tenure, much of this land is occupied by subsistence farmers whose tenure status is unclear.

Following evictions of these farm dwellers in the 1950s and 1960s, the government in 1967 introduced the Farm Dwellers' Act to regulate relations between farm owners and occupants. The act, however, only protects those who have a formal written agreement with the farm owner, and officially recognizes them as 'farm dwellers'. The act excludes protection for everyone else who finds themselves living on privately owned land with a verbal agreement, as was the tradition with a current or previous land owner, and authorities consider these occupants to be 'squatters' who lack even minimum security of tenure.

Eswatini began developing the National Land Policy in 1999, which has not yet been finalized. The 2006 constitution stipulates that the state shall 'endeavour to settle the land issue and the issue of land concessions expeditiously so as to enhance economic development and the unity of the Swazi people'. However, many land policy issues remain unresolved. Following the adoption of the constitution, the new Draft National Land Policy was introduced in 2009. In this document, the Eswatini government acknowledges the insecurity of all tenure types as an issue to be addressed. In 2013, the Draft Land Bill was introduced, which expressly repeals 19 archaic pieces of legislation, the oldest of which dates back to 1904. While steps had been taken to finalize both the draft land policy and the Draft Land Bill, neither has been passed. Delays in legal and policy reform have meant that the Eswatini government is yet to take the necessary steps to ensure

1 Meaning to worship

security of tenure and protection of the right to adequate housing, thus leaving hundreds of people vulnerable to forced evictions.

Evictions without due process in the Malkerns and Nokwane

In both the Malkerns and Nokwane, the residents affected by the forced evictions were largely subsistence farmers and casual labourers who claimed to have been living on the land for several years, if not decades. Family members were buried there. In both cases, some of the families claimed to have been allocated the land by a chief through the traditional system of land allocation known as *kukhonta*, described above, and others said that they had a verbal agreement with a previous owner of the land to live there. In both cases, the residents went through a protracted court process, which ultimately ended in their eviction and the demolition of their homes, as they were unable to provide any formal proof of security of tenure. At least 60 people were rendered homeless in the Malkerns and at least 180 people in Nokwane.

International human rights standards are unequivocal: protection from forced evictions is available to all, even to those without a legally recognized right to the house or land that they occupy. Further, the UN Committee on Economic, Social and Cultural Rights, in its *General Comment 7*, stresses that, even when an eviction is considered justified, 'it should be carried out in strict compliance with the relevant provisions of international human rights law and in accordance with the general principles of reasonableness and proportionality'. According to international human rights law, as outlined in General Comment 7, the threshold for lawful evictions includes seven elements: genuine consultation, adequate and reasonable notice, information on the proposed eviction, government officials present during evictions, evictions not to take place in bad weather or during the night, provision of legal remedies; and provision of legal aid. The committee also emphasized in *General Comment 7* that no one should be rendered homeless or vulnerable to violations of other human rights as a result of an eviction.

The responsibility for ensuring that forced evictions do not take place lies with the state. Where forced evictions are carried out by actors other than the state, such as private individuals or companies, the authorities have a duty to protect the affected people and intervene to prevent forced evictions. The duty of the Eswatini state to protect people from forced evictions also includes ensuring that safeguards of human rights are in place regardless of whether the evictions have been ordered by a public or private body.

The duty to engage in genuine consultations, provide adequate notice and ensure that no one is left homeless as a result of an eviction also lies with the Eswatini state. Amnesty International's finding is that the Eswatini government failed to ensure genuine consultation with affected people on alternatives to eviction and adequate and reasonable notice for affected people prior to the evictions. It also failed to provide alternative accommodation and compensation. The authorities failed to follow due process in carrying out the evictions in both the Malkerns and Nokwane. The resulting homelessness impacted not only the right to adequate housing, but a wide range of interrelated rights, including the right to education, access to livelihoods and food security. The factors outlined above and argued further in this paper support the conclusion that the government of Eswatini failed to meet the threshold of lawful evictions in the demolitions carried out in both Nokwane and the Malkerns.

Land governance: land as life and as a source of power

Land as a source of power

In Eswatini, the constitution of 2006 formally recognizes a dual land tenure system, consisting of Swazi Nation Land (SNL), held in trust by the king,[2] and privately-owned title-deed land (TDL):

> all land (including any existing concessions) in Swaziland, save privately held title-deed land, shall continue to vest in King in trust for the Swazi Nation as it vested on the 12th April 1973. (Section 211(1))

Today, the majority of the land in Eswatini is SNL, which includes, to a large extent, what was previously concession land. Concession land was land alienated to private companies and individuals for commercial purposes. The remaining land in the country is title-deed land, comprising privately owned land and Crown Land.[3] Crown Land is generally understood as land owned by government (Mushala 1992) but registered as TDL in the name of the king.[4]

This system of land governance is tied to the history and political economy of the country. Eswatini, which become a South African protectorate in 1894, was relinquished to Britain in 1903 following the

2 The king is also referred to as the *iNgwenyama* when performing traditional duties. For purposes of this report we will refer to the king as the authority, regardless of which role he is playing.
3 These proportions are according to a communication from the Ministry of Economic Planning and Development, received by Amnesty International on 8 August 2017.
4 Vesting-of-Land-in-King's-Order, Section Three. This accompanied the 1973 King's Proclamation.

Anglo Boer war. In 1907, the British administration passed the Concession Partition Act, which provided the initial legal basis for the current land tenure system in Eswatini. Through this act, one third of each land concession that was given to private companies or individuals was reserved for the sole and exclusive use of Swazis. This demarcated land, previously termed 'Swazi Areas', is what is today referred to as Swazi Nation Land (Armstrong 1986). The remaining two-thirds of each concession land was shared between the Crown (government) and the concession holder (Matsebula 1988, p. 184, Rose 1992, p. 3-4).

However, after Eswatini gained independence from British rule, King Sobhuza passed the Land Concession Order in 1973, by which the ownership of any concession land was transferred to the king.[5] Alongside this order, the king also passed the Vesting of Land in King's Order, through which any land vested in the Crown or government was transferred to the King, but also registered in the name of Crown land in the Deeds Registry Office (Vesting of Land in King's Order 1973, Section 3). This law also reinforced the king's continued hold over SNL, which he held 'in trust' for the Swazi nation (Vesting of Land in King's Order 1973, Section 6).

Experts explained to Amnesty International that the intention of these laws was to benefit the Swazi people by ensuring equality of access to land and adequate housing. Contrary to the colonial system, where Swazis were confined to limited land as part of concession land, under the King's Order, Swazis could now have access to more land in order to facilitate their right to an adequate standard of living. But, contrary to these assertions, Amnesty International found through its research that the Eswatini government has failed to respect and protect the right to adequate housing.

Swazi Nation Land (SNL)

There are two types of SNL – registered and unregistered (Armstrong 1986, p. 8). Registered SNL refers to previous or repurchased TDL bought by the Swazi monarchy and leased out to private companies to attract income, and administered by the Swazi government through a parastatal entity called Tibiyo Taka Ngwane (Wealth of the Nation). This is an entity set up by the royal family, initially with the purpose of controlling funds to buy back concession land to revert to Swazi Nation Land.

....

5 'The Concession land is to be held at the will and pleasure of the King: Notwithstanding anything in any other law any land held in Swaziland by a concessionaire, whose concession title or lease is still in force, shall be so held at the will and pleasure of the King on such terms as he may determine' (Land Concession Order, 1973, Section 3).

Unregistered SNL is held under customary land tenure and is allocated to individuals or families by chiefs (Armstrong 1986, p. 8, Mushala, Kanduza, Simelane, Rwelamira and Dlamini, 1998 (hereafter Mushala) ;). Tenure over unregistered SNL is not regulated by legislation, but rather by tradition, from which a number of issues arise. Tenure on unregistered SNL can also be acquired through inheritance (Mushala et al. 1998, p. 3).

Both registered and unregistered SNL can be expropriated by the government under the Acquisition of Property Act (10 of 1961), or by the king under the Swazi Administration Act (Armstrong 1986, p.9, United Nations Habitat 2013, p. 5). The constitution, however, provides protection against arbitrary deprivation of property, stating that the compulsory acquisition of land can only be made under certain conditions, which include 'prompt payment of fair and adequate compensation; and a right of access to a court of law by any person who has an interest in or right over the property' (Constitution of Swaziland 2006, Section 19).

Key to the concept of Swazi Nation Land is that it is communal land held by the king 'in trust for the Swazi nation' (Constitution of Swaziland 2006, Chapter 12, Section 211(1)). This system, reinforced by the constitution, is based on 'trust' – a patronage relationship, whereby the king holds land 'in trust' for the Swazi nation and accordingly allocates SNL to the people indirectly through chiefs. The constitution explains the critical role of chiefs as the 'footstools' of the king, who rules indirectly through them (Constitution of Swaziland 2006, Section 233(1)). The SNL allocations ensure a right to enjoy the use of the land, but the right cannot be bought, sold or used as collateral. In exchange, the recipients pay allegiance to their chief, usually in the form of tribute labour or unpaid labour, when requested. There is no formal legal security of tenure in this arrangement. There are no uniform official written records of these allocations. Under customary law, chiefs have the power to allocate as well as to banish people from land (Mushala et al. 1998, p. 9).

In accordance with Swazi law and custom, while SNL is purportedly communally owned, the king controls it all and rules indirectly through local chiefs, who in turn allocate land to families.[6] Through *kukhonta* residents may access SNL and 'a tributary relationship is thus established between the resident and the local traditional leadership, normally com-

6 While Swazi National Land is not owned, a person with a house built on SNL has lawful possession of the land on which the house is constructed, and a commercial farmer has no ownership over the land, only owning the produce from it (Gumedze 2014, p.6-8).

prising a chief' (Government of Swaziland 1996). In exchange for access to the SNL, the resident pays customary fees in the form of livestock and has to pledge allegiance to the chief – which may require tribute labour or other communal activities, as mentioned previously (Dube 2008, Nhabatsi 2016). This tributary relationship is problematic because failure to adhere to the chief's communal requirements could lead to eviction from the land. While banishment is not common, the chief's power over subjects creates a threat that can lead to insecurity and fear of homelessness (Mushala et al. 1998, p. 9; see also Dlamini 2020, Zulu 2010).

Lack of clarity in the trust relationship

While the 2006 constitution formally recognized a dual land tenure system, one of its weaknesses is that it does not clarify various key terms. The constitution outlines a 'trust' relationship regarding land.

However, the constitution provides no clarification about what holding land 'in trust' means, and the nature of the trust relationship between the king and the Swazi nation is therefore shrouded in uncertainty. The constitution does not elaborate on the obligations or entitlements that flow from this 'trust' relationship regarding land allocation and acquisition.

When Amnesty International asked a judge of the Eswatini High Court what the constitutional provision 'in trust for the Swazi Nation' means, the judge was uncertain: 'It has not been interpreted. I do not know' (Interview with a judge in Mbabane, 28 November 2017).

The lack of clarity in the constitution regarding the interpretation of the 'trust' relationship contributes to overall confusion and controversy on land ownership and tenure. In a context where there is great historical complexity around the transfer of land (from concession to SNL and TDL), and given that there are multiple archaic laws that govern land issues in Eswatini combined with a lack of clarity in the constitution, the failure of the Eswatini government to finalize a land policy contributes to the overall confusion, debate and controversy on land ownerships and tenure.

Title-deed land: lack of protection

While Swazi Nation Land constitutes the majority of the land in Eswatini today, the rest of the land is privately held title-deed land (TDL), also commonly referred to as 'farms'. A legacy of the mass granting of land concessions at the end of the 19th century was the creation of a system of farm dwelling, wherein Swazis continued living on concession lands converted into TDL[7] and were considered 'farm dwellers' or were commonly referred to as 'squatters' on these farms (Armstrong 1986, p. 23). Farm dwellers lived on TDL though oral agreements with new owners, requiring the tenants to provide certain services to the farm owner.

Following evictions of these farm dwellers in the 1950s and 1960s, the king eventually set up a Committee of Inquiry in 1967 which recommended the abolition of the farm dwellers system 'by forbidding the creation of new farm dwellers and gradually evicting the old ones' (Armstrong 1986, p. 23). This meant that the tradition of agreement between farm owners and dwellers was formally abolished, and the little security of tenure that farm dwellers had was eroded. However, since there was not enough SNL to resettle farm dwellers, the Committee of Inquiry proposed the purchase of farm land for resettlement and for limitations to be set on farm owners' ability to evict existing farm dwellers. In response to the Committee's report, the first Farm Dwellers Act 21 of 1967 was promulgated (Armstrong 1986, p. 23). However, the act did not resolve the 'farm dweller problem', as land available for resettlement was scarce and farm dwellers resisted resettlement (Armstrong 1986, p. 23).

The current Farm Dwellers Act was introduced in 1982 and aims to regulate relations between farm owners and others living on farms. According to this act, a 'farm' does not include SNL or Crown land (Farm Dwellers Act 1982, Section 2). The act recognizes 'farm dwellers'[8] as those who are afforded rights on privately owned TDL, through official written agreements signed with farm owners. This agreement provides a right to the umnumzane (head of household) and their dependants to reside on the farm for a period agreed upon between the farm owner and farm dweller (Farm Dwellers Act 1982, Section 4(c)). This act does not allow the farm owner to evict farm dwellers unless a tribunal is satisfied that conditions have been met, that alternative accommodation is provided to the farm dweller (without specifying who is responsible for providing it), that compensation is provided for disruption and transport and that the eviction cannot take place during the harvesting period (Farm Dwellers Act 1982, Section 10).

The act further established quasi-judicial bodies: a district tribunal

---

7 Including some which transferred to privately owned TDL prior to the enactment of the King's Land Concession Order in 1973, which prevented any concession land from being converted into title-deed land

8 According to the Farm Dwellers Act, a 'farm-dweller' means 'a person who resides on a farm other than the owner thereof; or a usufruct or fiduciary; or a lessee under a written agreement of lease; or the holder of a registered servitude which gives the right of occupation; or the manager or agent of a person referred to in the above, or a member of the family or a guest of a person mentioned in the above.'

responsible for officiating regarding the agreements as well as for first-instance jurisdiction over disputes, and a central tribunal which serves as an appellate body, to hear any appeals against decisions made by the district tribunal (Farm Dwellers Act 1982, Section 6). The central tribunal is also mandated to 'advise the Minister of Home Affairs as to measures to be taken for the gradual elimination of the existing system of farm dwelling' (Farm Dwellers Act of 1982, Section 6(a)).

Analysts have, for the past two decades, argued that 'the Farm Dwellers Act has done little to deal with ongoing struggles between "squatters" and landowners. The problem is often exacerbated when there is a change in ownership... ' (Levin 1997). The act, however, only protects those who have a formal written agreement with the farm owner; these it officially recognizes as 'farm dwellers. The act excludes protection for anybody else who finds themselves living on privately owned land with a verbal agreement, as was the tradition with a current or previous land owner, and authorities consider these occupants to be 'squatters' who lack any degree of security of tenure.

For example, one of the two cases documented in this chapter is the forced evictions in the Malkerns, where occupants were considered 'squatters' and therefore lacking a legally recognized claim to occupy the land as they claim to have had verbal agreements with the previous farm owner to settle on the privately held farm land.

In most cases, the informal arrangement continued for a number of years, and in some cases even decades.[9] However, with a change in ownership of the land, many were left with no protection. Since they are not considered formal 'farm dwellers' because of a lack of a written agreement with the previous farm owner, there is no legal protection afforded to them. These individuals are therefore vulnerable to forced evictions and other related human rights violations.

The Land Management Board

The constitution established the Land Management Board, which is responsible for 'the overall management, and for the regulation of any right or interest in land whether urban or rural or vesting in the King in trust for the Swazi nation' (Constitution of Swaziland 2006, Section 212(4)). The Land Management Board members are appointed by, and accountable to, the king (Constitution of Swaziland, Sections 212(1) and (5)). Since the board, which theoretically plays a critical role in

9 For example, the case of Mbondzela (near Gege).

both managing and regulating any right to or interest in land, is both appointed by and only accountable to the king, this raises serious questions about its independence.

Apart from establishing this board through the constitution, there is no subsidiary legislation outlining details of the board's mandate. The combined effects of the limited accountability and transparency of the board's functioning undermine both the legitimacy of and public trust in the board to fulfil its constitutional mandate.

Absence of land policy

Despite the constitution's acknowledgement that what is described as the 'land issue' has implications for both the economic development and unity of Swazi people, it has been almost two decades since Eswatini began developing the National Land Policy in 1999. It has not yet concluded. As a result, there are many land policy issues which remain unaddressed (United Nations Habitat 2013, p. 5-6). Following the enactment of the constitution in 2006 the Draft National Land Policy was introduced in 2009. In this policy document, the Eswatini government itself acknowledges that: 'the economic, social and environmental pressures on Swaziland land resources are severe. It was for this reason that government saw the need to formulate a land policy' (Draft National Land Policy 2009, p.1).

One of the key issues to be addressed, as highlighted by the government in this 2009 draft, was 'the insecurity of all tenure types' and the 'lack of transparency and accountability' on land allocation rights and procedures (Draft National Land Policy 2009, p. 5-6).

The deeds office, which registers title deeds, also acknowledges on its website that 'the absence of a National Land Policy hinders development on land generally for the whole country specifically where issues of access to land, land use and security of tenure are concerned' (Deeds Registry n.d.).

Following the draft land policy, a Draft Land Bill was introduced in 2013 which repeals 19 archaic pieces of legislation, the oldest of which dates back to 1904 (Draft National Land Policy, Second Schedule, p. 58). Although steps had been taken to finalize both the draft land policy and the Draft Land Bill, neither had been passed by the time parliament was dissolved in June 2018 in preparation for national elections in September 2018. In the absence of a draft land policy and land bill, the challenges identified by the Eswatini government, including the absence of guarantees of security of tenure, remain unresolved.

Despite these commitments and steps taken by the Eswatini government, delays in legal, policy and institutional reform combined with the lack of transparency surrounding these processes has meant that the Eswatini government is yet to take the steps necessary to guarantee security of tenure and the right to adequate housing.

Discrimination against women

The Eswatini constitution guarantees all citizens equal access to land, regardless of gender.[10] In addition, the equality clause in the constitution is non-derogable (Constitution of Swaziland 2006, Section 38). However, in practice, women in Eswatini have access to land mainly through their husbands. The traditional system of land allocation, *kukhonta* through chiefs, often disadvantages women-headed households. Chiefs traditionally allocate land to men, which means that women can only access land traditionally through the *kukhonta* process via their husbands or sons. Women who are unmarried, widowed or don't have sons are therefore unable to access land easily. Swaziland Rural Women's Assembly activists told Amnesty International: 'In Eswatini, the land belongs to the king. Although in the constitution women can access land, when it goes down to traditional structures, that doesn't happen, although you talk about the constitution (to them)' (Interview with Swaziland Rural Women's Assembly, Mbabane, 4 December 2017). This is because not all chiefs are familiar with the constitution and instead follow traditional practices, a system under which land is allocated through men.

Recognizing the gap between constitutional guarantees of gender equality and the traditional view of women and their place in Swazi society, some chiefs in close proximity to urban areas are more aware of the constitutional protection of equal rights for women, in particular women's right to *kukhonta*. Local rural activists also told Amnesty International that chiefs closer to urban centres were more open to allowing women to access land through *kukhonta*. However, as the majority of the population still live in rural locations, women-headed households, due to inherent discrimination in the *kukhonta* system, are at greater risk of prolonged homelessness after a forced eviction than those headed by men.

....

10 'Save as may be required by the exigencies of any particular situation, a citizen of Swaziland, without regard to gender, shall have equal access to land for normal domestic purposes' (Constitution of Swaziland 2006, Section 211(2)).

Culture of secrecy

There is a general lack of both public access to information and its proactive dissemination by authorities in Eswatini. There is no national legislation promoting access to information.

A human rights lawyer told Amnesty International that members of the public reported that they could not easily access information regarding the status of plots of land, unless they were title-deed holders and had the title deed in their possession. While conveyancing lawyers could access information regarding title deeds, it comes at a cost. Based on what lawyers told us, and as evidenced in the two case studies, this compounds uncertainty about whether a particular piece of land is in fact categorized as SNL or TDL. This causes friction between parties which manifests itself when a landowner (by virtue of a title deed) wants to evict families who believed they were living on SNL. When these cases reach court, judgments appear to favour title-deed holders who can prove land ownership. Those without title deeds are therefore often rendered homeless. The Malkerns case, described later in the chapter, exemplifies this situation.

Legal framework

Although the Eswatini constitution does not explicitly provide for the right to adequate housing, Section 19(2) of the constitution prohibits arbitrary deprivation of property and eviction from land without fair and adequate compensation. Despite this provision, Amnesty International found that people's experiences are that they are not being protected, indicating a disconnect between policy and practice.

The Eswatini government is obligated, under a range of international and regional human rights laws, to respect, protect and fulfil the right to adequate housing. While the constitution does not contain provision for the right to adequate housing, the state is still bound by this obligation, which arises from its ratification of a number of treaties. These include the African Charter on Human and People's Rights, the International Covenant on Economic, Social and Cultural Rights (ICESCR), the International Convention on the Rights of the Child, the Convention on the Elimination of All Forms of Discrimination against Women and the International Covenant on Civil and Political Rights.

Article 11 of the ICESCR guarantees the right to adequate housing. The monitoring body set up under the ICESCR, the Committee on Economic, Social and Cultural Rights, advocates a broad interpretation of the right to adequate housing 'as the right to live somewhere in security, peace and dignity'. The concept of adequacy of housing is given critical importance, and the committee has outlined certain key factors to determine adequacy: legal security of tenure, affordability, habitability, accessibility, location, cultural adequacy and availability of services, materials, facilities and infrastructure.

As a state party to the ICESCR, Eswatini is bound to ensure that forced evictions do not occur. The protection guaranteed in international human rights law is accorded to all, regardless of whether they own or occupy the land from which they are being evicted.

Under international human rights law, evictions may only be carried out as a last resort, once all other feasible alternatives to eviction have been explored and appropriate procedural protections are in place. Governments must also ensure that no one is rendered homeless or vulnerable to violation of other human rights as a consequence of eviction.

Adequate alternative housing and compensation for all losses – pecuniary and non-pecuniary – must be made available to those affected before eviction. The duty to ensure all these safeguards against forced evictions rests with the Eswatini state.

Evictions without due process

The Malkerns

Manzini is the commercial capital of Eswatini. The expansion of cities and towns into what were previously rural areas has led to increased demand for housing near urban areas. The Malkerns town in the Manzini region is a microcosm of this trend. It was declared a town in 2012 and since then has been managed by the Malkerns Town Board.

The Malkerns is home to approximately 4,050 inhabitants (Fakudza and FAO 2016, p. 27). Residents are mostly subsistence farmers and seasonal labourers in the fertile Malkerns valley, a predominantly agricultural district known historically for its fruit plantations, in particular pineapple cultivation and a fruit cannery (Fakudza and FAO 2016, p. 27). There is a growing demand from farm owners to subdivide the Malkerns land for housing estate development, combined with a need to protect the area's prime agricultural land.[11]

When Amnesty International arrived at Malkerns town in the Emphetseni farming area one week after the latest demolitions on 9 April 2018, children's shoes, school books, wires from mattresses,

11 As a result of these demands, the Ministry of Agriculture and the Ministry of Housing and Urban Development jointly declared the Malkerns a 'controlled area' (Fakudza and FAO, p. 20).

shattered glass and window frames were strewn about. Some of the affected families were still rummaging through the rubble, uncovering the doors to the homes they once lived in.

All of the affected families that Amnesty International spoke to expressed shock at the loss of their homes and the forced separation from their roots and family members' graves. The evictions also resulted in the loss of means to make a livelihood from the land. According to eyewitnesses, the Malkerns forced eviction was carried out by the deputy sheriff of the Mbabane High Court, accompanied by the police and executive members of a private agricultural company, Umbane Limited. The demolitions came after a protracted legal process.

In 1997, Umbane bought the title deed to the land in question from another private company, Usuthu Pulp Limited. Four homesteads housed 15 families who were living on the land at the time of the purchase, and contestation over rights began then. The new owners and the occupants of the land approached the courts to resolve the issue.

The chairperson of the company's operating committee told Amnesty International: 'We approached the seller after we realized there were squatters there. They (Usuthu Pulp) said the squatters had no right to be there' (Telephonic interview with Manana, chair of Umbane Limited's operating committee. 21 May 2018). However, the affected residents dispute that they were living on the land illegally, claiming that their forefathers had acquired the land from the chief through the traditional *kukhonta* process decades ago. Umbane Limited said they started engaging with the families living on the land as far back as 1999, when they visited each of the four homesteads and asked the families to move, which the families refused.[12] Consequently, in 2011 the company initiated a lawsuit for the residents' eviction. However, in a judgment delivered on 13 February 2013, the high court denied the eviction order on the basis that the occupants had settled on the land in 1957 and were therefore entitled to the common law principle of acquisitive prescription (Umbane Limited vs Sofi Dlamini February 2013). In terms of acquisitive prescription, continuous habitation may result in a statutory claim to land through title.

....

12 Since the purchase price had not been paid in full, Umbane Limited invited the families to join their group in purchasing the farm. Their offer was not accepted, however. This engagement took place between 1997 and 1999, according to Manana (Telephonic interview, 21 May 2018). However, the affected families disputed this, and told Amnesty International that the new owners of the farm (Umbane) did not give them the opportunity to purchase the farm since Umbane only became aware of the families living on the land after the transfer from the previous owners, Usuthu Pulp, was completed (Telephonic interview with Gavin Khumalo, 29 May 2018). In December 2011, Umbane Limited decided to sell the farm. A buyer was secured on the condition that the company must remove the 'squatters' before the purchase.

Unsatisfied with this outcome, the company appealed the judgment at the Supreme Court which ruled that acquisitive prescription cannot be held where there is occupation with the consent of the property owner. The court found that the residents were in occupation of the farm with the permission of the previous farm owner, Usuthu Pulp, and on this basis ordered the residents' eviction without alternative accommodation or compensation in a judgment delivered on 31 May 2013 (Umbane Limited vs Sofi Dlamini and Three Others May 2013). Umbane Limited thereby secured an eviction order against the residents of the four homesteads (Phakathi 2017).

In 2013, the UN special rapporteur on adequate housing wrote to the Eswatini authorities, warning that approximately 150 people would be affected by this forced eviction, and reminding them of their domestic, regional and international human rights obligations to protect the right to adequate housing.[13]

Since the supreme court's ruling in 2013, the community said they were seeking a remedy through traditional dispute resolution structures, including by presenting their case to the King's Advisory Council.

The affected community and Umbane Limited agreed that at least two consultation meetings took place,[14] during which, said the affected communities, Umbane Limited did not entertain the issue of compensation.

Consequently, the communities approached the Commission on Human Rights for assistance and, in 2016, the commission took the matter back to the high court in an attempt to seek alternative accommodation and compensation for the affected residents. In a judgment delivered on 4 April 2017, the high court denied the applicants' claim to compensation on the basis that 'In the constitution, reference to payment of compensation is made in cases where the state expropriates property for public purposes...' and held that the affected residents 'are evicted from a privately-owned farm and are not entitled to payment of compensation' (Eswatini High Court 2017).

Affected residents told Amnesty International on 12 December 2017 that the managing director of the company Tibiyo Taka Ngwane (Wealth of the Nation) convened a meeting between the affected residents and Umbane Limited at Tibiyo's headquarters. Umbane Limited

---

13 This communication highlighted that 'the Court did not take into account the rights recognized in the Constitution of the Kingdom of Swaziland', citing Section 211(3), as well as Swaziland's international obligations. (United Nations Office of the High Commissioner for Human Rights (2000-9).

14 The affected communities recalled three consultation meetings, while the company said there were two.

offered US$800[15] per homestead plus a cow by way of assistance. The company was clear that this was not compensation. The residents refused to accept it as this would amount to about US$160 to US$200 per family and was inadequate to find secure alternative housing. Affected residents told Amnesty International this amount would barely enable them to *kukhonta* for land in the Malkerns and would not enable them to build homes and other structures which they would lose. The company had given a deadline of 31 December 2017 for families to vacate the land. However, during this meeting, Umbane Limited agreed to postpone the demolition date to 31 March 2018. 'When March 31st came and they had not moved, that's when we planned to demolish,' said the operating chairperson of Umbane Limited.

Gavin Khumalo, the affected residents' representative, said the group did not find the company's offer of assistance acceptable, and instead requested the company to provide alternative accommodation. In his words:

> Our experience has taught us [that] to have land under a chief, it's not a guarantee that you will stay there forever. The experience we had was that even our fathers had been allocated the land through the khonta system, through the chief. It turned out that suddenly it became a farm while we were inside the land. There's no guarantee that land under a chief cannot be turned into a farm. Anyone who decides to make it a farm can make it a farm. If we have money, we would get Title-Deed Land and subdivide it for our farm. Then at least we would have a piece of paper – I am guaranteed that no one can move me from that piece of land, I'm entitled to it. It's registered under deeds office. (Interview with Gavin Khumalo, Malkerns, 17 April 2018)

The residents said they had asked the managing director of Tibiyo Taka Ngwane to convey this information back to the King and to appeal to him for assistance. They said they were awaiting a response when the evictions and demolitions took place on 9 April 2018 (Interview with Gavin Khumalo, Malkerns, 17 April 2018).

Adequate notice is a safeguard to prevent forced evictions. Some members of the affected community told Amnesty International that they were only informed verbally of the demolitions on 8 April –

....

15 The total amount of assistance was 10,000 South African Rand. At the time of the Malkerns eviction in April 2018, the exchange rate amounted to US$800.

giving approximately 24 hours' notice. The community leader said this information was only conveyed verbally by the station commander of the Malkerns police station, after the community requested a meeting because they had heard rumours of their imminent eviction. All residents interviewed by Amnesty International said they had not received any formal notice with detailed information prior to the demolitions and evictions. The authorities therefore failed in their obligation to ensure that the community was given adequate notice. This is contrary to requirements under international law and standards.

On 9 April 2018, the day of the demolitions, the chief offered the affected families temporary alternative accommodation in his residence; two families accepted and the majority subsequently found alternative accommodation at their own expense. After the demolitions, Umbane Limited had meetings with the residents in early May 2018. Having been left homeless, the families accepted the assistance of US$800. Since each homestead consisted of several families, the US$800 needed to be further divided amongst each family.

Amnesty International also found that even if the eviction had been legally justified, the authorities failed to put in place the safeguards required by international law and standards.

In line with procedural safeguards as articulated in international human rights law and standards, even where evictions may be justified, states are required to carry them out in strict compliance with the relevant provisions of international human rights law and in accordance with general principles of reasonableness and proportionality.[16] In the case of the evictions in the Malkerns on 9 April 2018, the authorities failed to provide the affected people with adequate notice and failed to ensure that no one was left homeless and vulnerable to other human rights violations as a result of the eviction, among other safeguards.

Evictions must always respect human rights and due process. Due process involves the right to be treated fairly, efficiently and effectively by the administration of justice. Due process protections, already described earlier in the chapter, include an opportunity for genuine consultation with those affected, adequate and reasonable notice to all affected persons before the scheduled eviction date, making information on the proposed evictions available to all affected in reasonable time, the presence of government officials during eviction, proper identification of all persons carrying out the eviction, no evictions at night

16 CESCR General Comment 7, paragraph 14

or during bad weather, and provision of legal remedies and legal aid to people who need it.

Nokwane

Nokwane is situated some 15 km east of Manzini town in the Manzini region in the centre-west of Eswatini. Once known for its pineapple plantations, Nokwane is today a 159-hectare construction site of the Royal Science and Technology Park, a government-led development initiative inaugurated in April 2018. The site is located on land where at least 19 homesteads once stood and from which at least 180 residents were forcibly evicted.

King Mswati III initiated the development of this project as part of the country's economic growth strategy, Vision 2022. Funded by the Taiwanese government, the project is now implemented through the Ministry of Information, Communications and Technology (Swaziland Government v Jabulane Dlamini December 2014). The park was established through the Royal Science and Technology Park (RSTP) Act 5 of 2012, and is officially classified as a public enterprise, or parastatal. It consists of two projects: the Bioscience and Technology Park in Nokwane, and the Innovation Park in Phocweni, a few kilometres from Nokwane.

At the heart of the dispute between the families and the Eswatini government is the tenure of the contested land – Farm 692 – and the accompanying rights. This dispute culminated in a protracted legal process. The court eventually ruled that the king owns the property in trust for the Swazi nation, and that the king allocated the land to the government through the Ministry of Information, Communications and Technology (MICT) via title deed 176/2005 for the construction of the RSTP (Swaziland Government v Jabulane Dlamini, 2014). However, the government and the families still contest the facts.

According to the government's version, the Ministry of Housing owned the land, which was initially earmarked for a township development programme. In 2006 they sold apportioned plots to multiple owners, who built temporary structures on the land (MICT memo 2017). The government later decided to instead use the land for the construction of the RSTP and wanted the land back. According to the ministry, the government provided alternative accommodation and fully compensated the owners of plots, who 'unintentionally created an opportunistic appetite for squatters in their vacant plots' (MICT memo 2017).

This account did not match the affected families' version. At least five people interviewed told Amnesty International that they were born on the land, which their parents had acquired through the traditional *kuk-honta* process. However, the ministry referred to the affected families as 'illegal squatters' (MICT memo 2017). The government's version, that the affected families only arrived after 2006 when the temporary structures were allegedly built by the owners of the subdivided plots, is not only inconsistent with the account of the affected families, but also in contrast to satellite imagery sourced by Amnesty International.

This imagery reveals that structures were present in the area from 20 October 2002 and 14 July 2015, and that from February 2015 they are missing. The imagery also shows excavators and bulldozers demolishing structures in 2014.

At least 19 homesteads were located on the disputed land. Affected families told Amnesty International that five of those were situated within the Royal Science and Technology Park (RSTP) boundaries, while 14 were outside. Initially, affected families said that government officials told them that only those families living within the boundaries of the RSTP would be affected by the development, but in the end all 19 homesteads – at least 180 people – located within and outside were forcibly evicted.

One family told Amnesty International that they were the first to be evicted, on 11 July 2012, because their house was in the way of the RSTP boundary wall construction. After a break of almost two years, according to affected families, forced evictions resumed on 25 September 2014, when three structures were demolished. The families told Amnesty International that only one of the homesteads demolished that day was situated inside the boundary of the RSTP, and two were outside. Families and eyewitnesses said that the principal secretary of the MICT was leading the delegation undertaking the demolitions, in the presence of a state law advisor from the attorney-general's office in the Ministry of Justice. Residents told Amnesty International that the demolitions lasted approximately two hours on that day. By December 2014, despite civil society's attempts to halt evictions from Nokwane, 19 homesteads – approximately 180 people – had been forcibly evicted and their homes demolished to make way for the construction of the RSTP.

Although the government held some consultations with the affected families, neither they nor the authorities have provided Amnesty International with dates or frequency of these meetings, or any details of what information was provided and discussed. Families were in agreement that, although meetings took place, there were inconsistencies in the information shared in the meetings by authorities regarding whose homesteads would be affected, as well as what the compensation would be.

Genuine consultation is one of the safeguards against forced evictions. However, all the affected families interviewed said that inconsistent information had been provided to them regarding details of the forced eviction. As such, they did not receive full, accurate and timely information in order to facilitate their meaningful participation. Some people told Amnesty International that they were simply told that their houses were to be demolished and that no opportunity had been given for raising concerns and comments. The meetings between government representatives and the affected families did not meet the threshold of genuine consultation as set out in Eswatini's obligations regarding international human rights law.

Initially, only those families located within the boundaries of the RSTP were told they would be affected by the development and compensated with alternative accommodation in nearby Bethany. However, all the families located within and outside the boundaries were ultimately evicted without any provision of alternative land or housing.

One of the affected residents told Amnesty International that, while they were offered an opportunity to *kukhonta* for land nearby, and made to pay US$7 for demarcating the boundaries of the land, they later found out that the same land had been given to another organization. In effect, therefore, the Eswatini authorities did not provide the affected families with alternative accommodation and their eviction left them homeless. This constitutes a forced eviction, in violation of international human rights law and standards.

Consequently, the Eswatini government approached the high court to seek the eviction of the residents (Swazi Government v 19 residents 2014). The high court granted an interim order which allowed the eviction of 10 families in Nokwane on 20 August 2014. The interim order was finalized by the same court on 8 September 2014. In response, the residents immediately launched an appeal (James 2014). Despite the pending appeal, which should have stayed the interim eviction order, the attorney general's office wrote to residents on 22 September, informing them that their homes would be demolished on 24 September. The residents launched an urgent application at the Mbabane High Court to stay the execution of the eviction order or to seek an interdict against demolitions of their homes pending the appeal. This application was dismissed by the Mbabane High Court on 24 September and, on the following day, 25 September, the forced evictions from Nokwane were initiated (James 2014). The attorney general's office effectively gave the residents two days' notice, which cannot be considered adequate. Adequate notice is one of the safeguards against forced evictions.

After the demolitions in September and October, the residents tried to appeal against their forced evictions. In December 2014, the Eswatini High Court found that 'the project is of national importance and the court cannot allow a situation where the project would fail just because of illegal squatters' (Swaziland Government v Jabulane Dlamini 2014). The high court ordered the eviction of the remaining families at Nokwane on the basis of 'overwhelming evidence' that the Eswatini government holds the title deeds to the farm. The court ruled that the land was SNL – the king, who owns the property in trust for the Swazi nation, allocated this land to the Ministry of Information Communications and Technology. The judge found that the residents failed to provide any evidence in the form of a legal agreement of how they managed to occupy the land (Swaziland Government v Jabulane Dlamini 2014). Although the residents tried to appeal against the eviction order, the Supreme Court of Appeal declined to pass judgment on the matter as demolitions had already taken place while the appeal was pending (Jabulani Dlamini & 9 Others v Eswatini Government 2015).

Families who were left homeless spent several nights in the open on the land where their homes once stood, before being assisted by a collective civil society initiative to access emergency shelter.[17] Some families lived in tents at the Lutheran Church in Manzini for more than a year until they dispersed and found alternative housing at their own expense. Some received donor assistance to secure the fees to acquire land through traditional means (*kukhonta*).

Conclusion

The above cases of forced evictions are a symptom of a deeper, underlying problem. At the heart of the matter is that many Swazi people – regardless of whether they are living on Swazi Nation Land, or on previous concession land that has now been converted to title-deed land – are not guaranteed security of tenure.

The forced evictions, in violation of international and regional human rights law, have led to homelessness, alongside a loss of sources

---

17 This included efforts by the Lutheran Church of Swaziland, the Swaziland Coalition of Concerned, the Council of Swaziland Churches, Lawyers for Human Rights Swaziland and the Red Cross

of livelihood and loss of and damage to belongings, as well as disruption of children's education. For those who have not been forcibly evicted but face imminent evictions in the Malkerns, Madonsa, Mbondzela and Vuvulane, the lack of adequate international safeguards against past forced evictions in Nokwane and the Malkerns has caused significant uncertainty and anxiety.

The cases documented demonstrate how the uncertainty over land ownership and tenure led to protracted legal battles which ultimately lead to forced evictions and homelessness.

In Nokwane, some residents believed they had settled on Swazi Nation Land, after paying allegiance to the area's chief. Others told Amnesty International they had been given permission by previous land owners, whom they understood to be the concession holders.

In the Malkerns, families who had been forcibly evicted and those facing imminent eviction were living on what they believed to be concession land, with the verbal permission of the previous landowner. While the concession land in some cases was legally converted to title-deed land, the residents said they were not aware of this arrangement and were not provided with adequate alternative accommodation or compensation when the new title-deed holder decided they no longer wanted the occupants on their land.

The cases highlight the failure of the Eswatini government to ensure that no one is rendered homeless and vulnerable to other human rights violations as a result of evictions. In the case of Nokwane, the Eswatini government failed to provide essential services to those affected by the forced eviction: food, potable water and sanitation, basic shelter and housing, appropriate clothing or means of livelihood. A collective civil society initiative ensured that those less able to provide for themselves, in particular older people, women-headed households and orphans, had access to basic services and food.

Amnesty International's research demonstrates that the existing legal framework in Eswatini fails to provide sufficient clarity and certainty regarding land ownership and other forms of tenure, which amounts to the Eswatini state's failure to meet both its regional and international obligations to take measures aiming to ensure residents' legal security of tenure. The current domestic framework provides fertile ground for forced evictions to take place. Justice is effectively denied and people are falling through the cracks.

References

Amnesty International (2018) 'They do not see us as people', London, Amnesty International

Armstrong, A.K. (1986) 'Legal aspects of land tenure in Swaziland', paper prepared as part of the Ministry of Agriculture and Cooperatives' research on Changes in Agricultural Land Use: Institutional Constraints and Opportunities

CESCR (1997) *General Comment 7*, Geneva, Office of the High Commissioner for Human Rights

Dlamini, J. (2010) 'Get out of my land!' *Times of Swaziland*, http://www.times.co.sz/news/21951-get-out-of-my-land.hmtl, accessed 2 February 2021

Deeds Registry, http://www.gov.sz/index.php?option=com_content&view=article&id=288&Itemid=386, accessed 2 February 2021

Dube, B.A. (2008) *Forced Evictions and Disability Rights in Africa*, Hauser Global Law School Program. University of New York, http://www.nyulawglobal.org/globalex/Forced_Evictions_Disability_Rights_Africa1.html, accessed 20 February 2021

Fakudza and FAO (2016) 'Malkerns Town Planning Scheme', Rome, Food and Agriculture Organisation

James, C. (2014) *Unlawful Evictions in Swaziland Signal More Disrespect for the Rule of Law*. Southern Africa Litigation Centre, http://www.southernafricalitigationcentre.org/2014/09/29/unlawful-evictions-in-Eswatini-signal-more-disrespect-for-the-rule-of-law/, accessed 20 February 2021

Levin, R. (1997) When the sleeping grass awakens', Johannesburg: Witwatersrand University Press

MICT (2017) 'Memo from Principal Secretary,12 August, Reference ICT/10/1. Eviction order of squatters at Mbanana Farm 692 at Nokwane', Mbabane, Ministry of Information, Communications and Technology

Mushala, H. M. (1992) "Legislation and soil conservation in Swaziland", University of Swaziland Research Journal no. 6, pp. 105-114.

Matsebula, J.S.M (1988). A History of Swaziland. Maskew Miller Longman

Phakathi, M. (2017) 'Kicking Swatis Onto the Streets', Open Society Institute of Southern Africa (OSISA) Blog, 24 July,

Swazi government (1996) 'Swaziland National Report', prepared for the City Summit, United Nations Conference on Human Settlements, Manzini http://uploads.habitat3.org/hb3/Habitat-II-NR-1996-Swaziland.pdf, accessed on 06/05/2021

United Nations Habitat. IFAD. Global Land Tool Network. Land and Natural Resources Tenure Security Learning Initiative for East and Southern Africa. Country Report Eswatini.

Zulu, J (2010) 'Don't bury dead at homesteads', *Times of Swaziland*, http://www.times.co.sz/news/21976-don-t-bury-dead-at-homesteads.html, accessed 19 February 2021

Legislation

Acquisition of Property Act 10 of 1961
Constitution of Swaziland (2006)
Draft National Land Policy, December 2009. Swaziland government.
Farm Dwellers Act of 1982
Land Concession Order, 1973
Royal Science and Technology Park Act 5 of 2012
Vesting of Land in King's Order. 1973

Cases

Case 1155/2014 Swazi Government (applicant) vs. 19 residents (respondents) and the Commissioner of Police (20th respondent). Mbabane High Court
Eswatini High Court Judgment. Case No 902/2011, p.3
Jabulani Dlamini and 9 Others vs. Eswatini Government (51/2014) (2015) SZSC 07 (9 December 2015)
Swaziland Government v Jabulane Dlamini & 19 Others (1155/14) [2014] SZHC401 (5 December 2014)
Umbane Limited vs Sofi Dlamini and 3 others (899/11,900/11,901/11 and 902/11) [2013] SZHC19 (13th February 2013)

PART III

Resistance and Struggles for Land Rights

CHAPTER 6

Civil Society struggles for peasants' rights over land in the Democratic Republic of Congo (DRC)

Blaise Muhire

Introduction

During the past two decades, peasants' struggles across Africa and elsewhere in the global South have been associated with land grabs and other harmful policies. These policies promote industrial agriculture on the one hand, and the failure of domestic policies to protect peasants and to advance food security at the local scale on the other hand. In the Democratic Republic of Congo (DRC), access to land as peasants' right has been hindered by several challenges from the 1960s to date, rooted in the colonial era. Some of these challenges are institutional and juridical; others are political and administrative. To address these challenges, a set of actors, which include the Congolese civil society organizations, believe that the violence around land access is inherent to inequalities caused by the ambiguities in the land laws and by the political use of these ambiguities by the elite to exclude peasants from access to land. Since the launch of the land reform process in 2012, very little has been achieved, and agricultural cooperatives across the country continue to fight for their rights.

While it is empirically justified that successful land reform would be a long-term solution for peasants' needs, the problem is that the success of the expected land reform continues to depend on the political will of the government. Moreover, in a context where land (mostly in rural areas) is accessed through patron-client networks, non-state initiatives (civil society) continue to be seen as a threat to the elite class for whom land reform is not a priority at all. In this chapter, I demonstrate how this elite's comfort lies in the legal and administrative land system which provides numerous juridical tools to dispossess land from communities and why the same elite hampers current efforts to reform the system.

While an important body of literature thoroughly discusses how, in the African context, contestations against land grabbing had led to agrarian reforms and changes in public policy (Locher, Steimann, and Upreti 2012, Rose 2002, Thaler 2013), other forms of dispossession are less explored. The aim of this chapter is precisely to examine *indirect dispossession,* namely the administrative and legal architecture of land governance as an analytical framework through which the elite indirectly and passively channels land dispossession over a long period.

The first part of this chapter presents the institutional and administrative land system in DRC. It shows how existing laws and structures in current land management are rooted in the colonial administration. The chapter also presents the reasons that the Congolese post-colonial government had not substantially adapted the land legal system to current realities – precisely, to provide a reliable and effective mechanism that would allow communities to secure land.

The second part uses a case study of Masisi Territory in the eastern DRC to illustrate how the difficulty for communities in accessing and securing land is mainly due to complex and contradicting land tenure systems since the independence of the country in 1960 (Mararo 1997, Tegera 2009). It emphasizes the 'passive dispossession' behind which the elite hides to grab large tracts of land at the expense of small-scale farmers. The last part examines current efforts by civil society towards fair agrarian reform and land tenure security that favours the peasantry while simultaneously describing major obstacles to these attempts. Information used in this chapter was collected from extensive field research conducted between 2013 and 2017 in Masisi (eastern DRC) and other specific studies currently going on. Data was collected using interviews, direct and participative observations and several focus groups, as well as fresh inputs from my current commitment to land issues.

Institutional and administrative organization of the land tenure system

The legal landscape of land management in DRC comprises of multiple coexisting regulation systems and both formal and informal mechanisms for settling the conflict, with custom as an important source of the regulation (Mukokobya 2013, p. 58). Research on legal pluralism in DRC has largely been oriented towards questions of land, emphasizing contradictions in the existing legal framework and the lack of a transparency in land acquisition procedures (Mugangu 2007, p. 386, Huggins 2010, p. 12). The major characteristic of legal pluralism in land tenure management in DRC has been the overlapping of laws within the existing legal framework as well as the conflict of competence between institutions in charge of the implementation of these laws.

Another problem is how these laws and institutions apply in rural areas where customary authorities continue to claim ownership of land and the authority to distribute it (Action Solidaire pour la Paix 2014). In this section, I intend to outline the structures and institutions related to land tenure management in DRC. Afterwards, I discuss the setting of land-related laws and show how violent conflicts around land are deeply rooted in and fuelled by a framework of laws and institutions.

As Figure 6.1 below, from the central government, illustrates, ministries dealing directly with land do not all follow the same logic in terms of lines of hierarchy. While the Ministry of Land functions with its local structures in a *'déconcentré'* [devolved] logic, the Ministry of Internal Affairs functions with a *'décentralisé'* [decentralised] philosophy.

To explain in more depth, *déconcentré* is a process of unitary state planning which consists of establishing administrative authorities representing the state in local administrative districts. These authorities are deprived of all autonomy and legal personality. They cannot be elected; instead, they are appointed by the national minister. Meanwhile, decentralization implies a unitary state management process that involves the transfer of administrative powers from the state to local entities (or communities) distinct from the state. These local entities have autonomy, and public authorities in these entities are elected representatives. In DRC, *déconcentré* entities have existed since the first and second republics, dating from the 1960s. Although the decentralization law has existed since the 1980s, the first substantial outcome was the creation of provincial government and assemblies in 2005. From then onward, both *déconcentré'* and 'decentralized' entities have co-existed and functioned in parallel, generating contested decision-making and perpetuating an ongoing crisis of authority between the two administrative systems.

Through the decree-law no. 081 of 2 July 1998, which provided for the administrative organization of entities, modified and completed by the decree-law no. 018/2001 of 28 September 2001, the government decided to create provincial governments and assemblies in 2005. With the creation of the provincial governments, each of which had a

Figure 6.1: Conflicts of competence in land management between state institutions

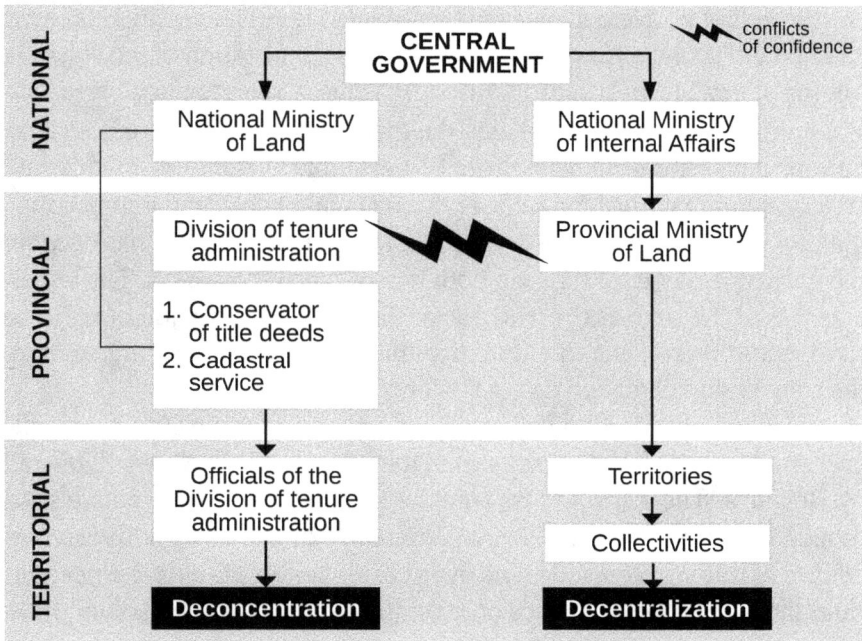

Ministry of Land and Customary Affairs, land tenure affairs came to be entirely managed by the National Ministry of Land via the Division of Land Tenure (see Figure 6.1 above). Since 2005, the national ministry has operated via the Division of Land Tenure while at the same time the provincial ministries of land affairs function in parallel to the Division. The decentralization structures are controlled by the provincial government whereas the devolved system is composed of the services that directly represent national ministries on the provincial and territorial level through a structure called a 'division' for each national ministry. However, the terms of collaboration and the limits of competences in land management between decentralized and 'deconcentrated' structures are not provided thus far by any of these laws. Before discussing the conflicting role allocation between decentralized and deconcentrated structures, it is useful to consider the organization of land tenure management might be useful to consider.

The problem with the legal framework on land tenure governance

In this section, particular attention is given to an analysis of crucial laws affecting the land tenure system: how they contribute to ongoing conflict while Big Men simultaneously benefit hugely from inherent ambiguities within the legal framework around the land tenure system.

The first post-independence land-related law, enacted in 1966, was called the 'Bakajika Law' and targeted the nationalization of the Katanga mining sector. It was only in July 1973 that a more general land law was introduced: this law remains the most important legal reference in current land tenure management. For example, Article 53 of this law clearly states that 'the land is the exclusive, inalienable, and imprescriptible property of the Congolese state'. In this regard, the state has become the exclusive owner of the land both in rural and urban areas. The exclusiveness of the state as the land owner thus begs the question of why the state would be so keen to emphasize this exclusivity since, in any case, the state is sovereign and can make any decision.

At the time this land law came out, only one decade after independence, many agricultural companies in the Kivu province were still owned by Belgians. The 1973 law became the legal device for claiming a state monopoly over all resources and particularly to get rid of both external control of mining companies and even customary supremacy over certain rural lands. The 1973 law not only reinforced the Bakajika law of 1966 but also opened up a legal avenue for political elites close to the regime to acquire huge plantations that once belonged to the Belgian companies. Another contextual factor regarding the land law of 1973 was Mobutu's 'Zairianization' ideology, active from 1975, of nationalizing all companies held by foreigners. Before discussing how this law contributes to the current violent conflict, an analysis of its key references is needed to understand how Big Men control land at all scales.

One of the problems with the land law is that it begins with the distinction between what it terms '*terres du domaine public*' and '*terres du domaine privé*'. 'Public land' means areas in which public services or specific activities by the state can be located, whereas 'private land' refers to areas in which the state can offer a plot of land to individuals or companies. The land under customary authority in chieftaincies has been defined as 'private land'. According to Article 53 of the land law, the state can grant land to any individual or company, both in public and private land areas. Here is where the current tensions between customary chiefs and public institutions are rooted. In designating customary land within the category of 'private' land, there is no longer any distinction between which kind of land customary chiefs can exercise their authority over and which land the state can use without interfering in customary land transactions. Customary chiefs continue to complain as public services in land tenure management continue to issue title deeds on customary areas based on Article 387, which stipulates that the 'land occupied by local communities enters, from the entry into force of the land law, into the public area'.

However, in promulgating the land law, parliament seemed to anticipate eventual tensions over Article 387, and in Article 389 provided details of how anyone could acquire a plot of land in areas where local communities were settled. This article states that a 'Presidential Ordinance will be issued to clarify the status of land occupied by local communities as well as customary competence on those lands' (Article 389). However, no ordinance has been issued since 1973. The remaining puzzle is how customary land areas (entities in which local communities are recognized to be subject to the chief's authority) should be managed in the absence of this ordinance.

For Mugangu (2007, p. 390), the question raised by this article is whether Parliament intended, through the promise of an ordinance, to maintain the status quo and to leave the issue of rural land tenure to a future law. He suspects that if the answer is yes, then it could be argued by the supreme court that, until the promised presidential ordinance is signed, this land must be managed according to the customary rules. In practice, public institutions continue to prevail and issue certificates, and thus to reinforce the dualism between customary authorities and public agents. Incidentally, this dualism is far from being resolved, even though the 1973 law apparently gives exclusive management of land to the state. An alternative pathway to resolution seems to be offered within the constitution of February 2006: Article 34 provides that 'public services of land management must respect all rights acquired in accordance with the customary procedures,' meaning that public institutions cannot issue any certificate to peasants who received land from customary chiefs. Unfortunately, Article 34 remains subordinate to Article 389 of the land law, which also refers to the presidential ordinance.

Considering that violence around land is reportedly experienced mainly at the local level due to the involvement of the local community, peacebuilding organizations have bought into a dichotomy between state authorities (legal and institutional frameworks) and customary authorities. In Masisi and Bashali chieftaincy specifically, there is a widespread narrative of land conflict, centred on the idea that land in Masisi belongs to autochthonous communities (Hunde, Nyanga and Nande). This is because, first of all, the demarcation between the two categories of land mentioned in the land law is not documented and mapped, meaning it is no longer possible today to locate the real boundaries between customary areas and public land areas. Second, there is a strong assumption held by customary authorities that the land in Bashali and Bahunde chieftaincies is exclusively customary property.

This dualism has extended beyond functioning as a narrative: it has been taken on board through several peacebuilding programs. Local committees formed by international NGOs in different villages of Masisi to promote dialogue and to resolve land-related conflicts reflect this binary conception: this is apparent when one looks at the composition of the members of those local committees. Each committee, for example, includes both customary chiefs and local state representatives, carrying the assumption that both parties can find common ground for transitional solutions to violence.

This dualism has been strongly emphasized in the existing literature concerning land in eastern Congo. However, the dualism has to be treated with a degree of caution. According to the Cadastral Service[1], not all land in chieftaincies is necessarily customary property as claimed by customary chiefs. This duality was already rooted in the colonial administration, under which customary entities were recognized as territories within which customary chiefs had the authority to distribute resources, mainly land, to community members. The problem is that, while recognizing customary authority over land, the colonial administration privatized thousands of hectares of land for farming in Masisi, regardless of whether or not this land was in customary areas. As shown by a report by Action Solidaire pour la Paix (2014, p. 55), the colonial administration had already divided a number of chieftaincies in Masisi into farming land in the 1950s. After independence, what the land law of 1973 did in nationalizing the land was to legally allow any individual or company to access any land anywhere through public institutions. It is in this context that, between 1970 and 1990, political and military elites acquired almost all the former colonial farms with fertile soils and, more importantly, ideally suited for cattle farming. To date, according to several Congolese civil society organizations working in the land sector, fewer than ten individuals among these elites own entirely the fertile lands in Masisi.

1 The technical body within the Division of Land Tenure responsible for land registration and valuation. Before a title deed is provided to anyone by the chairperson of the Division, the Cadastral Service has to offer a geospatial mapping to document the exact limit and location.

The case study: From land access to land dispossession in Masisi

The sense of dispossession in this context is related to inequalities between powerful individuals and small-scale farmers in access to land. The fact that the land tenure regime in DRC does not limit anybody with money from acquiring secured land (with title deed), small scale farmers are continuously being dispossessed of their 'non-secured' small plots (see Mathieu and Tsongo 1998). This situation is exacerbated by a lack of coordination or clear limits regarding competences in land tenure management. This was clearly explained by the president of a local peace court in Masisi:

> The real problem is the lack of coordination and transparency between public land management services. Most of the time, these services issue land title deeds to two or more persons but for the same plot of land. Other cases relate to conflicts opposing big landowners with title deeds to small scale farmers whose land is often received from local customary authorities, which means without titles. (Interview, Masisi, IV, 16 October 2014)

Still, in Masisi, a considerable number of the people who have received land from customary chiefs have managed to acquire title deeds from the cadastral services to cover their land legally. This quest for titles deeds has frustrated customary chiefs because they no longer receive a fee for the land covered by title deeds. In addition, the public authorities in the land tenure administration, both in Masisi and elsewhere in the country, do not make a distinction between land acquired in chieftaincies and land acquired in the public domain. In the customary domain, the chief can offer land to a family representative, not as a commercial transaction, but as a means of survival for members of local communities. Many of the people who received land from customary chiefs and later on managed to register it are somehow independent from customary authorities who continue to consider this way of accessing land a usurpation of customary authority and a hidden strategy of dispossession by the elites. Yet even some customary chiefs registered some parts of customary land in order to get title deeds; some even apparently procured title deeds in their own names and not for the people under their authorities.

As far as the political dimension of land dispossession strategy is concerned, the question becomes whether or not it would be useful to harmonize the coordination between public services and customary chiefs. In doing so, one would assume that there would be no overlapping authority in land tenure management, and that it would prevent land dispossession by the elites who corrupt public services. During a discussion with the provincial minister, he seemed to hope that the land reforms announced in 2012 would tackle this issue. It is also important to note that, although the provincial ministry of land is assumed to be playing a passive role as policy advisor, by contrast, the cadastral services are assumed to be playing a technical role. In practice, not only do the competences overlap, but the position and role of the chairperson of the cadastral services have also been subject to politics. For example, during the rebellion of the Congolese Rally for Democracy (CRD or Rassemblement Congolaise pour la Démocratie, RCD, in French) that controlled two thirds of the national territory from 1998 to 2003, the chairperson of the cadastral service was appointed by the rebel administration, not by the central government.

Several human rights activists had accused this rebellion of looting the Congolese natural resources. However, land dispossession had not caught the attention of these activists. In Masisi, for example, during the RCD rebellion the governor of North Kivu province allowed easy access to land and title deeds for his close collaborators, many of whom were among the political and military elites. This was made possible in two ways. First, by nominating a chairperson of the cadastral service, powerful individuals in the rebel administration and other close collaborators of the administration acquired huge tracts of land and legalized title deeds. An example of this is the Société Internationale de Commerce et des Industries Agricoles (SICIA), a former colonial plantation. This plantation, which is approximately 4,000 hectares, was divided into 28 plantations in 1998 with the authorization of the governor, and shared among only ten or so individuals (senior founder members of the RCD rebellion). In November 2014, when I visited this former SICIA plantation, I managed to meet with a group of people among the hundreds of families that were expelled between 2000 and 2002 by the new owners. Many of these families are still living in camps for internally displaced persons. Second, during the political negotiation between the RCD and the government in 2002, it was agreed that all juridical acts of the RCD administration, including court decisions, appointments to administrative posts and title deeds, would be considered 'legal' by the new government. This means that all title deeds obtained by powerful individuals during the rebellion's control were legalised and endorsed by the central government, regardless of the negative consequences on the small-scale farmers' households.

At the beginning of the government of transition in 2003, many former RCD elites gained administrative and political positions in higher institutions at the national level. These positions allowed them not only to secure their land in Masisi and elsewhere within eastern DRC but also to acquire even more land and to register this land at the national level. Some of them even gained land certificates in perpetuity. While the maintenance of this land system dysfunction seems to provide elites with avenues to dispossess land, peasants' contestations against dispossession have not been directly expressed by peasants themselves, as the peasant movement is not so organised. The next section will examine two main actors with different approaches, from whom one can better understand community responses towards land dispossession. The first actor is the community armed resistance and the second is civil society with its efforts towards a fair agrarian reform.

The Hutu and Hunde community resistance in Masisi

Masisi Territory ('territory' is the administrative name for sub-provinces) is inhabited by five community groups, the majority being the Hutu and Hunde. In the beginning of the 1990s, there was a group of young Hutu, many of whom were former combatants in local militias. They were informally organized in several villages in Masisi, without any particular name.

According to some influential local leaders, these young people became actively violent against some owners of large tracts of land in the areas where Hutu were living, claiming this was to protect the Hutu and *their* lands. When the Hutu peasants realized (at the end of the 1990s) that vast tracts of land were increasingly being purchased by some individuals (political and economic elites), which prevented them accessing land for their agriculture activities, violent resistance became their strategy to force landowners either to leave a piece of land to allow surrounding peasants to cultivate it, or to face violent eviction. This is what happened, for example, in 2011, when an individual purchased a farm in Kaniro (Masisi). This piece of land was at that time occupied by many Hutu families who considered it theirs even though none of them possessed any title deed.

When the new owner asked those families to leave the land without any negotiation, a group of Hutu young men killed more than 200 cows as a strategy to force the owner to leave the area. A local cooperative,

CAJEL, working in Masisi shared a report with me in which they noted that 19 cows were killed in July and 102 in August 2014. Between February and March 2015, 68 were killed in Bashali (one of the chieftaincies of Masisi). This strategy of killing cows continues to be used in Masisi by unidentified groups. CAJEL senior members suspected this killing to have been done by some local militia groups, as a strategy to force landowners to negotiate or leave the land.

Another community armed resistance is led by Hunde leaders, the People's Alliance for Free & Sovereign Congo (APCLS). Among many other political and economic grievances, APCLS leaders use the rhetoric of autochthony to claim exclusive ownership of the land in Masisi as customary land property. A collective discourse held by the Hunde community leaders suggests that the Hunde families are dispossessed from their land by foreigner communities, notably the Hutu, whose political and economic elite groups occupy strategic positions in higher institutions. What remains true is that Hutu elites are amongst the large-scale landowners, alongside the Tutsi in Masisi.

Since 1996, Masisi has hosted more than ten active armed groups with a particular emphasis on protecting land against dispossession. Although the quest for arable land seems to oppose local communities to each other (horizontally) through armed resistance, the confusion and dysfunction of the land management system remains the leading causes of the current chaos. So far, local resistance of these armed groups has not been proven to be a long-term solution either locally or at the national level. This is the reason civil society organizations across the country have started, since 2010, to play an active role in the current attempts towards an agrarian reform.

An example of a peasants' working framework: strategies and challenges

This section provides an example of a working framework for peasants' movements. There are many others across the country; this one will, hopefully, serve as an illustration of how peasants strive to protect their rights while facing the challenges related to overall land tenure governance in DRC.

The Federation des Organizations des Producteurs Agricoles du Congo au North-Kivu (FOPAC-NK) is a Congolese non-profit organization created in 2002 in the North Kivu province by several cooperatives of small-scale farmers. The mission was to ensure the representation of and advocacy for agricultural producers at the local, provincial, national, regional, and international levels. Its objectives are to:

- Strengthen the lobbying and advocacy capacity of FOPAC-NK to bring about changes in policies and practices in the agricultural sector
- Ensure exchanges of experiences among agricultural stakeholders and cohesion among the unions for better structuring and professionalization of agricultural producers
- Make agricultural education and information accessible in real time in a dynamic of interactive communication among producers
- Increase agricultural productivity through the emergence of the gender approach and young professional farmers
- Improve the management and organization of FOPAC-NK and its member organizations for better governance of agricultural producer structures
- Promote gender-based leadership and young farmers.

To reach the above objectives, FOPAC-NK focuses on lobbying and advocacy, a thematic concertation framework, information, education and communication, as well as building the capacity of its members. The idea of creating FOPAC-NK was motivated by several challenges faced by agricultural producers, including the difficulty of accessing the land and lack of land titles deeds to secure small farmers as the legal procedures are costly. At that time, these challenges were exacerbated by scarcity of arable land because of the vast expanses that have been converted into pasture for livestock, to the detriment of thousands of families who depend on subsistence agriculture for small areas. Thus, the mission of FOPAC-NK was to:

- Negotiate with the large land owners for them to put small plots of their lands at the disposal of the peasants to allow them to cultivate under certain conditions such as shelling or royalties
- Strengthen the capacities of members in production and marketing techniques
- Identify markets and inform cooperatives about potential customers
- Propose legal texts such as Édit , decrees or laws to the legislator in favour of farmers, even if the implementation of some of these texts still poses problems.

A concrete example of their influence at policy level is the Agricultural Code written and proposed in 2010 by members of FOPAC to the parliament and promulgated in 2012. According to the executive secretary of FOPAC-NK, during an interview in Goma,

> The idea with this law was to arrive at an agrarian reform because it offers technical provisions favourable to a reform that would favour hundreds of thousands of agricultural producers [having] difficulty access[ing] arable land. There is, therefore, a link between the Agricultural Code, the 1973 land law, [and] the land reform in the sense that the reform is a process and the agricultural code gives it content. (Interview, Goma, 4 December 2014)

To put it in context, this code was submitted to parliament in 2010, but nothing was done until a few months later before the general elections, including the presidential election. Thanks to a nation-wide mobilization, members of FOPAC across the country decided not to vote if the parliament did not choose the Agricultural Code. This pressure was significant and members of the parliament ended up voting for the code. The outcome was a kind of win-win situation, and for FOPAC it was at least a huge step in its fight. The problem with this code, however, is that it requires a roadmap to allow its implementation which must be approved by the parliament. Unfortunately, this roadmap does not exist yet, and the national committee in charge of proposing the draft seems to be less committed to the process. This lack of commitment hides a major stake, raised in the code mentioned above. In the first version of the Agricultural Code, Article 16 stipulates that in case of transfer of land to foreign investors, the Congolese government would hold more than 51 per cent of the shares. However, this article was later amended, and this time it indicated that individuals or companies can invest in all shares without the need to necessarily associate with government. FOPAC-NK and the other actors protecting the interests of agricultural producers across the country believe that the amendment to Article 16 opens up loopholes for land grabbing to the detriment of peasants, hence the need for advocacy. As a strategy, all FOPAC representatives across the country had decided to create a national platform called the National Confederation of Agricultural Producers of Congo (Confédération Nationale des Producteurs Agricoles au Congo, CONAPAC, in French) with its headquarters in the capital Kinshasa and representation in the provinces, namely in North Kivu, South

Kivu, Katanga, Maniema, Kassai Oriental, Kassai Occidental, Province Orientale, Central Congo, Ecuador, and Bandundu. CONAPAC, at its creation, was meant to be a platform organization that brought together provincial federations of agricultural producers and specialized agricultural federations either by sector of activity or by categories of agricultural producers. Provincial federations' members elect their leaders who represent them within CONAPC, through its various statutory bodies, including the general assembly, the board of directors, and the supervisory commission. The delegates of the provincial federations gathered in the general assembly define the general policy of CONAPAC, approve the various reports, elect the members of various statutory bodies, and create and define the tasks of the specialized or permanent specialized commissions. The next section shows how CONAPAC and its partners join existing efforts to influence the reform.

Towards agrarian reform: peasants' rights and the role of civil society organizations

In 2009, the Congolese organization, Forum des Amis de la Terre (FAT), benefited from financial support from the EU through a partnership with the French NGO CCDF-Terre Solidaire to carry out a study on conflict in Masisi and Lubero. This study aimed to understand land issues in North Kivu in order to, first, build the capacity of local Congolese organizations in land conflict management and, second, to come up with a strategy to address the conflicts around land. The two major recommendations made by this study were the implementation of local mechanisms for mediation and reconciliation of land-related conflicts and advocacy for land reform, and new modes of land tenure management. According to a local expert on land issues who I met during my fieldwork in Goma, the rationale behind this diagnostic was to advocate for a legal mechanism that would allow the protection of land used by small-scale farmers and families. He noted, for example, that:

> Land-related conflicts remain very [much more] important than other types of conflict in the eastern part of the country. It is for this reason that many UN agencies and international NGOs have been focusing on the prevention of violent conflict. (Interview Goma V 16 January 2015)

Notably, although different analyses of the conflict in Masisi and its surroundings strongly emphasize the three factors of violence, the focus on land issues has become a central theme in several programs implemented.

There is little or no consideration of the question of power and identity. Some of the project documents I collected from different organizations show this clearly. In 2013, for example, the United Nations Development Programme (UNDP), UN-Habitat and the Food and Agricultural Organisation (FAO) implemented a joint program titled 'Program of the securitization of land tenure for the integration and community recovery in eastern Congo'. The organizations behind this program made two main arguments. The first was that peacebuilding in eastern DRC depends on a durable solution to the problems caused by land issues. The second, along the same lines as the first, emphasizes that the recovery of land to meet the population's needs, particularly in rural areas, depends upon access through the use of 'secured' land and other natural resources. This program is premised on the idea that most small-scale farmers have only limited access to arable land; moreover, that the limited access to land they possess is in danger of expropriation by large-scale farmers known as *'grands concessionaires'* (major landowners). These two arguments, widely put forward by civil society organizations, both Congolese and international, since 2008, have led to the development of several initiatives around land questions both at provincial and national levels.

The first major initiative was the creation of group called *'Coordination Foncière'* (Land Coordination), a working platform that included UN agencies as well as Congolese and international organizations involved in land issues. This initiative was taken in 2013 by UN-Habitat in cooperation with the Ministry of Land Affairs of North Kivu. Members of the Land Coordination group meet once a month to share their experiences and to discuss how they can better coordinate their efforts on the ground. Although the provincial ministry leads regular meetings, UN-Habitat acts as the secretariat of the platform. It continues to show a strong interest in taking a leadership role, especially in policymaking. In 2013, for example, UN-Habitat drafted an *edit* (different from a law, an *edit* is a legal text equivalent to a law, but at the provincial parliament level), which proposed guidelines for collaboration between customary authorities and public institutions on land management. This edict successfully persuaded the provincial ministry to advocate voting for it in the provincial parliament so that the governor would sign it. When the minister was replaced, the legal procedure slowed down, and the edict is yet to be implemented.

Even so, international and Congolese NGOs remained concerned about land issues and continued to advocate for what could be a long-term solution and one which could involve the government of the DRC. It is from this perspective that International Alert (International Alert 2012, p. 49) expressed the need for what it termed a 'grounded approach to peacebuilding'. To this end, two Congolese organizations (Forum des Amis de la Terre, FAT, and FOPAC) received financial support from International Alert to carry out a series of concerted efforts at the 'local community' level, in both North Kivu and South Kivu provinces. Unlike the general land law (discussed above), the Agricultural Code is precise and focuses on the local mechanisms of conflict resolution. One of the members mentioned that:

> The Agricultural Code will provide effective tools to deal with the current land-related conflicts, namely when I see different stakeholders who are supposed to be working in the structures this law provides... (Interview Goma, 25 March 2014).

Different informants I met were, however, pessimistic about the chances of implementing the Agricultural Code if the central government does not support it through a deep reform of the land tenure system. Meanwhile, the necessity of pushing the government toward this desired reform is clearly expressed by international organizations through different funding programs. For example, to support this idea of 'securitization' of land, the United States Agency for International Development (USAID) granted UN-Habitat a fund to boost the land reform process. In the same period, the Global Land Tool Network (GLTN) followed the same example in funding UN-Habitat for one year to support land reform and other related initiatives. At the time I was collecting data during fieldwork, I was interested in the outcomes of these programs. Apart from a few workshops organized by these UN agencies, there was nothing concrete related to land securitization nor any appropriate step towards the promised land reform process on the provincial level.

These joint efforts finally led the Congolese government to announce a land reform process (discussed above). The first step was the organization of a national workshop on land reforms held in Kinshasa in 2012. During this workshop, participants identified three major concerns: the need to set up a legal mechanism that would promote the 'securitization' of small-scale farmers; clarification of the extent and limits of authority between public services at different levels; and the need to clarify the status of customary chiefs, as defined by Article 389 of the land law of 1973 and Article 207 of the constitution.

The second step in land reform was Decree No. 13/016 of 31 May 2013, issued by the National Ministry of Land for the establishment, organization, and functioning of the national committee in charge of the land reform process. While actions relative to this decree were supposed to end by 2017, the roadmap signed by stakeholders in Kinshasa during the national workshop has not been implemented yet. So far, neither the land code nor any of the edicts cited above have yet been approved by the parliaments.

Meanwhile, alleviating land-related tensions is one of the operating spheres; many international organizations have been trying to implementing projects within the most affected communities under the label 'tenure securitization'. By the 'securitization', these organizations mean bringing small farmers and large landowners to the same table to negotiate. The idea here is to come up with a deal whereby certificates can be delivered to a group of farmers at an affordable price. The first problem with the 'securitization' is that many farmers cannot afford the price, and the deals are usually temporary. FOPAC-NK finds this arrangement to be a kind of humanitarian intervention that does not protect small farmers from a long-term perspective. While FOPAC (through CONAPAC) intensifies the advocacy at different levels, some NGOs prefer to negotiate short-term solutions. FOPAC's strategy is a good example of how it is possible to focus on a long-term perspective amidst the legal and administrative adversities. The second problem is that these international organizations do not directly involve cooperatives of small farmers that work with FOPAC. There is an apparent lack of coordination, and often one can observe a duplication through activities in the field.

Such short-term solutions driven by a humanitarian philosophy are keeping people in dependency, and therefore hamper the long term vision FOPAC has been fighting for. One would agree that FOPAC still has a long way to go. Challenges and all kinds of adversities are complex and diverse. The basic land law is relatively old (more than 40 years old) and hardly addresses current challenges. Land governance in DRC has become, unfortunately, a field of humanitarian intervention and a target of foreign investors led by liberal economy through land exploitation.

In some African countries, experiences in land governance have shown that having policies is one thing, and implementing them is another (Boone 2007, p. 559). This is particularly the case for sensitive issues such as natural resources. Even though it is a commonplace to understand land reforms as a form of direct state intervention in property relations, the capacity of the state in most African countries to carry out land reform is severely limited, and especially so when it takes the form of redistribution or resettlement. Often, it is less the result of direct state action and more the result of the actions of private individuals within the state (Manji 2001, p. 328). As seems to be the case in DRC regarding the land reform process, initiatives and activities are largely carried out by local NGOs with the support of international organizations and UN agencies.

The Congolese government's role in this reform falls short of willingness to get fully involved. One of the reasons for this is the potential cost of reforms that may be too expensive to implement. Another factor is that political elite from Masisi may fear negative repercussions of land reform, since they are among the biggest landowners, even as they hold power in key institutions supposedly boosting the land reform process. At the present moment, the abundant legal ambiguity within the land tenure system seems not to be a concern for large-scale landowners. As long as the plurality of laws and institutional overlapping provide this maneuvering space, stakeholders behind land dispossession will continue to challenge normative approaches to account for the rationales of conflict dynamics in Masisi and other places in DRC.

Concluding thoughts

This chapter aimed to examine the form and the process of land dispossession using the case study of Masisi in the eastern DRC. Rather than other well-known forms of land dispossession, this chapter looks at *indirect* land dispossession. From a thorough analysis of the administrative and legal architecture of land governance as an analytical framework, this chapter demonstrates how the elite indirectly – but systematically – managed (and continue) to channel land dispossession over a long period. The elites use some articles in the land-related laws while instrumentalizing institutions dealing with land management (cadastral services and so on). By doing so, the elites buy large tracts of land at the expenses of small-scale farers (local communities) who need small tracts of land to fulfill basic needs for their survival.

This chapter discussed different forms of community resistance. Local leaders managed to bring together their community members in armed resistance through the formation of armed militias as a strategy to protect their land. As discussed, this armed resistance unfortunately fails to translate into a peasant's movement that can bring together issues related to land dispossession. Even in other regions of the country where there is no local armed resistance, the lack of a structured and coordinated peasants' movements means that there is insufficient demonstration of how land dispossession could be discouraged. Another form of resistance is non-violent, through advocacy. Despite current efforts to address land-related issues, many civil society organizations involved in defence of peasants' rights believe that improving governance over land tenure is the only solution to mitigate violence and to reduce inequalities among the population. By analysing the legal framework, this chapter warns that the current problems faced by peasants are caused by the legislator, to serve the elite. Even if several actors are pushing agrarian reform, it is worth mentioning that this reform contains political and economic implications, which justify why the government is reluctant despite the pressure from a wide range of actors. As long as *indirect* dispossession of land does not imply massive displacement and relocation of the population, the elites will continue to feel less concerned about local communities' collective rights to access land. The examples of local resistance discussed in this chapter show that there is a need for a more coordinated strategy that would navigate all scales, from the local to the national level.

References

Action Solidaire pour la Paix (2014) *Pour Que Les Bashali Fument Le Calumet De La Paix : Rapport De Recherche Action Participative Sur Les Conflits Inter-Paysans Liés À La Gestion Des Terres Rurales En Chefferie Des Bashali, Dans Le Territoire De Masisi (RDC), 2010–2014*, Série des Grands Lacs, Uppsala, Life & Peace Institute

Boone C, (2007) 'Property and Constitutional Order: Land Tenure Reform and the Future of the African State', *African Affairs*, Vol. 106, No. 425, pp. 557-586

Huggins C. (2010) *Terre, Pouvoir Et Identité. Les Causes Profondes Des Violents Conflits Dans L'est De La République Démocratique Du Congo*, London, International Alert

International Alert (2012) *Ending the deadlock: Towards a new vision of peace in eastern DRC*

Locher, M., Steimann, B. and Upreti, B.R. (2012) 'Land grabbing, investment principles and plural legal orders of land use', *The Journal of Legal Pluralism and Unofficial Law*, 44:65, pp. 31-63

Mararo B. (1997) 'Land, power and ethnic conflict in Masisi (Congo-Kinshasa), 1940's-1994', *International Journal of African Historical Studies*, 30(3): pp. 503-38

Mathieu P. A. and Tsongo M. (1998) 'Guerres paysannes au Nord-Kivu (République démocratique du Congo), 1937-1994'. *Cahiers D'études Africaines*, Vol. 38, No. 150

Mugangu M. S. (2007) 'La crise foncière à l'Est de la RDC', *L'Afrique des Grands Lacs. Annuaire 2007-2008*, pp. 385-414

Mukokobya M.R. (2013) *Pluralisme Juridique Et Règlement Des Conflits En République Démocratique Du Congo*, Paris, Harmattan

Rose, L.L, (2002) 'African elites' land control manoeuvers', *Etudes Rurales* (No. 163-164), pp. 187-213

Tegera A. (2009) *Les Banyarwanda Du Nord-Kivu (RDC) Au Xxème Siècle. Analyse Historique Et Socio-Politique D'un Groupe Transfrontalier (1885–2006)*, Paris, Université de Paris 1 Panthéon – Sorbonne U.F.R. D'Histoire

Thaler, K. (2013) 'Large-scale land acquisitions and social conflict in Africa', paper presented at conferences on Food sovereignty: a critical dialogue, Yale University, September

CHAPTER 7

Land Enclosures in Namibian Communal Lands: Popular Resistance and State Repression in N#a-Jaqna

Pablo Gilolmo Lobo

Introduction

The Namibian agrarian sector, except for the northern area, is mostly dedicated to extensive livestock farming. Due to its extremely dry conditions, livestock farming in Namibia requires exceptionally large farm sizes. For reference, in Otjozondjupa Region (where the case addressed herein is located), the average commercial farm is 3,327 hectares (Namibia Statistics Agency 2015, p. 19). Owing to the settler-colonial past, about 36 per cent of Namibian territory is not 'commercial' but 'communal' land (Mendelsohn, el Obeid, de Klerk and Vigne 2006, p. 13).[1] This communal status derives directly from the pre-independence division between white exclusive areas and 'native homelands'. Former 'native homelands' are now communal areas under state proprietorship and under the custodianship of traditional authorities (TAs). TAs have powers on land allocations, but always under the supervision of communal land boards (CLBs). CLBs are administrative bodies in which TAs, various government ministries and community members are represented.[2]

Livestock farming in communal areas is generally more arduous than on commercial farms because, in pre-independence times, the

---

1 By convention, in Namibia, 'commercial farms' are freehold farms in the formerly exclusively white areas, while 'communal' refers to former 'native homelands'. 'Homelands' (or, before 1964, 'native reserves') were the rural areas assigned for blacks before independence. Today, these areas are referred to as 'communal areas' or 'communal lands'. Even if private farming is also practiced in communal areas, this is seldom referred to as 'commercial'.

2 CLBs are composed of representatives of various ministries, the regional council, the concerned traditional authorities and conservancies, as well as the 'organized' farming community. Also four women must be part of the boards, two engaged in farming activities, and two 'who have expertise relevant to the functions of a board'. The attributions of CLBs are, among others, 'to exercise control over the allocation and the cancellation of customary land rights by Chiefs or Traditional Authorities' and 'to consider and decide on applications for a right of leasehold' (Republic of Namibia 2002:5).

white administration placed native homelands in areas with dryer environmental conditions and poorer pastures. Yet the social, economic, demographic and infrastructural conditions of these areas, marginalized by the political geography of white settler capitalism (WSC), are causes of hardship for their inhabitants as much as the harsh natural conditions under which they produce their livelihoods. Market-oriented (that is, commercial) livestock farming takes place in communal lands, but its contribution to national agricultural production is relatively small (Mendelsohn et al. 2006, p. 10). Furthermore, different and often opposed developmental visions, incompatible land-uses and overlapping claims on communal lands produce knotty conflicts, some of which we will explore in this short chapter.

In recent decades, conflict over communal lands in Namibia has taken its most visible expression in the form of *illegal fencing*. Traditional authorities, local rural entrepreneurs and urbanites, as well as the petty and bureaucratic bourgeoisies, are the main agents behind the accelerated and uncontrolled extension of illegal land enclosures (see, for example. Odendaal 2011, Werner 1997, 2011). The motive forces behind this enclosure movement are both 'internal' and 'external' to these areas themselves. The internal factor that fosters land enclosures is class differentiation at the local level. The external factor consists, mainly, of the above-mentioned action of incomers who enclose tracts of land on their own initiative, but also on state-driven development projects. These development projects come about under the aegis of both the Namibian government and international donors (see Gilolmo forthcoming).

The erection of fences in communal areas is forbidden since the promulgation of the Communal Land Reform Act (CLRA) in 2002 As per CLRA regulations,fences erected before 2003 may be authorised, but those erected after that date are generally regarded as illegal with only some exceptions. For instance, CLBs as well as government may grant exclusive access to tracts of communal land through leasehold agreements, thus allowing physically enclosing them (Republic of Namibia 2002). Both pre-CLRA fencing and approved leaseholds mean that enclosures of Namibian communal lands may also obtain from legal means. However, and beyond legalistic definitions, conflicts related to communal lands are invariably related to the fact that the different actors involved enjoy unequal access to the springs of state power. Concomitantly, the state, in making use of its protective and repressive capacities, performs different attitudes towards the different actors.

The problematic of enclosures in Namibian communal areas is not just about a legalistic issue regarding the pertinence of regulations, nor a problem of the applicability of norms, nor simply a question of effectiveness in policy implementation. Analytically, the illegal fencing phenomenon pertains to the field of historical socio-economic transformations. This means, first, that these transformations are deeply rooted in the shameful records of colonial history. Second that, due to post-independence political dynamics, the role that the state plays in these transformations generally, and in the illegal fencing phenomenon specifically, is characterized by an outstanding class bias. And, third, that, due to the interaction between the Namibian state and international donors, neoliberal notions of development dominate policy thinking and its implementation.

This combination of parameters (colonial inheritances, state-class lineament, and neoliberal development) has created the conditions for land-related conflicts to intensify, particularly in communal areas. Therefore, although these conflicts may appear as the result of internal class differentiation alone, they are inserted into the larger history of colonial / racial domination, and its neo-colonial and neoliberal form. Any comprehensive analysis of land enclosures in Namibia, and the resulting disputes within communal areas, must not be abstracted from a deeper inquiry about the overall social formation of contemporary Namibia as a historical inheritance and continuation of WSC.

Both before and after independence,[3] the different administrations controlling the territory of Namibia actively encouraged the individuation of communal lands, otherwise under so-called 'customary' land property regimes. Successive development projects, first in the 1970's but also after Namibian independence, have been the principal means through which individuation has been promoted by the state. Furthermore, the state has allegedly promoted land individuation through inaction and neglect of duty in facing illegal land appropriators. However, 'state inaction' is, perhaps, not a very exact phrasing for what is actually happening on the ground in N#a-Jaqna. Despite some showy actions on the part of security forces against some fencing episodes, the

---

3 Before Independence in 1990, Namibia was under South African rule, and its denomination was South-West Africa (SWA). Between 1884 and WWI, it was a German colony under the same name. However, for the sake of better readability, the territory will be referred to as Namibia all along in this chapter, irrespective of the historical period under discussion.

day-to-day experience narrated by those who suffer the illegal alienation of their lands is not one of simple state inaction, but rather of active
collaboration between the state security forces and the illegal fencers
– a story of violence, repression and impunity.

In this chapter, I shall explore several dimensions of the conflicts
produced by land individuation in N#a-Jaqna. First, I will summarize
the structural dimension: that is, the role that fences in general, and
enclosures in communal areas in particular, have played, historically, in
the political economy of WSC in Namibia. Then, in the context section,
I will provide some background information about the area of study.
This will include an explanation about the specific position that the
study area has come to occupy in relation to WSC; the process by which
the enclosures movement has penetrated into the area; and the different actors involved in land conflicts (the state, the TA, the communal
conservancy, and so on). Up to this point, the chapter relies mostly on
the theoretical and historical research I conducted for my PhD thesis
and on the existing academic literature about the history of N#a-Jaqna.

In the section following that, I will describe some of the ins-and-
outs of land politics within N#a-Jaqna that arose in the course of this
research. This section will show that, despite internal political divisions,
the external factors are the primary causes of land-related conflicts in
the area. Finally, in the last section before the conclusion, the chapter
will explore the responses that local residents perform in dealing, day
to day, with the enclosure of their lands. Framed as 'unorganized' forms
of resistance, the relevance of these actions to understand the material
dimensions of the conflict will become evident. These two later sections rely mostly on a series of unstructured interviews that I conducted
in the area in August 2018. Not all actors involved are represented in
these testimonies. For reasons related to my own personal security, or
to the unwillingness of certain actors to participate in this research, the
farmers who erect fences in the area were not interviewed, nor state
security forces.

I conducted a few but highly informative interviews in the villages
Omatako and Grashoek, as well as in the small settlement located at the
gate where the veterinary fence separates N#a-Jaqna from Okakarara
Constituency; this is the limit of the former Polize Zone (PZ). Few interviewees accepted their names being mentioned in an eventual publication: Glony Arnold, current chief of the !Kung TA ruling in Na#Jaqna
and one of her councilors, as well as the current vice-chairperson of the

Na#Jaqna Communal Conservancy. The rest allowed their testimony to be reproduced, but not their names to be mentioned. Perhaps this was because they spoke more freely, provided more sensitive information, or were simply afraid of possible consequences. In any case, the proportion desiring anonymity already reveals something about the conflictual situation in the area.

WSC in Namibia and the political economy of illegal fencing

Both legal and illegal enclosures have been mushrooming in Namibian communal lands, since at least the 1970s (Werner 1997). However, the fencing of large tracts of land is a phenomenon that holds the highest significance in the history of the country. During colonial rule, fences were in principle erected for farming purposes, but they were also a key device that entrenched the logics of white settlerism and apartheid on the physical space (see also Gordon 1998, Hayes, Silvester, Wallace and Hartmann 1998). WSC was (and arguably still is) a racialized socio-economic ensemble with several dimensions, including labour supply, socio-political control, agrarian development, exploitation of natural resources, and a myriad of subjective elements. The crafting and the historical evolution of WSC consisted, to a relevant extent, of the management of territoriality. Fences were placed on the ground as means to materialize the notions of private property, racial differentiation, ethnic containerization and colonial legality, as well as to set the conditions for the white-settler economy to prosper.

Arguably, thus, in the historical record of the *political geography of WSC,* an outstanding factor was the ability to impose a strong sense of *legitimacy of the fence* on the colonized peoples of Namibia. Fences were used to demarcate white farming clusters and thus set the pace of effective settler territorial expansion. But they also served to separate native populations under indirect rule from those under direct rule. An internal boundary known in Namibia as the Red Line was set during German colonial times (1898-1915), and maintained during South African rule (1915-90) (for a detailed history of the Red Line, see Miescher 2012). The Red Line also marked the limits of the PZ. But this internal boundary did not coincide with the separation between areas designated for whites and areas designated for 'natives'. On the contrary, some 'native homelands' were placed within the PZ.

Colonialism thus created two different political statuses among black Namibians. First, those 'homelands' located outside the PZ were 'self-governed' (their status can be assimilated into what is commonly regarded as indirect rule). Second, those 'homelands' located within the PZ were more tightly controlled by the white administration (although the label of 'direct rule' remains debatable). Furthermore, the Red Line had a veterinary function. The 'native homelands' within the PZ were, therefore, considered to be veterinarily safe, and so their livestock-derived commodities could be integrated into the national and international markets alongside commodities produced in the white farming sector. That is, the economic position of the 'native homelands' lying within the PZ was defined by virtue of the veterinary function of the Red Line and the market integration it implied.

Arguably, thus this separation gave rise to different economic roles for each 'homeland' within the larger structures of accumulation of WSC. Standard interpretations about the political economy of WSC affirm that all 'homelands' played the same role as cheap-labour suppliers for the white-controlled economy (see Hayes et al. 1998). Production means were available in the 'homelands' for black peoples to support their livelihoods. But these means only allowed them to cover part of their subsistence needs. This forced blacks to work for a wage in the white-controlled economy but, at same time, allowed white employers to pay them lower salaries. This is how the migrant labour system produced *super-exploitation* of the black workforce in white enterprises and in white farms (see Wolpe 1972).

Nonetheless, this structure of super-exploitation does not fit every Namibian 'homeland' equally. An alternative interpretation (one that I have reasoned through extensively elsewhere – see Gilolmo forthcoming) is that some of the 'homelands' located within the PZ never were, primarily, labour suppliers. As the structures of WSC matured in Namibia, some homelands adopted, instead, the role of supplying cheap young cattle (calves, heifers) for the white farming sector. This created another structure of super-exploitation, this time affecting 'independent' petty commodity producers rather than waged labourers. These cattle-producing 'homelands' thus acted as the 'base herd' for the white farming sector. In this way, therefore, cattle producers in these 'homelands' never obtained the full benefits of their labour; as petty commodity producers they also suffered super-exploitation. The white economy, and the white farming sector in particular, greatly benefited from both forms of super-exploitation (and they still do). Therefore, the agrarian structure of colonial Namibia was not double, as usually defined by paying attention to the differentiation between 'native homelands' and white areas. It was triple: two types of native reserves collaborated in different ways with capital accumulation that was invariably channelled towards the third and commanding pole: the white sector.

Because of the relevance they held for the economic survival of the white farming sector, the cattle-supply 'homelands' in the PZ were subject to state-driven development projects, at least from the 1970s (while marketing facilities for white farmers to obtain cheap calves were set as early as the 1950s). The aim was to improve cattle production in these 'homelands' so as to secure the supply cattle for the white farming sector. But, arguably, the aim of these development projects was also to keep the productive conditions precarious enough so as to ensure that the productive process could not be completed within these 'homelands' (Gilolmo forthcoming).

Most importantly, these development projects involved a shift in the land tenure regime (Gilolmo forthcoming). The most important pre-independence episodes of state-driven land individuation were implemented in the 'homelands' where cattle production was more active. These areas are nowadays the communal lands of the Otjozondjupa and Omaheke regions; before independence these areas were known as 'Hereroland' (see Figure 7.1).[4] Some authors benignly interpret these developmental interventions as a sign of genuine concern on the side of the white administration about 'native development' and 'self-reliance'. If they acknowledge that the aim of ensuring 'political control' was also involved, the economic dimension of these development projects (namely, the subordination of cattle production in 'homelands' to the requirements of the white farming sector) is totally ignored (as, for instance, in Werner, 1997). Whatever the case, deliberately or accidentally, the fact is that the kind of development induced by these state interventions remained subjected to the needs of the white farming sector, and produced an accumulation trajectory that worked to its benefit. Noticeably, it still does. And, most notably, these are precisely the areas where the private-driven spread of illegal fencing first began to take place and, also, where it has become the most extensive (see Gilolmo, forthcoming).

---

4 There is no space here to develop the complex historical process that led to the formation of this particular calf-supply function, but for reference it can be considered that such a triple structure consolidated during the two decades following the Odendaal Report of 1964 (see Gilolmo forthcoming).

Figure 7.1: Namibia – areas referred to in the text and the Red Line (shown with a dashed line)

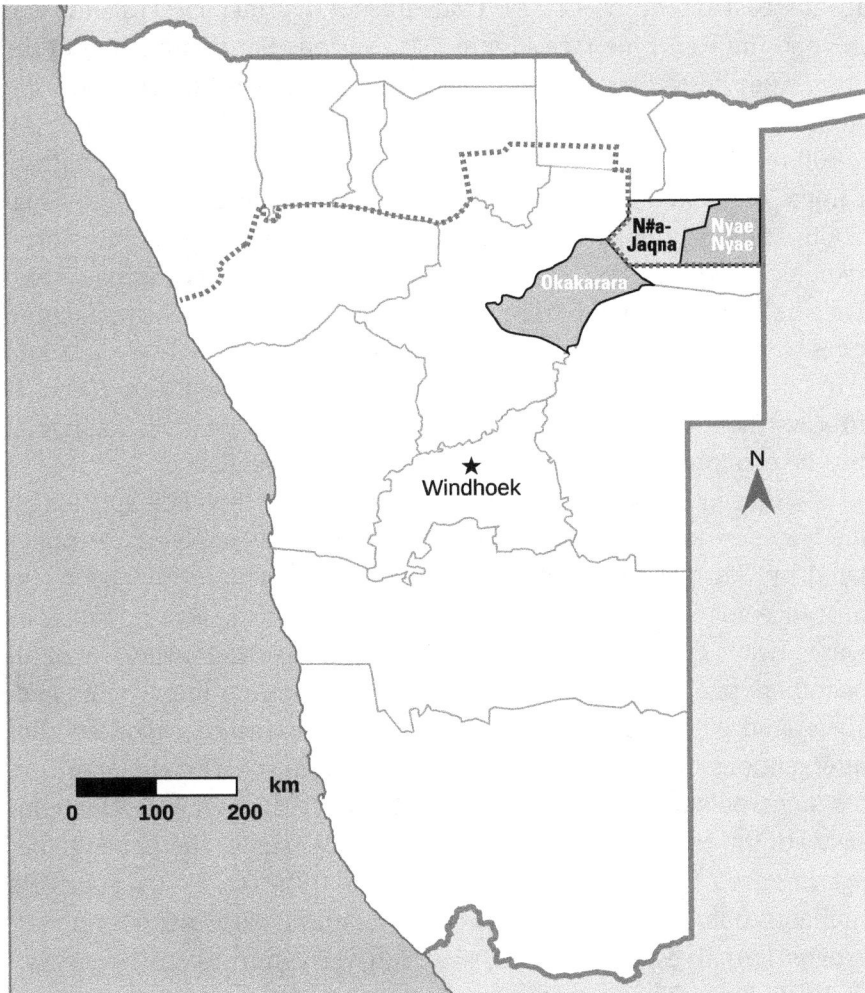

Context: N#a-Jaqna

The 'homelands' located beyond the Red Line, and thus outside the PZ, were left out of the developmental interventions of the pre-independence administration. But, due to private-driven expansion of the enclosure movement in communal lands, these former 'homelands' did not remain unaffected for too long. Our focus area in this chapter, Na#Jaqna, is one of such cases.

N#a-Jaqna, also known as Tsumkwe West, is a communal conservancy[5] proclaimed in 2003 and located in Otjozondjupa Region. It lays east of the Okakarara Constituency (former Hereroland) and beyond the Red Line (see Figure 7.1). Various San groups live in the area. They were brought here during the Namibian liberation war by the South African army, who employed them as field trackers. About 2,000 remained in the area after the war, mostly in abandoned military camps, but also scattered across a few remote settlements (Odendaal 2006). Some groups from the Kavango and the four north-central regions moved into the area after independence, as well as some Herero farmers from the neighboring constituencies. Currently the population goes up to 3,900.[6] N#a-Jaqna was mostly unoccupied before the South African army took it for its military operations (Odendaal, 2006). It follows that, besides these military functions, the area was tangential for the economic structures of WSC before independence.

Adjacent to N#a-Jaqna, the Nyae-Nyae Conservancy spreads all the way east to the Botswana border. Although Nyae-Nyae was populated by San peoples since immemorial times, it also had little significance for WSC. This is not surprising, since the San populations were always considered by racial doctrine as the most backward of all Namibian peoples (Gordon 2009). San peoples were literally 'hunted' all around Namibia and driven on to farms as resident workers, but interventions in their inhabited areas were more superficial than in any other 'homeland'. In Nyae-Nyae, the South African intervention consisted of the establishment of a town, Tsumkwe, in an attempt to gather the scattered San families living in the area. In the 1970s, a private 'philanthropic' initiative intended to transform these hunter-gatherer groups into livestock farmers, although with only relative success.[7] In 1991, Nyae-Nyae was the first Communal Conservancy to be proclaimed after independence. Behind this novelty there was the intention of some humanitarian NGOs to protect the most vulnerable of all Namibia's peoples, the San, as well as the drive of ecologist international organizations to conserve the wildlife of these areas.

....

5 After independence in 1990, an alternative development model was devised in Namibia: communal conservancies. These are a legal figure established by the Ministry of Environment and Tourism which allocates rights to manage natural resources and wildlife to local communities. Arguably, this implies a sort of demarcated territorial control, but its scope is limited to certain matters as well as restricted to conservancy registered members. Traditional authorities hold a post in the conservancy boards, but the degree of collaboration between the two institutions varies from case to case.
6 See Namibian Association for CBNRM Support Organisation (no date).
7 A documentary film by Adrian Strong, *Bitter Roots: The Ends of a Kalahari Myth*, is informative in this respect.

In parallel to the establishment of communal conservancies all around the country, the Ministry of Land Reform, with the financial and technical aid of a German cooperation agency, relaunched the individuation of communal lands in both Otjozondjupa and Omaheke. This development agenda is now termed small-scale commercial farming (SSCF) (Ministry of Lands and Resettlement 2012, 2013; see also Meijs , Hager and Mulofwa 2014). But, after independence, the model has also been expanded outside the former PZ.

Sandwiched between Okakarara (where farming in private enclosures and illegal fencing are widely extended) and Nyae-Nyae (the paradigmatic example of Namibian communal conservancies), N#a-Jaqna is trapped between the two development paradigms. In many Namibian communal areas, the communal conservancies cannot compete with the private-farming development paradigm. In N#a-Jaqna, soon after the proclamation of the communal conservancy in 2003, competition between opposed land uses and developmental agendas soon arose. Odendaal (2006) reports that the establishment of individual farming was envisaged for the area, although he does not specify a date nor a specific project. According to his account, the attempt became rather polemical. As a result, the government SSCF scheme in N#a-Jaqna has been suspended for the time being. Yet private enclosures and cattle invasions are still usual. More on the politics involved these phenomena will be analyzed in the section following this one.

Kahau Visser N!iaci summarizes the workings of the N#a-Jaqna Conservancy and describes the livelihoods of its inhabitants, as well as the main problems they experience due to the establishment of private enclosures (Interview 2). The conservancy has two main income sources: first, it runs two 'living museums', one in Grashoek and one in Omandumba (close to Omaruru, outside the conservancy's territory). Second is a partnership with a private tour operator (Thormählen and Cochran Safaris) which holds a tourist accommodation near the village of Manguetti Dune and works with trophy hunters. This operator pays the conservancy the amount of N$560,000 (Namibian dollars, the same amount in South African rands), three times a year, and employs 'some people' for its activities. The conservancy finds that, because of widespread fencing, trophy hunting activities are negatively affected. But livelihood activities of inhabitants are also undermined. Fences prevent them from collecting wood, food and medicinal plants.

However, as for traditional livelihoods, conservancy regulations are also regarded as a problem by some community members. Hunting is prohibited in the area except if the conservancy grants a permit. These permits are issued for trophy hunters, but not for community members who seek to get food in this traditional way. In fact, the conservancy has two rangers to prevent residents from hunting animals on their own. Some interviewees explained that, if found hunting, they would spend the night in police facilities (Interview 6; Interview 7). Arguably thus, the conservancy utilizes the notions of 'traditional livelihood' and 'San culture' in a biased way. This can be imputed to the strong role played by ecologist international organizations in conservancy matters. Conservationist interests negate, to an extent, the traditional livelihoods of inhabitants, who suffer from conservancy regulations, especially in times of need. More on the ways in which community members try to continue with their traditional livelihoods and try to resist the limitations imposed by both enclosures and conservancy regulations will be tackled in the fifth section, later in this chapter.

The politics of private enclosures in N#a-Jaqna

It is well known that the lands of N#a-Jaqna are periodically invaded by cattle herds from the surrounding areas. Still, the major problem raised by interviewees was the presence of incoming farmers whose illegal fences restrict access to large tracts of communal land. In 2013, some police action was taken against these illegal fencers (*The Namibian*, 2013; see also Na Jaqna Conservancy Management Committee, 2018). However, the problem is far from being solved as it appears that police action was taken only as long as public controversies lasted.

The extent of private enclosures in N#a-Jaqna is difficult to estimate. Media reports affirm that, in 2016, the courts ordered 22 of these illegal farms to be vacated. However, there are currently up to 34 of these enclosures pending a resolution of the High Court of Namibia. This number was offered by several interviewees at different moments. But those are just the enclosures whose perpetrators' identities are known to the communities. This piece of information is necessary in order to bring them before the courts. All interviewees, with the interesting exception of the !Kung traditional authority, affirm that a much larger number of illegal fences is present in the area.

Kahau Visser N!iaci, current vice-chairperson of the N#a-Jaqna Conservancy and a particularly well informed community member, affirms that they are currently busy trying to collect the names of the perpetrators of 170 more enclosures in order to add them to the court case (Interview 2). Still, Glony Arnold, current chief of the !Kung TA, affirmed that 'the Land Board, and the TA, in 2016, removed all the [illegal] fences' (Interview 1). But according to N!iaci, as well as to three other anonymous respondents, the 170 illegal farms are just an indeterminate fraction of the total number of enclosures currently existing in the area. Judicial processes are being pushed by the conservancy (with no participation from the TA), but these processes are just slower than the spread of enclosures themselves (Interview 2). As noted above, it was obviously impossible, for reasons of personal security, to interview any of the farmers who come into N#a-Jaqna to erect illegal fences, so their views are not included here.

Nonetheless, the spread of illegal fencing is not only related to agents external to the area; it also involves local actors and relates to intra-community politics as well as to the state's development plans. The individuation of land for the development of private farm-units was first proposed, and rejected, 'long [ago], when the late Chief [Arnold, father to Glony] was still alive'. The rejection was due to claims made by conservancy members that the demarcated area was reserved for a wildlife zone (Interview 1). During the interview with the current Chief Glony Arnold, it was revealed that the state recently approached the TA to propose again the establishment of individual farms in the area, and that last year, KFW, a German development bank, 'took over the project' (Interview 1). Information in the media corroborates this point (Zungu, 2018). According to the chief, the proposal was to establish nine farms of 2,500 hectares each, and includes the building of water infrastructure.

However, it appears that the community is still divided about the implementation of this development initiative, and different members of the TA are divided as well. Sara Zungu, one of the senior councillors of the !Kung TA who is also the chairperson of the communal conservancy, is the main voice opposing the creation of private farms in N#a-Jaqna. According to Chief Glony Arnold and one of her councillors, Zungu has been acting 'on her own' (Interview 1). It was not possible to interview Zungu, but her position is well known through the media. In an interview published in *Namibia Economist* on 14 June 2018, she accused the EU and the KFW of funding the sale of land in N#a-Jaqna (Zungu, 2018). Visibly upset, the chief complains that Zungu 'just ran to the newspaper [saying] that there is illegal fencing', instead of informing the TA office first (Interview 1). Internal political quarrels within N#a-Jaqna's traditional power structures are not new, though. The late Chief Arnold died in 2012, and his daughter Glony Arnold succeeded him in 2015. Several councillors, including Sara Zungu, opposed the undemocratic way in which the new chief came into office (The Namibian, 2015).

Several statements made by various interviewees suggest that these conflicts relate to different visions about promoting livestock farming, and private farms, in N#a-Jaqna. Different claims of represen-tation of community members also apply: Sara Zungu claims to speak on behalf of the community in opposing the establishment of enclo-sures, while the chief and some of her councillors affirm that communi-ties are in favour of such a development agenda. From the interviews I could conduct, the division in the larger community corresponds quite tightly to the class configuration of the San community itself. This was all most apparent when observing the personal interests that some of the TA board members have in the establishment of farms. The coun-cillor who was present during the interview I conducted with the chief did not hesitate to express his personal interest in the establishment of individual farms as proposed by KFW:

> "They [those who oppose the SSCF project] do not want the places to be fenced for us to put our cattle there. [But] my uncle is a farmer, with a lot of cattle, [and] I am also a farmer. My grandmother have a kraal there, and my mother in law have a kraal; [there is] a lot of people farming" (Interview 1).

In sum, there are indeed San residents who are in favour of the establishment of individual farms for commercial farming to be launched in the area. Some '24 to 40' San own cattle in N#a-Jaqna (Interwiew 1). Although not very useful as an estimate, it is enough to understand that farming is envisioned by those better-off residents as well as to perceive that the differences in land-use visions are not brought about by external agents only. Indeed, class-related internal political divisions exist and are quite significant. However, the bulk of land-related conflicts result from incoming farmers willing to take advantage of the farming potential of the area. After all, the nine farms proposed by KFW under the new version of the SSCF project cannot be compared to the about 200 illegal farms reported by some respondents (34 in the court case plus 170 more in the process of being included). According to several interviewees, some of these 'newcomers are

Herero', but most of those who seek to set up permanent farms come from the four north-central regions or from Windhoek (Interview 3; Interview 4).

Picture 7.1: On the main road, eastwards on the way to Tsumkwe, SWAPO flags on a farm gate warn about the political connections of the land grabbers

Popular resistance and state repression in N#a-Jaqna

In this scenario, two instances are perhaps the most decisive for the future course of events: on the one hand, the actions taken by community members outside of official channels and besides litigation; on the other, the reactions of the police to the erection of fences as well as their repressive response to communities' actions. In N#a-Jaqna, organized forms of resistance against illegal enclosures are limited to the judicial actions already discussed above.

The presence of Sara Zungu, who aims to make visible the existing land conflicts in N#a-Jaqna in the media, represents a form of organized activism. The same applies to the protests that were organized in 2013 when an episode of cattle invasions in the area jumped into the media and the police were thus forced to intervene. Besides these, the actions taken by residents against the illegal enclosure of their lands can be framed as what has been termed elsewhere unorganized forms of resistance (trespassing, squatting, poaching, stealing) (c.f. Moyo and

Yeros 2005, p. 40). These forms of resistance do not fit 'classic' definitions of social movements as structured organizations with a political
agenda and a defined strategic outlook. Instead, in the case of 'covert
and unorganized' resistance, action is taken in the form of spontaneous responses against perceived aggression in a context in which the
capacity to agitate in the wider political arena is limited. But this type
of resistance is not apolitical: it seeks to undermine the material assets
of those who act against the sources of livelihoods of affected communities. And it has the potential to explain what is behind the expressed
views of the actors involved in conflicts in which access to the public
arena is unequally distributed.

In N#a-Jaqna, inhabitants in different villages attest that sometimes they invade illegal enclosures in order to gather food, firewood,
medicinal plants and herbs, and even to steal or kill livestock (Interview 3; Interview 4; Interview 6). These forms of unorganized resistance are, in their own view, the only alternative left for them, given
that no other sources of livelihood are available. In Grashoek, where
private enclosures have encroached closely on the areas surrounding
the village, Kahau Visser N!iaci narrated: 'In 2016 the tourists were not
moving so much so there was not a lot of income, we could not afford
food, so this wild food is all that we are eating in this area' (Interview
2). 'Wild food' sources include attempts to hunt wild animals and are
thus prosecuted by conservancy-hired rangers (Interview 6; Interview
7). This is all the more significant since the conservancy supposedly
exists to support the livelihoods of the very same people who act
against its regulations. And conservancy members are also the most
active in trying to stop enclosures. It all suggests that different visions
within the conservancy itself (namely the views of residents and local
board members versus the views of Windhoek-based ecologist organizations) are also at stake.

Notably, a resident affirmed during an informal conversation that,
sometimes, locals even set the bush on fire. This goes against conservationist efforts and also reveals the contradictions existing between
ecological concerns and livelihood needs. Fires are part of traditional
hunting techniques. But since conservancy regulations prevent them
from practicing traditional hunting, residents do not show concern
anymore about the sustainability of hunting methods. They rather use
fire as a way to destroy the resource base for the farming activities of
illegal fencers (Interview 7). This all suggests that the combination of

illegal fencing and conservancy regulations add to each other in weakening the livelihoods of residents. Thus, consciousness of sustainable management of natural resources gives way to these kinds of actions, now aiming to expel illegal fencers by setting pastures on fire.

In a clear indication of the level of land-related conflicts in N#a-Jaqna, these actions on the part of residents are usually retaliated against. Most strikingly, village residents are often subject to threats and violence. Threats include warnings of 'shooting' in case of trespassing illegal fences. Episodes of armed men wandering around in villages were narrated as well. In one of these cases, 'a young farmworker pointed a gun on somebody's neck'. Beatings and other violent incursions also occur often. Sometimes, these cases are not reported to the police because the affected person does not will to do so. But in other cases, villagers inform the police about these violent episodes. The answer they get from the police officers are that the illegal fencers are acting within their own right because village residents cannot invade 'private property'! (Interview 2; Interview 7).

For obvious reasons, no police official could be interviewed in this research; and, obviously as well, official police discourse does not acknowledge any such episodes of violence and police inaction. In any case, the police response shows that fences, despite being erected illegally, enjoy a high degree of legitimacy in the eyes of security forces, or at least of those policemen who are on the ground day to day in N#a-Jaqna. Land grabbers enjoy legitimization of their illegal actions (including erection of fences but also direct violence and armed threats). The police see in them a rightful defence of private property. The police also seem to deeply disrespect San residents owing to their poverty and, what is more worrying, to their ethnicity. Some respondents reported episodes of police abuse that included arbitrary beatings and ethnicist insults (Interview 6; Interview 7). The San perceive that the 'protection' of illegal fencers is related to an ethnicism that works against their interests as well as against their dignity as a people and as the true owners of the land. The police, moreover, may arrest San residents on the grounds that the latter attack private property, act violently or hunt wild animals. An estimate of the number of arrests was impossible to obtain, but interviewees showed great concern about imprisonment and complained that their youth were 'spending their lives in police cells' (Interview 5; Interview 7).

Conclusions

Conservancies and SSCF are two contrasting development agendas
for communal lands in independent Namibia. However, illegal fencing
mediates between the pre-independence development agenda (which
supported the privatization and insertion of communal farming into
the wider complex of WSC) and the developmental duality of post-
independence times. Arguably, illegal fencing emerges from, and again
devolves into, the state's involvement in the private-farming development paradigm. Noticeably, though, both conservancies and SSCF are
state-driven development initiatives, if yet conflicting or even mutually
exclusionary. However, the extent to which each of these developmental models work in the interest of the inhabitants of N#a-Jaqna remains
highly debatable.

The privatizing developmental paradigm is not peculiar to
Namibia, though. All around Africa, land privatization is usually seen
as a matter of land tenure security – that is, as a necessary condition
for the take-off of African agriculture, because it provides the certainty
and bankability required to foster investment and productivity. In that
tale, the spontaneous 'development' of land enclosures is nothing more
than a locally-driven extension of capitalist farming into communal
areas. In this view, the expansion of illegal land enclosures belongs to
a process of local capitalist development and, thus, it should be encouraged in spite of its inevitably uneven effects. In such a framework,
obviously, there is no room to think about the consequences of enclosures on local livelihoods, and even less room to understand the forms
of resistance deployed on the ground, either in organized or unorganized forms. Equally important is to inquire about the reactions of the
state apparatus towards these forms of resistance, especially at the level
of security forces and the judiciary.

Communal conservancies are not proving to be a suitable alternative. It is claimed that they are a 'culturally appropriate' development
initiative, but evidence shows that conservancy regulations undermine
San traditional sources of livelihood to the benefit of income-generat-
ing activities like trophy hunting and tourism. That the San inhabitants
of N#a-Jaqna do not benefit from these activities to any extent com-
parable to the profits obtained by tour-operators and the managers of
trophy hunting activities is rather clear.

Land individuation is only for those who are in a position to
provide themselves with individuated land – and such a position does

not only depend on availability of capital, but also on personal connections and police protection. In such a scenario, it remains difficult to see how the privatization of land may benefit the San peoples of N#a-Jaqna in any form. These doubts about the possibilities for local residents to benefit from the development of private farming apply both to the enclosures built by private initiatives as well as to the role of the state, which finds this illegal movement to be coherent with its own developmental goals and thus aims to drive it with the aid of KFW. That the state backs the individuation of land does not guarantee that it will benefit the majority of N#a-Jaqna inhabitants, as the conflicts at the level of local politics show.

Fences, in spite of being erected illegally, are rarely prosecuted by the state apparatus. On the contrary, those who cut fences or invade into enclosures are prone to spend the night locked in the police station for destroying or invading 'private' property. This should open a reflection on the anomaly apparent in the fact that fences, despite being illegal, hold such legitimacy before the eyes of state authority while, at the same time, those who do not respect the integrity of these illegal fences are treated as criminals. The class character of the enclosure movement, but also the history communal lands in WSC, need to be taken into account in order to understand such an anomaly. At the same time, San traditional livelihoods are restricted on behalf of their own protection and to the benefit of private actors in the tourism sector. In any case, the vast majority of the San population in N#a-Jaqna is losing effective control over their lands and means of livelihood, either by virtue of legal and illegal fencing or by virtue of a biased conservationist model.

References

Gilolmo, P. (forthcoming) The *Human Right to Development in Namibian Eastern Communal Lands. Super-Exploitation and Land Privatization in a Former Native Reserve* (tentative title). PhD Thesis. University of Coimbra

Gordon, R.J. (1998) 'Vagrancy, law and "shadow knowledge" internal pacification 1915-1939,' In Hayes, P., Silvester, J., Wallace, M., and Hartmann, W. (eds) (1998), *Namibia Under South African Rule. Mobility and Containment 1915-46*, Oxford, James Currey, pp 51-76

Gordon, R. J. (2009) 'Hiding in full view: the "forgotten" Bushman genocides of Namibia.' *Genocide Studies and Prevention: An International Journal*, 4(1):29-57

Hayes, P., Silvester, J., Wallace, M., and Hartmann, W. (1998) *Namibia Under South African Rule. Mobility and Containment 1915-46*. Oxford, James Currey

Mendelsohn, J., el Obeid, S., de Klerk, N. and Vigne, P. (2006) *Farming Systems in Namibia*, Windhoek, Raison

Meijs, M., Hager, C. and Mulofwa, J. (2014) 'Local level participatory planning; an approach towards tenure security and development planning', paper presented at the 2014 World Bank Conference on Land and Poverty, Washington DC, March 24-27

Miescher, G. (2012) *Namibia's Red Line: The History of a Veterinary and Settlement Border*, New York, Palgrave MacMillan

Ministry of Lands and Resettlement (2012) *Road Map for the Development of Small-Scale Farming Areas on Communal Land in Namibia*, Windhoek, MLR

Ministry of Lands and Resettlement (2013) *Local Level Participatory Planning for the Development of Infrastructure for Small Scale Commercial Farming in the Communal Areas of Namibia*, Windhoek, MLR

Moyo, S. and Yeros, P. (2005) 'The resurgence of rural movements under neo-liberalism', in Moyo, S. and Yeros, P. (eds.) *Reclaiming the Land. The Resurgence of Rural Movements in Africa, Asia and Latin America*, London, Zed Books, pp. 8-66

Na Jaqna Conservancy Management Committee (2018) 'Why is illegal grazing, fencing and settlement on San land, not a priority?' *The Villager*, 12 September, https://www.thevillager.com.na/articles/13832/why-is-illegal-grazing-fencing-and-settlement-on-san-land-not-a-priority/ , accessed 8 February 2021

Namibian Association of CBNRM Support Organisations (no date) *N#a-Jaqna Conservancy* http://www.nacso.org.na/conservancies/na-jaqna , accessed 8 February 2021

Namibia Statistics Agency (2015) *Namibia Census of Agriculture 2013/2014. Commercial, Leasehold and Resettlement Farms*, Windhoek, Namibia Statistics Agency

Odendaal, W. (2006) *San Communal Lands Contested: The battle over N#a Jaqna Conservancy*. http://www.lac.org.na/projects/lead/Pdf/bushmanland.pdf

Odendaal, W. (2011) 'Land grabbing in Namibia: a case study from the Omusati region, northern Namibia', paper presented at the International Conference on Global Land Grabbing, Institute of Development Studies, University of Sussex,, 6-8 April. http://www.the-eis.com/data/literature/Willem%20Odendaal.pdf

Republic of Namibia (2002) *Communal Land Reform Act*, Windhoek: Office of the Prime Minister

The Namibian (2015) '!Kung San deplore biased intervention', 5 March, https://www.namibian.com.na/index.php?id=134330&page=archive-read, accessed 8 February 2021

The Namibian (2013) 'Illegal farmers stay put in Tsumkwe', 14 June, https://www.namibian.com.na/index.php?id=110883&page=archive-read, accessed 8 February 2021

Werner, W. (2011) '*What Has Happened Has Happened'. The Complexity of Fencing in Namibia's Communal Areas*, Windhoek, Legal Assistance Centre

Werner, W. (1997) 'From communal pastures to enclosures: the development of land tenure in Herero reserves', NEPRU Working Paper no. 60, Windhoek, Namibia Economic Policy Research Unit

Wolpe, H. (1972) 'Capitalism and cheap labour-power in South Africa: from segregation to apartheid'. *Economy and Society*, 1(4):425-56

Zungu, S. (2018) 'Bushmen accuse EU and German Development Bank of funding the sale of their land', *Namibia Economist*, 14 June, https://economist.com.na/35984/speak-your-mind/bushmen-accuse-eu-and-german-development-bank-of-funding-the-sale-of-their-land/, accessed 8 February 2021

Interviews

Interview 1: Interview with Chief Glony Arnold and Senior councillor, from the !Kung Traditional Authority. Omatako, August 9, 2018.
Interview 2: Interview with Kahau Visser N!iaci, Vice-chairperson of the N#a-Jaqna Conservancy. Grashoek, August 8, 2018.
Interview 3: Interview with anonymous respondent 1. Grashoek, August 7, 2018.
Interview 4: Interview with anonymous respondent 2. Grashoek. August 7, 2018.
Interview 5: Interview with anonymous respondents 3. Omatako, August 8, 2018.
Interview 6: Interview with anonymous respondents 4. Omatako, August 8, 2018.
Interview 7: Interview with Anonymous Respondent 5. Grashoek, August 10, 2018.

CHAPTER 8

The Madagascar-WISCO deal and resistance to it: outstanding questions and lingering concerns

Boaventura Monjane and Tsilavo Ralandison

Introduction

In 2008, Wuhan Iron and Steel Corporation (WISCO), a state-owned company and one of China's top steelmakers, and the president of Madagascar at that time, Marc Ravalomanana, entered negotiations to allow the company to exploit iron ore deposits[1] located in Madagascar's northwest regions of Boeny and Melaky (Bachelard and Marcus 2012, Carayol 2010, Pellerin 2012, Schiller 2013). This project is often known as the Soalala mining project, named after a culturally and ecologically-rich coastal town from which the extracted iron would be exported. In response, a coalition of five civil society organizations (CSOs) in Madagascar[2] criticized the contracts' opacity in a communiqué (SEFAFI 2009). The coalition demanded that the negotiations stop in a letter addressed to the Minister of Mines (Pellerin 2009, Yves 2008).

Two years later, the central government, which at that time was being led by President Andry Rajoelina, issued exploration (and possibly, exploitation) permits[3] to the WISCO Group, a consortium of companies led by WISCO (42 per cent of the total investment), followed by the Guangdong Foreign Trade Group Co. Ltd, also referred to as the Guangxin Group (38 per cent) and the Hong Kong-based Kam Hing International (20 per cent). The permits gave them the right to the iron deposit for 30 years. The total area affected is 43,214 hectares, with a

---

1 The prospective deposit contains approximately 800 million tons of iron ore reserves available for exploitation (World Bank 2015).
2 The coalition was led by Sehatra Fanaraha-maso ny Fiainam-pirenena (SEFAFI, the Observatory of Public Life), and included Conseil National Économique et Social de la Société Civile (CONECS, the National Economic and Social Council of Civil Society), Comité de Développement Economique (EDC, Economic Development Committee), Fédération des Exploitations Miniers (FEDMINES, Federation of Mining Operations), and Komity Mpanara-Maso ny Fifidianana - Fanabeazana Olompirenena (KMF/CNOE, National Election Observation Committee – Citizen Education).
3 There appears to be no consensus in the literature about what kind of permit and how many were issued. This is discussed later in the chapter.

planned investment estimated at US$2 billion. Once operational, the project would represent Madagascar's largest mining project (Chen and Landry 2016). With an estimated total inflow of US$8 billion, it would mean the most significant foreign investment in the country's history (Schiller 2013).

Thirteen years have passed since the permits were issued, and, to the best of the authors' knowledge, little has been written about the project itself and reactions to it up until now. The objective of this chapter describes what we have found out about the project's activities and the kinds of resistance that have been carried out since 2010. Information about the project is mainly based on Internet research. Information about the resistance activities is primarily based on interviews conducted in 2015 and 2019 in Madagascar with community members, local government, and CSO representatives. About the project, we found that it has carried out exploration activities and that, at the time of writing, the project seems to be dormant but not abandoned. About resistance activities, we found that questions and concerns, such as those related to the lack of transparency about the project, raised at the local and national level, appear to remain unanswered and ignored. If the project were to resume and questions and concerns continued to be unanswered and ignored, resistance may resurface. This future scenario concerns us, especially when considering contemporary authoritarian political dynamics that undermine collective and individual agency, particularly in rural areas. Thus, as we come to terms with the events that have unfolded over the last few years and consider the broader political processes, what strikes us the most is not so much the particulars about the project and the types of resistance that have taken place, but the looming uncertainties.

This chapter is organized as follows. First, we present information about the project over the last ten years. Second, we present some information about resistance activities at the local and national level. Third, we summarize the key points and offer some general remarks and questions for further consideration. It is important to note that this contribution is not a comprehensive account of the project, nor is it an exhaustive description of the types of resistance activities related to the deal. It does, however, offer a first attempt to document recent activities related to the WISCO deal. That said, this piece only scratches the surface, and more extensive field research would be required before presenting any firm conclusions about the project or the responses to it. While further research is essential, the authors felt compelled to write about this case now, given its magnitude and the concerns that have been raised about it, and to do so in a way that triggers further thought and reflection about these types of projects and related resistance activities.

The project: questions and concerns

Up until now, project details continue to be mostly unknown. First, it remains unclear what kinds of permits were issued. According to the government decree, which was presented in a 2013 statement published by two CSOs called SIF[4] and Collectif Tany[5] , which had been contesting the project, it appears that the WISCO-led consortium received permission to both explore and exploit the deposits (SIF and Collectif Tany 2013). However, others reported that only exploration permits were issued (Iloniaina and Lough 2013, Reuters Staff 2011) or a mining research permit (EITI 2018).

It also remains unclear what the central government received in exchange for the mining rights. Some claim that the WISCO Group gave a US$100 million signing bonus, which was directly managed by the president's office (Bachelard and Marcus 2012). However, WISCO executives reportedly disputed that they paid US$140 million, not US$100 million (Africa-Asia Confidential 2012). The International Monetary Fund (IMF) reported that the 'US$100 million ... fee was reclassified as rent' (IMF 2018).

Once this exchange became public knowledge, it raised major concerns about how the money would be used, with some speculating that it would be used to prop up the unelected transitional government, thus prolonging the political crisis that was happening at the time. It was indeed a considerable sum for the government, representing about 15 per cent of total public expenditure (Sellström 2015). Eight years later, before being re-elected in the 2018 presidential elections, Andry Rajoelina spoke to an audience of Malagasy diaspora in France, reportedly saying that the '$100 million' was used in a transparent way (*La Gazette de la Grande Île* 2018).

There are also questions about how the arrangement was agreed upon and if local communities were involved in the decision making.

4 SIF is short for Sehatra Iombonana hoan'ny Fananan-tany (in French, Solidarité des Intervenants sur le Foncier, in English it is Solidarity of Stakeholders on Land). SIF is a national platform in Madagascar that brings together non-governmental organizations (NGOs) and civil society organizations (CSOs) that are working to protect Malagasy farmers' rights. It was established in 2003 (Fert n.d.). One of SIF's objectives is 'to ensure the best possible application of the 2005 land reform' (Terre Solidaire 2015).
5 Collectif Tany (Collectif pour la Défense des Terres Malgaches) is a France-based association that was established in 2008 and is made up of Malagasy citizens who 'oppose the theft of Malagasy citizens and peasants of their lands' (Collectif Tany 2008).

It appears that those who have been or will be affected by the project remain in the dark. In 2011, WISCO conducted public consultations as part of its environmental and social impact assessment (ESIA) to obtain an environmental permit. However, based on the actions taken by CSOs in Madagascar, it appears that locals were not privy to project information, and many lived in fear of losing their land.

In recent years, it also remains unclear what the project's status is. By the end of the year 2013, it was reported that the project was suspended 'because it did not fulfil some construction commitments made to the government in exchange for the permit' (Chen and Landry 2016). Exactly which commitments are they remain unknown. Around the same time, it was also reported that WISCO, along with other mining companies in the country, had been scaling back exploration activities (Iloniaina and Lough 2013). Falling global commodity prices – specifically of metals, due to reduced demand for steel in China (Africa's top mineral buyer) – and political uncertainties with the changing of presidents in early 2014 were the two main reasons cited for why WISCO and others became dormant (Jorgic and Rabary 2015). Since then, it appears that financial and political challenges have continued and that the project has not advanced beyond exploration (Ali, Sturman, and Collins 2018).

When trying to get a sense of the project's status today, we could not locate any information that confirms whether the WISCO-led consortium is still suspended, on-hold or if it has been abandoned. Based on the fact that we could not find any reports or statements from WISCO or its partners about leaving the project nor from the central government about annulling the permits, it might be safe to say that the project is on standby and will resume activities when conditions are favourable. This idea is supported by some recent engagements between Madagascar's central government, the WISCO Group, and China's central government. In August 2014, Madagascar's prime minister and his wife met with shareholders of the Guangxin Group.[6] In March 2017, Madagascar's president from 2014 to 2018, Hery Rajonarimampianina, visited Beijing and signed a memorandum of understanding with the Chinese government to jointly advance China's Belt and Road Initiative (Lintner 2019).

....

6 Guangxin Group (Guangdong Guangxin Holdings Group Ltd) is a provincial state-owned enterprise, operating as an investment holding company (Bloomberg n.d.). It was formerly known as Guangdong Foreign Trade Corporation and 'has now transformed into a competitive international conglomerate with distinct industry chains and the power of integrating international resources' (Guangdong Guangxin Holdings Group n.d.).

Resistance activities: defending local land rights

In response to community concerns previously described, in 2012, Fikambanan'ny Tantsaha eto Madagasikara / Coalition Paysanne de Madagascar (FTM/CPM) began helping peasant farmers obtain land certificates to help them defend their right to their land.[7] *'We are strongly fighting land grabbing, and we are mobilizing the peasants to resist and protect their rights. What we are fighting for is that local community life improves and that the right to their land is guaranteed,'* said a CPM technical assistant.[8]

One of their first initiatives was to identify which land was being occupied. Together with SIF, CPM conducted a survey in 2013 to determine current land occupations. The survey was done on only 50 per cent, 15 per cent and 2 per cent of the total land for Ambohipaky, Ankasakasa, and Bekodoka, respectively (SIF and Collectif Tany 2013). Funding cuts prevented the survey from being completed. That said, what the survey showed was that the areas destined for WISCO to mine were located on occupied land, Ambohipaky appearing to be the most affected as it is the main town of the commune (see Figure 8.1 below).

Based on this information, CPM began working on setting up local land offices (*guichet foncier*, in French) where land occupants can apply for a land certificate.[9] The certificate is a legal document that validates one's property rights. Although the certificate differs from a land title, it offers another way to formalize land rights that is more accessible than the titling system.

CPM worked with the local authorities in three communes: Ambohipaky, Ankasakasa, and Bekodoka. Since the communes did not have the means to take on this initiative[10], CPM, which received funding at that time from a Canadian NGO, Development and Peace, offered support. With financial resources and buy-in from the land administration and regional authorities in hand, the project was discontinued by newly elected mayors following the 2015 communal elections.[11] Until now, no land registration office has been set up, and no certificates were delivered.[12]

....

7 FTM/CPM is a platform of farmers organizations in Madagascar that was established in 2001. For some years it was a member of La Via Campesina.
8 Interview in Antananarivo, August 2015.
9 Interview with CPM's president in Antananarivo, 5 October 2019.
10 The cost of creating a local land office is between US$9,000 and US$35,000 (Andriamanalina et al. 2014); it costs around US$2,500 to US$3,500 a year to run a land office, about 15 per cent to 20 per cent of the communal budget (Andrianirina et al. 2013).
11 Interview with CPM's president in Antananarivo, 5 October 2019.
12 Ibid.

Figure 8.1: Overlay of the mining parcels and current land occupation

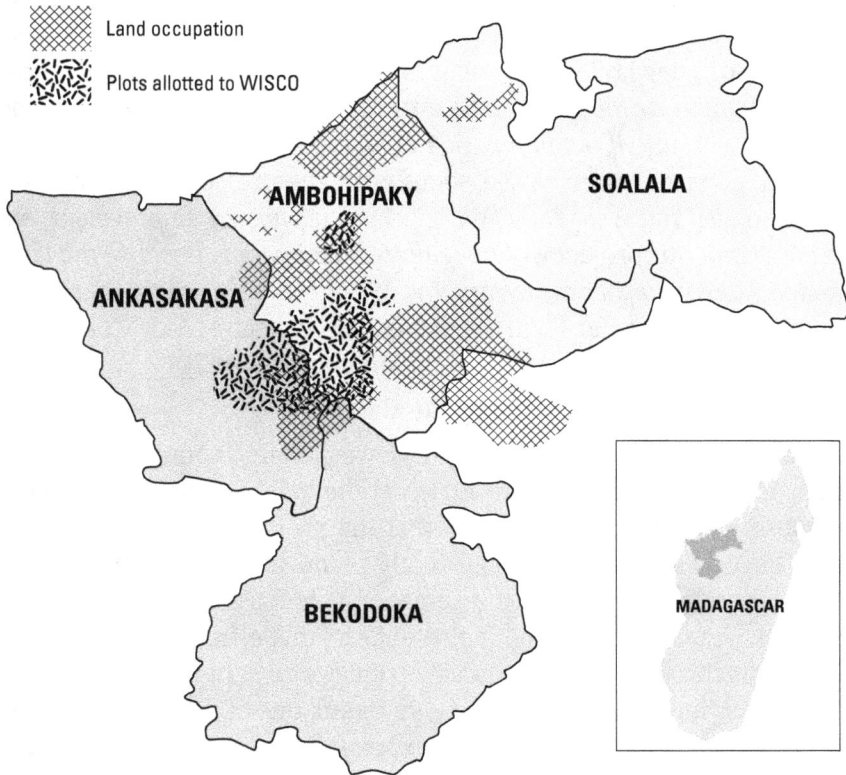

Source: Collectif Tany 2013

Alongside CPM's efforts, other CSOs were forging alliances and raising awareness about the lack of transparency surrounding the project. In July 2013, SIF reported that the affected population was not aware of the details of the ESIA results nor about the mining operation itself (SIF 2013), raising questions about how the ESIA was carried out.[13] Then, in September 2013, SIF and Collectif Tany, and the mayors of Ambohipaky and Ankasakasa (two of the communes directly affected by the project) claimed that almost none of the population in the communes had any knowledge of the borders of the mining site and demanded transparency on all aspects of the project.

Since the project was suspended in 2013, the momentum surrounding land rights initiatives seems to have slowed. Despite this, interviews conducted by the authors reveal that resistance and concerns

----

13 National legislation requires that the environmental and social impact assessment (ESIA) be publicly disclosed.

still exist. For example, in 2014, a local group of citizens wrote a letter to WISCO which read, '*You work in Anketika without authorization, then you are considered thieves.*'[14] In 2015, frustrations and fears were also found: '*They [WISCO] promised to build roads, schools, and hospitals. Albeit those infrastructures are necessary, our livelihoods will no longer be possible if the mining is in place. This will create poverty.*'[15] In 2015, concerns were raised about what the project represented for local peoples' futures: '*They [WISCO] are promising employment, but we know that this project will not employ local people because the level of education of our people is very low. We only have primary schools.*'[16] Perhaps in response to local resistance and concerns, WISCO moved away some of its equipment from the mining sites in 2017.[17]

Looking ahead

This chapter presents what information we gathered about the WISCO-led project and the activities initiated at the local and national level in response to it. In sum, it appears that the project has not progressed much beyond exploration and currently seems to be on standby. As for resistance-related activities, the demand made for greater transparency seems to remain outstanding. It also appears that efforts to defend local land rights through obtaining land certificates remain incomplete.

Reflecting on the information we found, one of the most troubling aspect, we think, is the uncertainty expressed by those we interviewed. The letter to WISCO also indicates a degree of fear in the community about the project. The fears inflicted on communities are perhaps one of the most pernicious, yet overlooked, aspects of these types of transnational deal. Even if greater transparency and land rights are secured, such kinds of land deals alone are intimidating. Even when they are merely announced to the public, social and political tensions can happen. Thus, we think it is important to note how these deals can create fear and produce a lasting alienating effect.

As noted in the introduction, we recognize the importance of understanding what has transpired over the last thirteen years. Still, we feel it is also worth drawing attention to what is on the horizon. If the project goes ahead and if public questions and concerns are ignored, what will happen to those directly affected by the project and those who want to help protect them? Given the authoritarian tendencies

14 Fieldnotes
15 Interview with a farmer in Ambohipaky in 2015.
16 Interview with a commune head in 2015.
17 Interview with CPM president via Skype on 23 June 2020.

in Madagascar's political structures that are unleashing tensions that undermine collective and individual agency, we think that it is necessary to consider what these transnational deals represent in a context where various forms of domination and repression exist.

It is also important to note how large-scale, transnational land acquisitions in Madagascar, such as the WISCO deal, are continuing. For example, in 2020, a memorandum of understanding was signed between Madagascar's central government and United Arab Emirates-based Elite Agro LLC to use 60,000 hectares for grain production (Ngounou 2020). Another example is Singapore-based Reenova's rare earth project, which involves a concession area covering approximately 23,800 hectares. In 2020, Reenova reportedly applied for an exploitation permit (Malagasy News 2020). Alongside this, resistance movements such as those carried out to contest the mining projects led by Rio Tinto and Base Resources are severely repressed, leading to criminalization (see, for example, Carver 2019, CRAAD-OI and Tany cited in Huff and Orengo 2020, Solly 2017). In other words, while Madagascar still attracts capital-intensive, large-scale projects backed by high-profile national and transnational companies, those who raise questions about transparency, accountability, safety, and ethics can face severe repercussions. Such dynamics particularly concern us and warrant immediate and closer attention to the processes that are facilitating these deals and projects.

References

Africa-Asia Confidential (2012) 'Miner's missing millions,' 30 July, https://www.africa-confidential.com/article-preview/id/10769/Miner%e2%80%99s_missing_millions, accessed 1 October 2020

Ali, S. H., Sturman, K., Collins, N. (2018) *Africa's Mineral Fortune: The Science and Politics of Mining and Sustainable*, London: Routledge

Andriamanalina, B., Burnod, P. and Andrianirina Ratsialonana, R. (2014) 'A land reform that survives the political crisis,' *Contemporary Africa*, 251 (3), p. 149-151

Andrianirina N., Andrianirina Ratsialonana R., Burnod P. (2013) 'Malagasy local land offices: what are the determinants of their integration in the local governance?' paper presented at the World Bank Annual Conference on Land and Poverty 2013, Washington, April 8-11

Bachelard, J.Y. and Marcus, R. (2012) 'Madagascar' in Dizard, J., Walker, C., and Tucker, V. (eds.) *Freedom House: Countries at the Crossroads 2011: An Analysis of Democratic Governance*, Vol. 11, Lanham, Maryland, USA, Rowman & Littlefield Publishers, p. 363-382

Bloomberg. (n.d.) Guangdong Guangxin Holdings Group Ltd. https://www.bloomberg.com/profile/company/GDFTGZ:CH, accessed 13 July 2020

Carayol, R. (2010) 'Un contrat dur comme fer', *Jeune Afrique*, 24 June https://www.jeuneafrique.com/196319/economie/un-contrat-dur-comme-fer/, accessed 2 October 2020

Carver, E (2019) 'Madagascar mine ignites protests, community division,' *Mongabay*, 2 July, https://news.mongabay.com/2019/07/madagascar-mine-ignites-protests-community-division/, accessed 10 February 2021

Chen, Y., and Landry, D. (2016) 'Where Africa meets Asia: Chinese agricultural and manufacturing investment in Madagascar,' Working Paper No. 2016/5. China-Africa Research Initiative, School of Advanced International Studies, Johns Hopkins University, Washington, DC. http://www.sais-cari.org/publications accessed 4 September 2020

Collectif Tany (2008) 'Qui sommes-nous?' Collectif pour la Défense des Terres Malgaches - TANY, 28 December. https://terresmalgaches.info/qui-sommes-nous/article/collectif-pour-la-defense-des-terres-malgaches-tany, accessed 15 August 2020

EITI International Secretariat (2018) *Validation of Madagascar Report on initial data collection and stakeholder consultation*, Oslo, Extractive Industries Transparency Initiative (EITI), 12 March, https://eiti.org/document/madagascar-validation-2017, accessed 1 October 2020

Fert (n.d.) 'Meeting with the president of the Solidarity of the stakeholders on land (SIF) in Madagascar,' Fert: Paris. https://www.fert.fr/rencontre-president-solidarite-intervenants-foncier-sif-madagascar/, accessed 1 October 2020

Guangdong Guangxin Holdings Group. (n.d.) Guangxin Today - About us, https://www.gdghg.com/en/news/detail.asp?nid=28, accessed 10 April 2020

Huff, A. and Orengo, Y. (2020) 'Resource warfare, pacification and the spectacle of "green" development: Logics of violence in engineering extraction in southern Madagascar,' *Political Geography*, vol. 81, 102195

Iloniaina, A. and Lough, R. (2013) 'Analysis: Madagascar faces a struggle to restore mining industry,' *Reuters*, 2 December, https://in.reuters.com/article/us-madagascar-mining-analysis-idINBRE9B10F320131202, accessed 1 October 2020

IMF (2018) 'Republic of Madagascar technical assistance report - government finance statistics,' International Monetary Fund Country Report No. 18/283. Washington, DC. https://www.imf.org/en/Publications/CR/Issues/2018/10/03/Republic-of-Madagascar-Technical-Assistance-Report-Government-Finance-Statistics-46265, accessed 10 July 2020

Jorgic, D. and Rabary, L. (2015) 'Madagascar faces uphill struggle to revive bruised mining sector,' *Reuters*, 25 August, https://www.reuters.com/article/madagascar-mining-idUSL3N10W42720150825, accessed 1 October 2020

La Gazette de la Grande Ile (2018) 'Publi-reportage: Andry Rajoelina, À cœur ouvert et en accord avec la diaspora malgache', 25 September, http://www.lagazette-dgi.com/?p=19438, accessed 23 September 2020

Lintner, B. (2019) *The Costliest Pearl: China's Struggle for India's Ocean*, London, Hurst

Malagasy News (2020) 'Terres rares d'Ampasindava: Reenova veut passer au stade d'exploitation', 23 September, https://malagasy.news/economie/terres-rares-dampasindava-reenova-veut-passer-au-stade-dexploitation/, accessed 10 February 2021

Marcus, R. and Ratsimbaharison, A. (2005) 'Political parties in Madagascar: Neopatrimonial tools or democratic instruments?' *Party Politics*, 11, no. 4, p. 495-512

Ngounou, B. (2020) 'Madagascar: NGOs oppose the transfer of 60,000 ha of land to Elite Agro LLC,' *Afrik21*, 5 February, https://www.afrik21.africa/en/madagascar-ngos-oppose-transfer-of-60000-ha-of-land-to-elite-agro-llc/, accessed 10 February 2021

Pellerin, M. (2009) 'Madagascar : un conflit d'entrepreneurs. Figures de la réussite économique et rivalités politiques,' *Politique Africaine*, 113, p.152–65

Pellerin, M. (2012) *The Recent Blossoming in Relations between China and Madagascar*. Paris, Institut Français des Relations Internationales, https://www.ifri.org/sites/default/files/atoms/files/noteafriquempelleringb.pdf, accessed 10 September 2020

Reuters Staff (2011) 'China's Wuhan to explore for iron in Madagascar,' *Reuters*, 6 April, https://www.reuters.com/article/ozabs-madagascar-mining-20110406-idAFJOE7350FD20110406, accessed 24 August 2020

Schiller, C. (2013) 'China and Madagascar: engagement, perceptions, and developmental effects,' Ph.D. Thesis, SOAS, University of London, https://core.ac.uk/download/pdf/42547063.pdf, accessed 2 October 2020

SEFAFI (2009) 'La société civile et sa fonction d'interpellation', *Madagascar Tribune*, 24 October, https://www.madagascar-tribune.com/La-societe-civile-et-sa-fonction-d,12939.html, accessed 2 August 2020

Sellström, T. (2015) *Africa in the Indian Ocean: Islands in Ebb and Flow*, Leiden, Koninklijke Brill NV

SIF (2013) 'Quelques cas illustrant l'accaparement de terre à Madagascar selon la solidarité des intervenants pour le foncier', *Farmlandgrab.Org: The Global Rush For Farmland And Peoples' Struggles Against It*, 24 July, https://www.farmlandgrab.org/uploads/attachment/Quelques%20cas%20de%20LG%20VF%20.pdf, accessed 5 July 2020

SIF and Collectif Tany (2013) *Projet d'exploration et d'exploitation de gisement de fer* à Soalala et Besalampy, Collectif pour la Défense des Terres Malgaches - TANY, 13 September, http://terresmalgaches.info/IMG/pdf/Communique_Soalala_13sept2013.pdf, accessed 5 August 2020

Solly, R. (2017) 'Saving civilization: the 2017 Rio Tinto AGM,' *London Mining Network*, 19 April, https://londonminingnetwork.org/2017/04/saving-civilization-the-2017-rio-tinto-agm/?mc_cid=19f2e983d3&mc_eid=cffc734cf6, accessed 11 February 2021

Terre Solidaire (2015) 'Madagascar, une plateforme associative se mobilise autour de la réforme foncière', *Terre Solidaire*, 5 March, https://ccfd-terresolidaire.org/projets/afrique-subsaharienne/madagascar/madagascar-une-4965, accessed on 5 October 2020

World Bank (2015) *Economic contributions from industrial mining in Madagascar—Research summary*. Antananarivo, World Bank Group, http://documents1.worldbank.org/curated/en/263731468179369566/pdf/100345-WP-P131522-mining-research-summary-Box393222B-PUBLIC-ENG.pdf , accessed 5 August 2020

Yves, B. (2008) 'Sauvegarder la souveraineté nationale et les intérêts du plus grand nombre, Madagascar: Table ronde pour une nouvelle politique manière', *Témoignages*, 27 November , https://www.temoignages.re/international/madagascar/sauvegarder-la-souverainete-nationale-et-les-interets-du-plus-grand-nombre,33778, accessed 10 August 2020

CHAPTER 9

Film review: land struggles and repression in Zambia, eSwatini and Mozambique

Sara Lagardien Abdullah

The African context is one marred by the vestiges of colonial rule, with the most prominent reminder of age-old systematic and structural processes of dispossession being visible through the state of land across the African continent – who owns it and who has access to it. Traversing through the Southern African Development Community (SADC) region, the documentary film *We Rise for Our Land: Land Struggles and Repression in Zambia, eSwatini and Mozambique* – produced as a sister project of this book– seeks to facilitate the movement of these conversations to the forefront of our public conscience. In its articulation of agrarian reform in the aforementioned countries, *We Rise for Our Land* engages aptly with the worrying realities of our present, where people are continually subjected to land dispossession, whether it is through the destruction of homes, evictions, or the ongoing degradation of the environment to the extent that it becomes uninhabitable. At the forefront of social movements agitating for change are women who are acutely invested in establishing a world where they are empowered with the land.

The fight for land justice is indubitably entangled in the neoliberal stronghold of bureaucracy and extended colonialism, which has made the road to agrarian reform one bestrewn with obstacles. In spite of their efforts to establish this world – one divorced from archaic notions of land ownership that have governed agrarian reform for time immemorial women continue to face ongoing harassment from law enforcement whilst persisting in their pursuit of justice.

In the postcolonial dispensation that defines Africa in its present, land remains politically charged – an inescapable consequence of the lack of agrarian reform across the continent. In his exposition of land policy under the colonial state, Shinichi Takeuchi (2014) details the strategic land dispossession of Africans beginning with the inaugural policy of despoliation 'through which vast lands were transferred from Africans to the colonial states, white settlers, and private chartered companies' (2014, p. 98). The systematic seizing of land at the onset of colonialism established itself most prominently in settler colonies. Missionary schools, present in the film, reflect this enduring legacy, a disturbing reminder of colonialism's entrenched character. A. J. G. van der Borght (2009) confirms that the church was allocated land by the colonial regimes through the process of expropriating the grazing land of traditional communities – displacing these communities in the process.

A guiding philosophy of colonialism, Christianity legitimised the settler-colonial project, with consequences extending into the present. Inheriting a past of this nature, postcolonial African states have faced innumerable predicaments. Attempting to build on the deeply fractured terrain of postcolonial Africa has been hindered by state dysfunction whereby the introduction of democracy has, to a significant extent, been fictitious on account of actions authorised by the state undermining civil liberties (Takeuchi 2014). In agreement with Takeuchi, Wandile Dlamini, a member of the Swaziland United Democratic Front, expressed that:

> African governments continue using and not necessarily transforming the land question. Land currently continues to be owned by private farm owners, who, most of the time, are of foreign origin. They are white and, of course, there's been a huge emergence of black private ownership in the form of prince[s] and princesses. (2020, 13:48)

It is evident that authoritative figures across Zambia, eSwatini, and Mozambique operate in isolation from the communities they are entrusted to serve. In addition to inheriting this legacy, Africa is now faced with the prevailing order of neoliberalism, producing an iteration of development that undermines livelihood strategies and individuals' autonomy as well as their control over their land (de Wet 2011).

With land dispossession frequently occurring under the guise of development, it is imperative that this mode of invading the land is assessed and critiqued as evidence of development that excludes those who it claims to be for – as an unconsented imposition, exploiting communities' lack of civic education. It is out of these historical and contemporary conditions that social movements seeking to hasten agrarian reform have emerged.

The role of women in catalysing the actualisation of land justice in Zambia, eSwatini and Mozambique forms part of a long tradition of women at the front line of agrarian reform advocating radical transformation. Rural women's participation in La Via Campesina, an international peasant movement in resistance to the neoliberal globalisation of agriculture, attests to this tradition. Representing an estimated 200 million farmers across 81 countries, Via Campesina comprises 182 local and national organisations, with women, who have contributed to gender issues being addressed and to espousing an integrated approach to land justice, being an integral part of the movement. Writing about rural women's involvement in Via Campesina, Annette Aurélie Desmarais states that 'women insisted that food sovereignty could only be achieved through women's greater participation in policy development in the countryside' (Desmarais 2003, p. 143) - evidencing that selective justice is no justice at all. In eSwatini's not-so-distant past, women were not allowed to own land using their own surnames – they had to do so through a husband or a son.

However, through effective organising and mobilisation, these policies have shifted to recognise women as autonomous individuals. Dlamini addresses the patriarchal tradition rife in eSwatini – a sentiment that is shared across contexts – by observing that the profoundly sexist and patriarchal system centres and protects men, disregarding women in the process and subjecting them to greater vulnerability. Echoing Desmarais' insight, Salma Ismail notes that 'a woman's viewpoint is critical to any understanding of development strategies' (Ismail 2003, p. 103), an ethos that reverberates throughout the film.

A woman community activist and a staff member of the National Farmers' Union (UNAC) in Maputo, Mozambique, Flaida Macheze, elaborates on the significance of agrarian reform: 'For me the issue of land is fundamental. It is fundamental because the land is the only wealth that peasant families have in Mozambique.' In conjunction with land being a site of agency for individuals, land – particularly but not exclusively in rural areas – carries considerable ancestral significance, cradling an intimate relationship between people and the land as a locus of liberation and autonomy. Engaged in a social pedagogy – a teaching praxis that nurtures a lifelong holistic and relationship-centred approach to knowledge sharing and production – these communities have succeeded in fostering a compelling learning environment 'from their own experience, and from dialogue and critical reflection, which leads to social action and solving problems' (Ismail 2003, p. 105).

The dearth of civic and popular education in Zambia, eSwatini, and Mozambique – including about the law of the land – has resulted in people losing their land. The work initiated and sustained by women in these communities seeks to combat the scarcity of knowledge through the conscientisation of communities, motivated by the eventual attainment of land and liberation.

The continuation of mining and the rise of corporate entities' presence across Zambia, eSwatini and Mozambique have had detrimental effects on the livelihoods of individuals as well as on the condition of the natural environment. With the degradation of water sources, including damage to and pollution of the Mushima stream in Zambia by the mining company Vedanta, and the global escalation of climate change, a deliberate and urgent engagement in an ecocentric land ethic holds innumerable possibilities for an alternative: a human community integrated with the agroecosystem (Merchant 1992).

The work of women such as Lonhlanhla Mthethwa, a farmer, community activist and member of the Swaziland Rural Women's Assembly, who cultivates indigenous farming practices, proposes a mode of nurturing the land as a radical way forward, motivated by the bridging of these divides as crucial to healing society (Escobar 2011). The emergence of social movements has evidenced resistance to state-sanctioned violence imposed on peasant farmers, displaying a glimmer of hope amidst an unjust reality.

The bureaucratic processes that have become synonymous with agrarian reform across Africa suggest that agrarian reform in its predominant manifestation is a project preoccupied with 'personal enrichment by those closer to political power or those in political office' (Gumede 2015, p. 21) rather than a commitment to the collective upliftment of the common people. The khonta system in eSwatini, a land tenure system where the chief allocates communal Swazi national land to an individual for personal use – the end product of several procedures – is an example of the often futile endeavour to ensure that agrarian reform is delivered.

Notwithstanding these multiple procedures, the person does not own the land but is allowed to use it for any purpose and pass it on to their beneficiaries for use, explains an elder of the Manzini community, Celani Ernest Mkhonta. Historically, cattle were used as a trade-off to access land. However, in eSwatini's present, it is uncommon for families to own cattle. Money is then used, with people spending around SZL20,000 (US$1,190) for a hectare of land that will continue to be held in trust for the Swazi nation by the king. Reflecting on the absurdity of the *khonta* system, Wandile Dlamini asserts that 'when you die, they grab the land back.'

The Mozambican context is no different. The land and its associated resources are the sole property of the state, and thus the private ownership of land is nonexistent (Kathrada 2014). Despite the nonexistence of private land ownership, jural systems such as the 1997 land law insist on complicating this process. Monetary fees are involved in purchasing the paper that 'grants private persons the right to use and benefit from the land' (Kathrada 2014) — the DUAT (Direito de Uso e Aproveitamento da Terra, translated as the Right to Use Land). Peasant farmers do not have the financial capacity to purchase the DUAT, placing people in a lifelong state of limbo and making them more susceptible to vulnerability and dispossession. In accordance with the concerns expressed above, Zambia's bureaucracy has exposed the state's fervent disregard for the livelihoods of those on the economic periphery.

Echoing this concern, Nsama Musonda Kearns, the executive director of Care For Nature Zambia, urges individuals to move beyond activism into the realm of politics, stating that 'land is controlled by people who are involved in politics' – resolute in her belief that agrarian reform in Zambia will only materialise once the grievances of those on the margins are represented in political discourse and decision-making processes.

We Rise for Our Land has affirmed that an engaged pursuit of agrarian reform requires extensive civic and popular education, particularly in rural areas. It is imperative that we take seriously the work of social movements in actively imagining and creating a world where agrarian reform is not a pipe dream, but an attainable reality – a transformative and promising locus of thriving material conditions – and stand in solidarity with those on the front line.

References

Desmarais, A.A. (2003) 'The Via Campesina: peasant women at the frontiers of food sovereignty', In *Canadian Woman Studies/Les Cahiers de la Femme*, 23(1): 140-5

De Wet, J. P. (2011) '"We don't want your development!" Resistance to imposed development in northeastern Pondoland', in T. Kepe and L. Ntsebeza (eds) *Rural Resistance in South Africa: The Mpondo Revolt after Fifty Years*, Leiden, Brill

Escobar, A. (2011) 'Sustainability: design for the pluriverse', *Development* 54: Issue 2, pp.137–140. https://doiorg.ezproxy.uct.ac.za/10.1057/dev.2011.28

Gumede, V (2015) *Inclusive development in post-apartheid South Africa, Vusi Gumede Research and Publications,* https://www.vusigumede.com/content/2016/academic%20paper/Inclusive%20development%20in%20post.pdf, accessed 9 March 2020.

Ismail, S. (2003) 'A poor women's pedagogy: "When ideas move in people's hands and hearts, they change, adapt and create new solutions"', *Women's Studies Quarterly,* 3 & 4, pp. 95-112.

Kathrada, Z. (2014) 'Acquiring land rights in Mozambique', *Financial Institutions Legal Snapshot,* https://www.financialinstitutionslegalsnapshot.com/2014/08/acquiring-land-rights-in-mozambique/, accessed 25 June 2020

Merchant, C. (1992) 'Sustainable development', in *Radical Ecology: The Search for a Liveable World*, New York, Routledge (pp. 211-233)

Takeuchi, S. (2014) 'The evolution of land policy in African state building', in K. Otsuka and T. Shiraishi (eds.) in *State Building and Development*, New York, Routledge, pp.95-113

Van der Borght, A.J.G. (ed.) (2009) *The God-Given Land: religious perspectives on land reform in South Africa*, (Savusa poem proceedings series, no. 2), Amsterdam, Rozenberg Publishers

PART IV

*Land Occupations
and Alternatives*

CHAPTER 10

Land struggles over agricultural land in Zimbabwe: the case of Chisumbanje

Steve Mberi and Freedom Mazwi

Introduction

Zimbabwe inherited a racially skewed, bimodal agrarian structure at independence in 1980, composed of about 6,000 large-scale commercial farms (LSCFs), plantations and agro-industrial estates on one hand, and close to a million black peasant farmers on the other (Moyo 1995). By 1999, about 4,500 LSCFs controlled a total of 11 million hectares of land, constituting 35 per cent of prime agricultural land, highlighting unequal land ownership patterns. What was clear in Zimbabwe's post-1980 case is how the Lancaster House Agreement entered into by the liberation parties – the Zimbabwe African National Union – Patriotic Front (ZANU-PF) and the Zimbabwe African People's Union (ZAPU) – and the British government had failed to reverse land inequities (Moyana 2002).

With the adoption of a structural adjustment programme in the 1990s, massive retrenchments led to enormous loss of formal employment among working people due to deindustrialization, leading to the intensification of an urban to rural migration (Moyo and Yeros 2005). The market-assisted land reform which had been agreed on at the Lancaster House conference yielded abysmal results, as, by 1999, only 3.4 million hectares of land had been transferred to a small proportion of indigenous blacks, thus further fuelling a land and agrarian crises in the countryside (Moyo 2013). Meanwhile, the evidence among poorer communities showed an increase in illegal and underground land occupation (Moyo 1998). The outcomes of the market-assisted land reform and the socio-economic crises triggered by SAPs have been extensively discussed (see Moyo 2011a, Moyo and Chambati 2013, Moyo and Yeros 2005). At a social movements level, the dire socio-economic conditions and failure to redistribute land resulted in the mobilization of forces from below, through various groups such as the landless, workers, peasants and the war veterans, into land occupations from 2000 to 2003 (Moyo and Yeros 2005). While the state's initial response was to thwart the self-allocation of land, it eventually gave in to the land occupation movement by enacting the necessary laws and deploying state infrastructure to facilitate the Fast Track Land Reform Programme (FTLRP) (Moyo and Yeros 2007). The FTLRP resulted in more than 130,000 A1 peasant households and 30,000 middle to large capitalist A2 households benefitting[1] (Moyo 2013). A study by Moyo, Chambati, Murisa, Siziba, Dangwa, Mujeyi and Nyoni (2009) shows that more than one million people directly or indirectly benefitted from the FTLRP.

Despite the FTLRP altering the agrarian structure from bimodal to trimodal and enlarging a black peasant base, the land reform policy by the government of Zimbabwe was not clear on the redistribution of large-agro industrial estates, conservancies and forest plantations (Moyo 2013). Evidence has shown that large-agro industrial estates, land owned by churches and state-owned land were largely spared from the FTLRP (Moyo 2011a). While Zimbabwe represents a case of radicalization through its redistributive land reform after 2000, there have been worrying cases where the peasantry have either been threatened or evicted by the state acting largely in favour of agrarian and mining capital (Chambati, Mazwi and Mberi 2018). This is largely because the major challenge faced after the FTLRP in Zimbabwe has been how to finance agrarian production, given the capital flight, the attendant international isolation and an expanded peasant base (Moyo and Nyoni 2013).

In this chapter, we examine the trajectory of primitive accumulation and disarticulation of the peasantry in Chisumbanje by examining the differentiated practices of land alienation and dispossession of agrarian communities by capital, and the consequent obliteration of livelihoods of the peasants and agrarian productive forces. The chapter then assesses the consequences of these processes and responses from social movements to the land dispossessions and how the state, through its various apparatuses, sought to intervene through alterna-

----

1 The A1 scheme was meant to expand the smallholder-farming sector to cater for the landless, unemployed and disadvantaged peoples, with A1 beneficiaries allocated 5 to 6 hectares of arable land for farming and 7 to 15 hectares per household for grazing. The A1 model has two sub-schemes; the 'villagised' and 'self-contained', with the former scheme replicating earlier Model A resettlement schemes in which land beneficiaries live in a closed village and allocate households arable land and common grazing lands that are outside the village. The self-contained farms resettled individual families on one piece of land, to contain their homestead, some land for crop cultivation and also some to provide pasture for livestock production. The A2 model encompasses individually held farming plots that range in size from the small scale A2s of 50 hectares to the large scale A2 units at around 400 to 1,500 hectares.

tive strategies. While Zimbabwe's land reform was progressive in its redistributive agenda, some contradictions have emerged. The chapter concludes with proposals to guarantee secure land rights and adequate compensation for smallholder farmers.

Primitive accumulation: perpetuation of land concentration by white capital

Waves of accumulation

The recent foreign land acquisitions in Africa are rarely examined in terms of their diverse historical and sub-regional contexts of colonial rule and capitalist penetration to decipher the varied forms of dispossession and the state ideologies and projects which enable land grabbing, as well as the diverse sources of popular struggles against it.

The first wave of land expropriations by the colonialists in Africa can be traced back to the 1930s, both in settler-colonial Africa, on an extensive scale, and in non-settler colonial Africa on a modest scale in dispersed reserves (Amin 1972, Moyo 2010). After independence there were attempts by African states to amend foreign land control and land concentration that followed land expropriations through resettlement, narrow land redistribution and, at a higher level, nationalisation (Shivji 2009). In the mid-1980s, a second erratic, dispersed and smaller scale wave of land expropriation emerged at a time when the neoliberal structural adjustment programmes were introduced (Moyo 2008, 2010). In the early 1990s, the national land policies were reformed, which prompted land privatisation (see Manji 2006, Moyo and Yeros 2005), opening up for land concessions (Moyo 2011b). The third contemporary and expansive wave, which involves a myriad foreign capitals and local elites in liaison with comprador states (Petras 2008), is present in numerous former non-settler and settler African countries through land purchases and long leases (see Grain 2009), for mining and diverse resource concessions. The Chisumbanje case falls within this third wave of accumulation, as explained later in this chapter.

Accumulation by dispossession

Historically, the trajectory of a highly skewed agrarian structure in then-Rhodesia began in the 1890s, as a result of the dispossession of the indigenous natives of their land and natural resources, which subsequently led to racially discriminatory land tenures (see Moyana 2002, Moyo 2011b, Palmer 1977). The dispossession process resulted in the natives being crowded into Communal Areas, formerly called Tribal Trust Lands, with marginal and unfertile soils (Shivji, Moyo, Ncube and Gunby 1998).

Mining and the import substitution industry were hinged on migrant black labour largely subsidised by a peasant sector. This structure of the economy tended to perpetuate class inequalities underpinned by race. For the agricultural sector, landlessness on the part of the black peasantry and land concentration by white large-scale commercial farmers became key features after the dispossession. After 1965, there was an increased number of dams and rural electrification, among other infrastructures provided through state support, to improve large scale-irrigated estate farming (Moyana 2002, Rukuni, Tawonenzi and Eicher 2006). The broader aim was to reduce wheat and sugar imports by promoting a nascent agrarian capitalist base (see Moyo 2011b). During the 1970s, the state established farm estates under the Agricultural Rural Development Authority, formerly known as the Tribal Trust Lands Development Authority. The Cold Storage Commission was amongst other parastatals established, with eight of them covering 52,264 hectares under leasehold lands belonging to communal areas (Moyo 2011b). By 1999, the state had more than 250 large farms and estates supported by the Bilateral Investment, Protection and Promotion Agreements (BIPPAs), amounting to about 500, 000 hectares (3 per cent of the large-farm area and 1 per cent of the agricultural land) was under foreign ownership (see MoFA 2007).[2]

Highlighting land dispossessions during the neo-liberal era in Zimbabwe was the ownership of vast tracts of land by transnational corporations. Before the FTLRP of 2000, South African based transnational corporations (such as Hippo Valley and Triangle Sugar Corporation) owned private estates alongside other local and European white capital, such as Tanganda Tea, Mazoe and Ariston Holdings (see EU 2007, Moyo 2011b, Moyo and Nyoni 2013). The local agribusiness corporations and estates were largely dominated and owned by pioneer white capital, with some in possession of licenses for mining. Seven wildlife conservancies were created in the drier lowveld region by various large scale farmers involving European shareholdings by 1999, covering more than 900,000 hectares (Moyo 2011b). Preceding this, from the late 1980s into the 1990s, 70,000 hectares were largely under foreign ownership via 16 private forest plantations under companies such as Allied Timbers, Border Timbers and Mutare Pulp and Paper mills, among others, with the state-owned plantations covering only

....

2 Nine European countries held 65 per cent of these farms while US nationals, Malaysian, Indonesians and South Africans held 33 per cent.

36 per cent (40,000 hectares) (see Bradley and McNamara 1993). And by 1999, just before the radical land reforms, there existed more than 100 timber outgrowers (FAO 2001).

In total, about 4 per cent of the national agricultural land, amounting to one million hectares, was under large farming estates, with about 80 per cent under private ownership (GoZ 2009, Moyo 2011b). Grain (2009) posits that such foreign land ownership and the land concentration that ensued in Zimbabwe was by far the greatest compared to the current land grabbing happening in some African countries with no settler-colonial history.

Historical overview of Chisumbanje

Chisumbanje lies some 100 km downstream of Birchenough Bridge on the east bank of Save River, in the south-eastern lowveld region of Zimbabwe. It is located in the Dowoyo communal land. It is in agro-ecological region V, characterised by hot and short rainy season lasting from late November to March and long, dry but cool winters that are frost free and ideal for cane production. The hot climatic conditions are ideal for sucrose development and maturity. Maturity of sugarcane in such areas can be attained in twelve months, as opposed to eighteen months in other regions.

Chisumbanje was established as an experimental station by the Ministry of Agriculture in 1953, for agricultural production potential evaluation through soil analysis under intensive irrigation. A potential 40,000 hectares of irrigable soils was confirmed in 1964 by the research station, and in 1966 the Chisumbanje Development Company (Pvt) Ltd was registered to stimulate the obligation to irrigation development on the 40,000 hectares. An American company, EL Bateman Inc, was then consulted in 1979 to do a study for the establishment of a 15,000 hectare sugarcane estate, which was finalized, but due to the liberation war the proposed project was set aside (Green Fuel, n.d.).

After liberation in 1981, the Agricultural Rural Development Authority (ARDA) was established by the Ministry of Agriculture, with the key obligation of planning, coordinating, implementing and promoting agricultural development in Zimbabwe. ARDA entered into lease agreements with the local rural district council (RDC) and awarded ownership of the Chisumbanje estate, which it started leasing from the RDC in the 1980s.

Chisumbanje estate has maintained an estimated arable area of 40,000 hectares, of which 4,500 hectares are used annually for dry land

(2,000 hectares) and irrigated (2,500 hectares) cropping. The major crops on the estate include sugar cane, maize, seed maize, wheat and tomatoes. Sugar cane alone takes up to 1,100 hectares and production is up to 132,000 tonnes annually, which used to be transported to the Triangle mill, located 123 km away, but has been processed within the estate since 2011, after the establishment of the Green Fuel ethanol processing plant.

For some time now, the government has been driving a radical expansion of ethanol production in the Chisumbanje area, with the targets being motivated by concerns about high oil prices on international markets due to the 2007/8 energy and financial crises, dwindling foreign exchange inflows as a result of crippled foreign direct investments, export opportunities and curbing climate change (see Cotula, Dyer and Vermeulen 2008). Biofuel production is not a new phenomenon in Zimbabwe, as it started in the 1970s, leading to the country's drive to blend petrol with ethanol processed from sugarcane in 1980. Ethanol blending with petrol, pegged at 12 to 15 per cent, went on until 1992 before the El Niño-induced drought struck the country, reducing production of sugarcane and ultimately temporarily halting the ethanol production and petrol blending (see Mujeyi and Moyo 2010). In 2004, actual production of ethanol was slightly above 20 million litres, having declined from a total capacity of 35 million litres in 1983 (Earth Policy Institute 2005). For a long period until 1992, ethanol-blended fuel was available on the market, with the first ethanol processing plant in Triangle having been in operation for more than three decades (Mujeyi and Moyo 2010).

After the FTLRP of 2000, there has been a resurgence in the ethanol expansion drive necessitated by fuel shortages in the country and foreign exchange crises which led the state and private domestic white capital to offer enormous tracts of land for investment in agro-fuel production. This has resulted in the government entering into a partnership agreement to produce sugarcane for processing into ethanol with two private investment companies on its two large estates under ARDA in the lowveld, on a 20-year lease agreement (see Mujeyi and Moyo 2010). The project is a joint venture between the government (through ARDA) and private investors Rating Investments Ltd and Macdon Investments Ltd. It initially ran on a 'build, operate and transfer agreement' (BOTA) basis where the investors were to develop ARDA's land and infrastructure over a period stated in the agreement (20 years in this case) before handing it over (Mujeyi and Moyo 2010). This was, however, changed to a joint venture partnership amongst ARDA, Green Fuel and Macdom in 2012, based on the initial commercial value brought to the project to date (Green Fuel n.d.). Plans involved the establishment of 40,000 hectares of sugar cane for processing into ethanol for blending with fuel over eight years by developing 5,000 hectares each year. Currently, Chisumbanje Estate occupies 9,375 hectares, which falls within the 40,000 hectare concession under lease agreement between ARDA and the RDC (Green Fuel n.d.). The more-than US$300 million ethanol processing distillery plant which was constructed on site at the Chisumbanje estate began operation in October 2011, with a capacity to produce 120 million litres of anhydrous ethanol per annum, and 18 megawatts of electricity (*Herald* 2015).

Study methodology

The study employed a qualitative approach to explore and deepen understanding of the impact of land dispossessions on the local communities affected in the Chisumbanje area. Secondary literature was also used to explore how the Green Fuel developmental project affected the peasantry's ways of life in the area. Due to the Covid-19 pandemic, some interviews with stakeholders were carried out telephonically, although some were conducted before the pandemic in 2019. Interviews were held with key personel. These include Platform for Youth and Community Development (PYCD) representatives, traditional leaders, councillors and headmen who represent a wide section of the communities affected in the Chisumbanje area. The focus on the local traditional leaders was rooted in the fact that these play a crucial role as custodians of various facets of life of the communities. Information from the investors in the project was gathered through secondary sources from other studies done in the same area within the past six years. All the information gathered was analysed and triangulated with the secondary sources to inform the discussion of the issues raised in this chapter.

Land reform and the state's agro-industrial project in Zimbabwe

The redistribution of land during the FTLRP entailed popular struggles from below for access to land through the 'illegal land occupations' which were ultimately supported and then co-opted by the state (Moyo 2011, 2013). The co-option happened through the formalization of such occupations, as well as bureaucratically regulated land expropriations for allocation to selected beneficiaries by the state (Moyo 2013). This process was heavy with partly competing agrarian reform projects, in terms of the social reproduction of the peasant and working classes and the accumulation strategies of former and remaining white capitalist and black capitalist farmers and the largely transnational-corporation estates, whose contradictions created specific land and agricultural policy struggles.

The state's key strategic mechanism on the estates in Chipinge, particularly Chisumbanje, Chiredzi, Masvingo and other areas in the lowveld involved the expansion of agro-industrial estate farming, with the involvement of public trust land alliances owned by Development Trust of Zimbabwe (Moyo and Nyoni 2013). This constituted part of the larger agrarian reform process and an extension of the state's role and capacity to pursue an articulated development strategy based on expanded production of food for local markets and import substitution for key imports such as fuel, maize and wheat (see also Moyo 2011a).

The estate-based development strategy, which geographically was focused on the regions of the southern lowlands previously dominated by the transnational corporations' estates, was continually under gross attack by sections of the peasantry who occupied private and state owned estate lands (Moyo 2011b). Exerting pressure on this land as well were black provincial political and business leaders and some 'elites' who sought to control the regional expression of the state's development strategy, based on promoting a national bourgeoisie, expanding state capital and autonomy, and 'including' as many small and middle level farming families as possible (Moyo 2011b).

Land struggles and socio-political movements in Chisumbanje

The continued organisation of rural movements in the Chisumbanje area marks an extreme example of dispersed struggles from below over land in Zimbabwe, which reflects deeper social deprivation under hostile economic conditions created by neoliberal economic and political reform (see also Moyo 2011a). The dynamics of land reform in this context are complex and variegated, and can best be understood in political terms – that is, in terms of a protracted struggle of peasants, poor urban workers and other rural groups for access to land, and in terms of the reaction of the dominant landholding class to this struggle, as well as the responses of the state.

Although there was a downscaling of larger farms, including estates, after the FTLRP, the Green Fuel estate of Chisumbanje is cumulatively encroaching, remaining extensive and divesting the peasant, poor and landless families' access to sovereign livelihoods and land.

Lately, there have been wrangles between the villagers and the Green Fuel estate agents over boundary issues. The later have been accused by the former of encroaching on their land, and dispossessing them, prompting the villagers and traditional leaders to protests and threatening to take legal action (Interview with PYCD, May 2020). On the other hand, Green Fuel, through Macdon Investments, which is owned by a domestic white bourgeois, Billy Rautenbach, accuses villagers of encroaching into its estate, which is being leased from the ARDA (Interview with PYCD, May 2020). Although the government committed itself in 2010 to compensate the displaced villagers affected by the ethanol project, no meaningful strides have been made to date, with the land disputes being far from over (Interview with a chief, August 2020).

The legitimacy of the Green Fuel project was anchored on the promise of enhancing the welfare of the public through sharing surplus value with the communities, providing employment and enhancing food security (see Moyo 2011a). However, to date, villagers lament the lack of meaningful employment opportunities created for local people by the ethanol-producing company. It is worth noting that state-owned estates have always been contentious because of their ties with colonial dispossessions, alleged corruption and ineffective management. The ongoing experience with the white 'investor' of the Green Fuel ethanol project has further exacerbated negative perceptions about large-scale oriented agriculture.

Lately, there was an emergence of farmer organisations such as the PYCD, representing the local black farmers, which arose because of the continued escalation in struggles between the latter and the white capitalist outgrowers in the Chisumbanje area (Interview with traditional leader, September 2020). Apart from PYCD, there is an organised group of farmers numbering 116, women's advocacy farmers and war veterans who have also emerged to challenge the land displacements (Interview with traditional leader, September 2020). White capital, as represented by Macdon Investments, continues to dispute the rights of villagers to the land, and farmer organisations' movements have challenged the takeover of their land through litigation and continued resistance to the land evictions. The latter has entailed approaching local government officials through traditional leaders.

Relocation, displacements and resistance by the communities

Although there are nebulous claims about the decline in the current rate of displacements of late, a cloud of insecurity still lingers over the welfare of the villagers living in Chisumbanje area, with more than 1,000 peasants having lost their land. They have been affected in various ways. Before the coming in of Green Fuel, smallholder farmers in the areas were engaged in cotton and maize production. The former was being produced under contract with The Cotton Company of Zimbabwe, Cottco. With the coming of Green Fuel, smallholder farmers were displaced and allocated half a hectare of land as compensation. As the displaced smallholder farmers reported their experiences with Green Fuel:

> The allocated plots are located more than 15 kilometres from our homes and [are] inadequate to support our families, with little input support from the government. During the peak demand, irrigation water is not available to smallholder farmers. Some displaced smallholder farmers migrated to the neighbouring Mozambique as the available 0.5 plots were not enough for all displaced households.

Similar experiences were reported with another agricultural investor in the Checheche area in the same district. Some civil society organisations and independent media allege lack of consultation and have bemoaned the exclusionary nature and the top-down nature of the deal, since information surrounding the investment contracts is not in the public domain. Moreover, they even blame the government for flouting its decrees and guidelines with regard to the relocation and displacements of the settlers (see also Mujeyi and Moyo 2010).

In a study by Konyana and Sipeyiye (2015), the state, through ARDA, claimed that the local villagers in Chisumbanje were aware of the establishment of the Green Fuel project and were warned against erecting any permanent structures or planting crops in the area as it was approved for the ethanol project. In this regard, the state remains adamant that some displacements did not warrant any compensation as the villagers were forewarned. The villagers, however, justify their occupation of the land and contestations with the investors as emerging from the late onset of the project, which took far too long to commence. This led to violent clashes between the villagers contesting the evictions and the local investors. It is important to note that the villagers have also claimed ancestral links to the pieces of land they are being evicted from, a claim which makes it difficult to ignore the farmers (Interview with villager, January 2020). Ancestral-link claims to land are not uncommon in Zimbabwe, as post-FTLRP studies in Zimbabwe have clearly demonstrated that demand for land during the FTLRP was partly driven by ancestry and historical links (see Moyo et al. 2009, Scoones, Marongwe, Mavedzenge, Murimbarimba, Mahenehene, and Sukume 2010).

This push has not gone unchallenged by the villagers in Chisumbanje, but has been met with various forms of resistance. Worth noting has been the organization of numerous social forces from diverse localities in Chisumbanje. The persistence of land concentration and accumulation by the foreign, multi-racial local elites and the state, despite the successful land redistribution exercise after 2000, continue to be resisted in the Chisumbanje area through various mechanisms, such as organised community rural movements and, at a low level, illegal land occupations, which are condoned by some state sections (see Moyo 2011b). These rural movements in Chisumbanje have emerged to become the most important social forces against the dispossessions. Such rural movements, which are of diverse political character, share a common base of dispossessed peasants and unemployed workers, who have previously used land occupations and other tactics to confront the neoliberal state (see Moyo 2011a).

Although the local traditional leadership from the Chisumbanje area support local development in their area (see the study by Konyana and Speyiye 2015), they lamented lack of consultation by the government and investors before the establishment of the project, and also felt coerced to come to terms with the project and create space for it. This kind of approach caused a spike in the resistance to the establishment of the Green Fuel project, as is the case elsewhere in African communities, with the socio-ethical sources of such resistances tied to the land ownership concept by the local people.

Contrary to the views regarding consultations by the local traditional authorities, the state authorities involved in the ethanol project claim that the local villagers were always kept aware of developments in the project's establishment through the same community leaders, and from the chiefs, headmen, the district administrator (DA), ward councillors, and members of parliament for the area. This highlights that divergent views emerged amongst the political entities, local traditional leaders and state authorities, which is also synonymous with the findings of a study by Konyana and Speyiye (2015), where the DA asserted illegitimacy of the compensation claims made by the locals, citing their encroachment into lands reserved for the project since the colonial period. The political dimensions also took centre stage as indicated by the polarisation between the ruling party, ZANU-PF, and the opposition party, the Movement for Democratic Change (MDC), with the villagers who were resisting displacement and claiming compensation being aligned to the opposition party because of its perceived history of fighting the regime, and those vying for the project establishment labelled mainstream ruling party supporters (field observation).

Contestation over land and compensation

High level arguments and contentions emanating from the Chisumbanje Estate villagers and movements against domestic white capital investors revolve around the land question. The villagers have always been sceptical about the large scale investments, which they argued have propensities similar to land grabbing, as happened in other settler colonial states such as Mozambique, Namibia, and so on, and enormously affected the peasantry's land tenure security, impacting on their livelihoods (see Moyo 2007, Scoones et al. 2012). Furthermore the contestations continue to escalate through scepticism regarding the undermining of food sovereignty of the local peasantry through rekindling the food-fuel argument, as land for food production is given over to agro-fuels for ethanol production. Since 2009, biofuel production has been increasing, with negative implications, however, for the land tenure security of the local communities (see Moyo 2011b), as well as food security and social and cultural dimensions of land use.

The rush to embrace agro-fuel, which has been necessitated by the desire to reduce dependence on fossil fuel, has been done without a careful analysis of the potential threats and risks associated with it, resulting in the emergence of conflicts between the local communities and investors (Mujeyi and Moyo 2010). The agro-fuel production has enunciated the neglected debate on the land and agrarian question, with Mujeyi and Moyo (2010) identifying specific questions around the following issues:

- Can bio-energy fulfil the promises claimed by its proponents? Can it become an environmentally sustainable, economically viable, pro-poor source of energy?
- Is bio-energy an extension of unequal or unfair trade and market fixing (export-oriented or 'cash cropping')?
- Is it another avenue for land alienation or concentration?
- Is it an expanded basis for extraction of value from labour?
- To what extent is it a new platform for (exporting) ecological despoliation?

- Is it not another instrument for 'recolonisation' of developing countries or resource control in them by developed countries?
- Is it a new instrument for smallholder exploitation?

Amidst the villagers' resistance to displacement and relocation, the investors decided to come up with a compensation plan for the villagers. The compensation plan included money payouts equivalent to the value of improvements on the land lost and a five hectare irrigated plot for the displaced (see also Konyana and Sipeyiye 2015). Nonetheless it still remains a contentious issue, as the villagers continue crying in desperation about how the Green Fuel investment invaded their land, left by their forefathers, without notice and compensation (Manono 2018).

Concluding remarks

Although Zimbabwe embarked on a radicalised path which redistributed land to the landless, the case of Chisumbanje illustrates some contradictions which emerge in attempting to embark on such a process in a neoliberal economy. Domestic elite interests are pushed through the state and these tend to go hand in hand with private capital thus threatening land access for peasants. The case of Chisumbanje highlights the potential of 'large-scale land investments' to drive the peasantry into precarity as demonstrated by the inability of the latter to engage in food and cash-crop production. This raises questions about whether 'large-scale investment' in agriculture is the panacea to the agricultural financial crisis in Zimbabwe. Despite the massive attack on the villagers by the state, peasants have shown resistance by way of organising themselves as social groups to challenge land displacements. This has entailed villagers organising themselves to meet with state bureaucrats, in an attempt by the latter to rescind the 'land investments' as well as the use of litigation. The instrumentalisation of litigation is yet to bear any fruits as the country is grappling with challenges of independence of the judiciary. Emanating from potential displacements resulting from large scale land investments, there is a need to guarantee secure land rights for smallholder farmers. In addition, there is need for adequate and comprehensive compensation of displaced smallholder farmers to ensure minimal livelihood disruptions. Compensation given to farmers in Chisumbanje has been shown to be largely inadequate.

References

Amin, S. (1972) *Neocolonialism in West Africa*, Hammondsworth, Penguin Books

Bradley, P.N. and McNamara, K. (eds) (1993) *Living With Trees: Policies for Forestry Management in Zimbabwe*, World Bank Technical Paper No. 210. Washington D.C., World Bank

Cotula, L, Dyer, N. and Vermeulen, S. (2008) *Fuelling Exclusion? The Biofuels Boom and Poor People's Access to Land*, London, International Institute for Environment and Development

Earth Policy Institute (2005) *Homegrown for the Homeland: Ethanol Industry Outlook 2005*, Washington, DC, Renewable Fuels Association

EU (2007) *Zimbabwean Adaptation Strategy to the European Union: Sugar Regime Reform, Final Report. February*, Brussels, European Union

FAO (2001) 'Forestry out-grower schemes: A global overview; Report based on the work of D. Race and H. Desmond', Forest Plantation Thematic Papers, Working Paper 11, Rome, Forest Resources Development Service, Forest Resources Division, FAO

GoZ (2009) 'Memorandum to cabinet by the Minister of Lands and Rural Resettlement Hon. H. M. Murerwa (M.P) on the update on Land Reform and Resettlement Programme. Ministry of Lands and Rural Resettlement' (September), Harare, Government of Zimbabwe

GRAIN (2009) 'Grabbing land for food', *Grain Seedling* January 2009

Green Fuel (n.d.) *Milestones*, http://www.greenfuel.co.zw/milestones/

Konyana, E. and Sipeyiye, M. (2015) 'Complex moral dilemmas of large scale projects: The Case of Macdom-ARDA Chisumbanje ethanol plant project in Chipinge, South-Eastern Zimbabwe,' *International Journal of Sustainable Development*, 18(4), pp. 349-60

Manji, A. (2006) *The Politics of land reform in Africa: from communal tenure to free markets*, London and New York, Zed Books

Manono, E. (2018) 'Chisumbanje villagers open up on land dispute', *The Zimbabwe Sentinel*, 13 November, http://www.zimsentinel.com/chisumbanje-villagers-open-up-on-land-dispute/, accessed 22 November 2020

Mazwi, F., Chambati, W. and Mutodi, K. (2018) *Contract Farming Arrangement and Poor- resourced Farmers in Zimbabwe*, Harare, SMAIAS Publications

MoFA, (2007) *Current Status on the Bilateral Investment Promotion Partners Agreements (BIPPA) Farms*. Harare, Ministry of Foreign Affairs

Moyana, H. V. (2002) *The Political Economy of Land in Zimbabwe*, Gweru, Mambo Press

Moyo, S. (1995) *The Land Question in Zimbabwe*, Harare, SAPES Books

Moyo, S. (1998) *The Land Acquisition Process in Zimbabwe (1997/8)*, Harare, United Nations Development Programme (UNDP)

Moyo, S. (2008) *African Land Questions, Agrarian Transitions And The State: Contradictions Of Neoliberal Land Reforms* (CODESRIA Green Book Series), Dakar, CODESRIA

Moyo, S. (2010) 'Rebuilding African Peasantries: inalienability of land rights and collective food sovereignty in Southern Africa?' Harare (mimeo)

Moyo, S. (2011a) 'Three decades of agrarian reform in Zimbabwe', *Journal of Peasant Studies*, 38(3), pp. 493–531.

Moyo, S. (2011b) 'Land concentration and accumulation after redistributive reform in post-settler Zimbabwe', *Review of African Political Economy*, 38(128), pp. 257–76.

Moyo, S. (2013) 'Land reform and redistribution in Zimbabwe since 1980', in S. Moyo and W. Chambati (eds), *Land and Agrarian Reform in Zimbabwe: Beyond White-Settler Capitalism*, Dakar, CODESRIA, pp. 29-78.

Moyo, S., and Chambati, W. (eds) (2013) *Land and Agrarian Reform in Zimbabwe: Beyond White-Settler Capitalism* . Dakar, CODESRIA.

Moyo, S and N. Nyoni. (2013) 'Changing agrarian relations after redistributive land reform in Zimbabwe', in S. Moyo and W. Chambati, (Eds.), *Land and Agrarian Reform in Zimbabwe: Beyond White-Settler Capitalism*, Dakar, CODESRIA, pp. 195-250

Moyo, S., and Yeros, P. (2005) 'The resurgence of rural movements under neoliberalism', *in* S. Moyo and P. Yeros (eds) *Reclaiming the Land: The Resurgence of Rural Movements in Africa, Asia and Latin America*, London, Zed Books

Moyo, S. and Yeros, P. (2007) 'The radicalised state: Zimbabwe's interrupted revolution', *Review of African Political Economy*, 111, pp. 103-21.

Moyo, S., Chambati, W., Murisa, T., Siziba, D., Dangwa, C., Mujeyi, K. and Nyoni, N. (2009) *Fast Track Land Reform Baseline Survey in Zimbabwe: Trends and Tendencies, 2005/06*, Harare, African Institute for Agrarian Studies (AIAS)

Mujeyi, K., and Moyo, S. (2010) *Land and Bio-Fuels Industry Development in Zimbabwe*, Harare, African Institute for Agrarian Studies (AIAS)

Palmer, R. (1977) *Land and Racial Denomination in Rhodesia*, London, Heinemann Educational.

Petras, J. (2008) *The Great Land Give away: Neo-colonialism*, New York, Voltaire Network.

Rukuni, M., Tawonenzi P. and Eicher E.K., with Munyuki-Hungwe M. and Matondi P. (eds) (2006) *Zimbabwe's Agricultural Revolution Revisited*, Harare, University of Zimbabwe Publications

Scoones, I., Marongwe, N., Mavedzenge, B., Murimbarimba, F., Mahenehene, J. and Sukume, C. (2010) *Zimbabwe's Land Reform: Myths and Realities*, Harare, Weaver Press / Jacana Media and James Currey, UK

Scoones, I., Marongwe, N., Mavedzenge, B., and Murimbarimba, F. (2012) 'Livelihoods after land reform in Zimbabwe: understanding processes of rural differentiation', *Journal of Agrarian Change*, 12(4), pp. 503-27

Shivji, I. (2009) *Where is Uhuru? Reflections on the Struggle for Democracy in Africa* (edited by Godwin R. Murunga), Cape Town, Dakar, Nairobi and Oxford, Fahamu Books

Shivji, I.G., Moyo, S., Ncube, W. and Gunby. D. (1998) 'National land policy draft. A draft discussion paper prepared for the Government of Zimbabwe', Harare, FAO and Ministry of Lands and Agriculture

The Herald, (2015) 'Green Fuel invests $300m into Chisumbanje ethanol project', 15 October, https://www.herald.co.zw/green-fuel-invests-300m-into-chisumbanje-ethanol-project/, accessed 22 November 2020

Interviews

Interview with PYCD, May 2020, telephone interview with the PYCD director

Interview with a chief, August, 2020, telephone interview with chief (name withheld for anonymity)

Interview with a villager, January 2020, face to face interview with Chisumbanje villager (Name withheld for anonymity)

CHAPTER 11

Can land occupations achieve 'land reforms from below'? Evidence from southern Malawi

Justin Alinafe Mangulama and Wu Jin

The past five decades have witnessed an increasing number of peasants encroaching into idle estate land in Thyolo and Mulanje districts, southern Malawi. A study was conducted to understand land occupations in the white-owned tea estate land in Thyolo, Malawi. This region is popularly known as *'Matipate'*[1] among the peasant communities. A study was conducted to understand the livelihood activities of the land occupants, peasant accumulation, and whether the occupations can achieve land reforms from below. We found that peasants in the occupied land have been differentiated socially, and there was emerging 'peasant capitalism', with fewer farmers who owned more land than the rest employing a relatively larger amount of labour, and relying on multiple income generating activities with close links to local markets, a phenomena popularly known as 'straddling'. Accumulation of land by the rural capitalists involved 'leasing' land from fellow occupants as well as employing more labour during the occupation period to 'clear and control' more land for social reproduction. The peasants who occupied land from the estates were better off than their counterparts who did not occupy any land. The study uncovers that the occupations are steps or efforts by the peasantries to achieve 'land reform from below.' We argue that, although the land occupations in Thyolo and Mulanje have potential to achieve land reforms from below, the scale at which this is happening is low, as the majority continue to swim in extreme land poverty. Hence state interventions are needed to solve land woes.

....

1 Matipate is a local name referring to occupied estate land. The peasants referred to it as *Matipate*, from the English word 'Multiparty', meaning that many people from different villages surrounding the estates were involved in the cultivation of the idle estate land.

Setting the scene

In the past decade, an increasing number of peasants in Thyolo, a southern district of Malawi, have occupied white-owned tea estate land. While Kanyongolo (2005, p. 4) has termed the phenomenon land occupation, Chinigo (2016a) has argued that it is a trend which can be better described as 'repeasantisation' in rural Malawi. Peasants in the Thyolo and Mulanje tea growing areas continue to struggle when it comes to accessing arable land. The land question in southern Malawi is not only an important and very sensitive topic but also a highly politicized one (Chinigo 2016a, 2017). This is the case because 85 per cent of Malawians are directly or indirectly employed in the agricultural sector. Agriculture contributes 90 per cent of export earnings in the country and 39 per cent of GDP; it accounts for 85 per cent of employment and 65 per cent of total rural income (Chirwa 2008, Chinsinga 2011, Kanyongolo 2005). Efforts to resolve the land issue have amounted to a long discussion by land policymakers, as decades have gone by and little has been done by way of policy to respond to the area's land tensions.

Land conflicts in Africa are not a new phenomenon. By 2000, land-related conflicts had escalated in Zimbabwe, Côte d'Ivoire, Nigeria's Delta region, and Malawi (Moyo 2007, Chinigo 2016a). The surge in land-related conflicts in Africa reflects the failure of African states to decisively deal with the land-development nexus (Moyo 2007, Chinigo 2016a). Therefore it is not surprising that in 2020, British settlers owned enormous tracts of land in southern Malawi, acquired in the 1890s during the colonial era. In race terms, white farmers of British origin own the majority of the tea estates in Thyolo, Malawi.

Since 1891, when Malawi became a British protectorate, estate farming and small-scale farming were maintained as dual agricultural systems (Machira 2009, p. 368, Peters 2007). Much more emphasis was put on estate agriculture than on the smallholder counterpart. Chinigo (2016b) explains that this was done on the pretext that revenues from the estate agriculture would stir other sectors of the economy. This hardly happened, as it was an incomplete capitalism, which created a dispossessed proletariat with neither jobs nor land in the estates. Despite promises by the authoritarian administration of Kamuzu Banda of multiparty democracy, the land question has not been solved. The situation is more pronounced in south Malawi. Demographically, the population of Malawi has risen at a rate of 2.9 per cent per year, as seen in the 2018 Malawi Population Census (National Statistical Office 2018). Most populated districts in Malawi are in the southern region where, ironically, there is an artificial shortage of land as a result of a failure to implement land reform. It is stated that more than 24,000 hectares remain idle in Thyolo alone.

This is the land the peasants are occupying. Though the actual figures for land covered by estates in Mulanje and Thyolo[2] district remain unknown, it is reported that approximately 75 per cent of arable land is covered by the tea estate plantations in Thyolo alone (Chinigo 2016b).

The Malawian constitution prohibits any type of encroachment on private land estates. However, the land occupations in southern Malawi continue to increase at an alarming rate. There are frequently stories of land clashes and occupations in Thyolo. Hence, this chapter is not going to discuss further on the legality of the land occupations in southern Malawi. Many of the works on land occupations dwell on the legality of the occupations, tenure regimes and the recent land grabs in Malawi.[3] It remains unclear, however, whether the land occupations in southern Malawi can achieve 'land reforms from below,' and this chapter seeks to explore this latter issue.

Theoretical reflections – access to land and livelihoods

The link between land and livelihoods in Malawi, as is the case in so many sub-Saharan African countries, is predicated on the fact that farming was the most important means of subsistence for the overwhelming majority and that access to land is critical. The country's main development challenges, related to the agricultural sector, are presented particularly in rural areas. In Malawi, for instance, agriculture contributes to 90 per cent of the country's export earnings, adds 39 per cent of GDP, accounts for 85 per cent of jobs and 65 per cent of total rural income (Kanyongolo 2005, p. 5; see also Chinsinga 2011, Chirwa 2008). Studies of land livelihoods therefore need to be carefully considered and understood to advance rural development in the countryside.

While numerous scholars have theorized various understandings of the 'peasant mode of production' (Hyden 1980, Waters 2007), the

2 In this study, southern Malawi and 'Thyolo and Mulanje districts' will be used interchangeably because many of the tea estates in southern Malawi are found in these two districts.
3 Many studies on land related conflicts have centered on the green-belt initiative in Salima, Malawi. The Government of Malawi has appropriated huge tracts of land for foreign capitals for sugar and mango production. Scholars have expressed that the situation has necessitated state-sponsored land grabs.

general sense that emerged was that 'the peasant economy was related to the broader political economy by extracting surplus value from rural areas, by restricting peasant access to resources (mainly land) and by involving very unfavourable ties between rural people and the market and the state (Bebbington 1999, p. 2024). Accordingly, the peasants have provided the economy not only with cheap food but also with cheap labour, as many lack access to enough land and therefore resort to selling their labour to reproduce themselves (Bebbington 1999, Mueller 2011). The theories of social differentiation and the concepts linked to the structure and exercise of power at different levels are very important in order to understand the prevailing conditions in rural areas and agrarian sectors. Viewed broadly, various factors such as socio-economic and demographic factors affect differentiation. Although the notion of rural differentiation was theorized in various ways, the unifying argument was to refrain from treating 'peasants as if they were homogenous categories' (Isaacman 1990, p. 13). The earliest analysis of agrarian differentiation was the debate between the Marxists and the neo-populists, often personified as the 'Lenin-Chayanov debate', on the 'agrarian question' in rural Russia (Bernstein 2009).

Based on empirical analysis, Lenin (1967) differentiated peasants by their incomes, ownership of means of production and degree of reliance on wage labour. These differentiated classes were the rich, middle and poor peasants. The rich peasants (rural 'capitalists') were those who actively engaged in agricultural commodity markets: they owned large landholdings, produced predominantly for the market and relied on hiring wage labour. The middle peasants only owned enough land for the subsistence needs of their families. Finally, the poor peasants were those who participated in wage labour markets because they lacked access to land as a means of subsistence (Byres 1986).

Methodological reflections

This study was about understanding livelihood activities, peasant capitalism, and land reforms from below in southern Malawi. The study also looked into the state responses to the political processes in the Malawian countryside. The study largely employed a qualitative research design. This approach is meant to ensure a comprehensive understanding and interpretation of the phenomenon under investigation, which in this case is to analyze the political processes and resistance over land in southern Malawi. Narratives were used extensively in this study.

The study was conducted in Chibwana and Chaona villages, in the Southern Region of Malawi in Thyolo District. The study villages were selected because they were located outside Comforzi and Makwasa tea estates, where many peasants were fighting to repossess idle land on the estates. Most people within the villages surrounding the tea estate eked out their livelihoods through small scale farming, with few working on the tea estates as labourers. Thyolo is one of the regions where population densities are among the highest in Africa. It has 433 people per square kilometre[4] (National Statistics Office 2018:15). One was, therefore, likely to find a rich source of landless or near-landless people who could be studied in relation to the objectives of this study. Many peasants grew crops such as maize, millet, sorghum, cassava, potatoes, cowpeas, pigeon peas, sugarcane, tea and vegetables like lettuce and cabbage. Some kept livestock such as chicken, pigs, goats, cattle, and doves. Being a rural area, literacy levels among the people were low. Many of the people in these villages (both landed and landless or near-landless) had to find other creative sources of income, as farming from their small landholdings could not meet their daily needs. Some of the farmers resorted to cultivating their crops on estate land that had remained unused for three or four decades.

In total, we interviewed 60 households in Chaona Village and 50 households in Chibwana Village, making 110 in total. Amongst these household interviews that were conducted, 33 were with female-headed households, representing 30 per cent; 77 were male-headed households representing 70 per cent of the total sample. We stopped interviews in the villages after we noticed that the responses provided were the same (saturation point). We also interviewed 15 other households who did not have land in the estates. The aim was not for comparison per se, but to have an in-depth understanding of alternative narratives pertaining to the occupation processes.

Benefits derived from accessing the plantations' land resources
Increase in farmland and household incomes

The first thing we noticed was that the land parcels that the land occupants got from the estate land were larger than the average land holdings among the peasantry in the region.

....

4   By 2007, the population density for Thyolo was 255 people per square kilometer. It increased to 433 people per square kilometer in 2018 (see also National Statistics Office 2018, p. 15).

Table 11.1 New (occupied) farmland sizes
in Chaona and Chibwana villages

No. of households	Amount of land (hectares)	Percentage of households (%)
8	More than 2	7.27
4	2.0	3.64
3	1.8	2.72
13	1.5	11.82
14	1.3	12.73
10	1.0	9.09
58	0.5	52.73

Source: fieldwork in 2018

The average landholding sizes per capita in Malawi are estimated at 0.178 hectares in the southern region compared to 0.257hectares and 0.256 hectares for central and northern regions respectively (Chinsinga, 2011). It can be seen from the *Matipate* case above that the amount of land per household on the encroached estate lands was a bit higher than the average land area per household in the southern region where this study was conducted.. We can see from Table 11.1 above that the peasants in Chaona and Chibwana villages owned more than the average amount of farmland. With a higher percentage of the Malawian population living and working in rural areas, availability of farmland is key to people's livelihoods.

The second benefit from social reproduction in the newly occupied land was an increase in household incomes. We found that the majority of the 110 respondent indicated that they gained considerable incomes from selling surplus food (see Table 11.2).

We can see that though people lost land to the tea plantations in the colonial era, about a century ago, they are now reclaiming it and the land occupations are increasing on the estate land. This might also reveal that there is a scarcity of other non-farm activities that they can venture into in this region apart from the land occupations. Being a rural area, located in one of the least developed countries in the world, the figures portrayed above – minute as they may look – provide the peasants with some assistance to maintain a livelihood

Table 11.2: Estimated annual peasant incomes

No. of households	Percentage of households (%)	Estimated Annual Income (MWK)*
9	8.2	100,000 to 200,000
30	27.3	200,001 to 400,000
37	33.6	400,001 to 600,000
26	23.6	600,001 to 800,000
8	7.3	Above 800,000
110	100	

Source: fieldwork in 2018

*The estimated annual incomes are in Malawian Kwacha (MWK). These incomes were estimated from the sale of surplus food from the occupied land only. It excluded incomes from remittances, wage employment, gifts from relatives and other social networks. Incomes from other non-farm income activities were also excluded from the estimates. The exchange rate in that period was US$1=MWK 735

Aiding direct employment opportunities

The respondents explained that access to estate land has offered them access to self-employment, and it would be difficult for them to be employed in other non-farm activities. Results showed that 92 households, representing 83.63 per cent of the land occupants, explained that they were full-time farmers on the occupied land and have been so for the past decade. The rest – 18 households representing 16.67 per cent – reported that they considered agriculture in the newly occupied land as part-time employment, as they had other profitable business ventures. The majority of households remarked that they are principally farmers, and that their key problem has been access to land. Land occupation on the tea estates offered them a new lease on life to eke out a living from agriculture.

The study wanted to find out whether the food crops harvested by the land occupying households suffice for the whole farming season. The study found that the majority (80 per cent) of the respondents harvested enough maize for the whole year from the occupied land, while 20 per cent of the respondents reported did not harvest enough. It can be shown, however, that the majority of the respondents' households were able to produce more from their farms for subsistence, leaving aside more to sell and buy other basic needs. Although the majority did not own huge land or harvest for sale, they still had access to food. It is evident that subsistence farming has been made possible because of the land occupations. Land access in Thyolo is a serious concern as the region has the highest population density in Africa, as mentioned above (Machira 2009, p. 378). The land occupations have been used as a strategy for coping with food insecurity in the area. One village leader in Chaona had this to say:

> Before the land occupations, just like when the estate managers decide to slash our crops in that land, the people in this village suffered a lot. Many things changed when the people started the land occupations. Now we have choices of food. Apart from maize, sugarcane, bananas, cassava and groundnuts are easy to get in the village – all these thanks to the idle land in the estates. (Interview with local leaders, Chibwana Village, Thyolo, 2 July 2018)

From the above empirical evidence, it can be seen that majority of the households were able to access food in times of need from the agricultural activities on the occupied land. It must be mentioned that for many rural Malawians, shortages of food translate to shortage of maize, which is used to make the local staple food called *nsima*.[5] Most rural Malawian families experience an acute shortage of maize in the period between November and March (Mangulama 2015). The households that managed to occupy idle land from the estates were able to compare the times before and after the land occupations. Even if they had no maize, they were able to sell other crops such as tomatoes and vegetables to buy maize for *nsima*.

Most of the land occupiers in southern Malawi used the occupied land parcels for crop production. Farming requires inputs. Most rural Malawian farming households rely on the Farm Input Subsidy Program (FISP)[6] to access inputs such as improved seeds and chemical fertilizers. The study revealed that the FISP faces logistical and technical glitches such as late delivery of farm inputs to rural areas, diversion of inputs and corruption, unscrupulous traders inflating the buying prices and omission of deserving beneficiaries, among many other problems in the area the study was conducted. The majority of the respondents (82 per cent) reported that they use part of the proceeds to reinvest in agricultural production on the occupied land. It should be noted,

5 This is the staple food in Malawi as well as other countries such as Zambia, Tanzania and Mozambique. It is commonly served with relish such as vegetables, meat and legumes.
6 The agricultural sector in Malawi has benefited from fertilizer subsidies since 2006. The initial investment in FISP was US$50 million for this ambitious programme, solely to import improved seeds and fertilizers for distribution to farmers at subsidized prices through coupons (Juma 2011). Since that time, Malawi has recorded an increase in its maize harvest, but FISP still encounters many problems and many question its sustainability.

though, that a considerable number of the respondents indicated that they feared that their tenure was not secure enough for them to invest more in the land. However, for simple things such as the fertilizer sub-sidies, the respondents indicated that they did invest such to increase their annual harvest.

Returning to the FISP issue, targeting of beneficiaries has been problematic. During the fieldwork, only a few people had access to the FISP. One also had to have a higher social capital with the village leaders and officials from the Ministry of Agriculture to get a coupon for FISP. There has been a huge debate in Malawi on the viability and sustainability of FISP for small-scale farmers. Although this is not a review essay, central to one side of the opposing stances is the claim that FISP is a money drain, not sustainable, and that it makes farmers over-reliant on government for obtaining farm inputs. The other side maintains that FISP should be provided annually without strings attached. Another debate has been whether FISP should target fewer small-scale farmers or whether it should be a universal subsidy, which anyone with financial muscle can access. Both have pros and cons which this chapter will not explore further as it will diverge from the core objectives of the chapter.

The agricultural activities in the study area helped the peasants to obtain agricultural inputs with ease. This has been possible in three ways. In the first place, the estate land had been idle for long time. So after the peasants cleared the land and cultivated the area, the soil was still alluvial. They were able to grow crops and harvest relatively well with little chemical fertilizer. Secondly, peasants who were unable to buy agricultural inputs in the initial years of cultivation invested more in quarry stone production (for construction), livestock and crops that needed less or no fertilizer, such as sugarcane and groundnuts. After trading these, they then accumulated some capital that they could use to purchase chemical fertilizer to boost crop productivity.

The farmers who had no access to FISP stated that they used the money they got from selling surplus produce to re-invest in buying farm inputs because they usually payed more money than the intended prices of the FISP due to the abovementioned problems. It was found during interviews that the land occupiers were able to buy extra ferti-lizer since the provision under the FISP was sometimes not enough. Mwiinga (2014) found that rural areas of Malawi's neighbour, Zambia, share many similarities in terms of agricultural activities. He found that the majority of the farmers in Kanakantapa, Zambia, faced challenges with accessing farm inputs such as fertilizers. Some of the problems were in the identification of FISP beneficiaries, as those who deserved to get farm input subsidy were left out.

More than half (68 per cent) of the households interviewed in our study reported that they used some of the money from their businesses to buy pesticides to prevent post-harvest crop losses. There is evidence from many African countries that a considerable proportion of food crops are damaged after harvest. Li et al. (2012) found that, in sub-Saharan Africa, many smallholder farmers experienced significant post-harvest losses owing to, among other causes, poor storage and pests. The proceeds from the occupied land in southern Malawi are helping the farmers to safeguard their harvest, thereby allowing them to keep it for a relatively long period of time and contributing greatly to their household food requirements. It can be seen that the new land occupants are not only diversifying their income sources by 'straddling', but are also re-investing in smallholder farming, which remains the backbone of many rural peoples' livelihoods.

Helping children, parents, orphans and other dependents

We found that the land occupants in Thyolo used part of the proceeds from agriculture on the occupied land to help their dependents. Dependents included children, wives, parents, orphans and other extended family members in need. Of course, one can argue that the dependents also have a key role to play in the agricultural production because, for families that do not hire labour, family members work in the fields. The contribution of the proceeds from the *Matipate'* to the livelihoods of the land occupants' households cannot be underestimated. It was revealed in this study that the majority of the land occupants' households had four dependants, excluding the household heads. The majority (99 per cent) of the respondents explained that they offer monetary support to their dependants. The village leaders estimated that, in the region where the study was done, about 1,000 households were involved in land occupation, at various scales. Excluding the household heads, this translates to around 4,000 dependents' livelihoods being supported from the land occupations in the study area alone.

Housing units from proceeds from the occupied land

The study found that 40 land occupants in Chaona and Chibwana, representing 36.26 per cent of the respondents, indicated that they have either built or renovated their houses from the incomes that they have acquired from selling surplus food from the estate land and trading other resources such as quarry or forestry resources from the estate land. This might seem a small number, but building a house in these villages where poverty is rampant is a dream come true to many. Most of the households that boasted building a house for themselves used iron sheets for roofing, a symbol of affluence in the study areas.[7] When asked, one respondent named Sinoya (a pseudonym) had this to say on the benefits that have been accumulated after they occupied land from the estates:

> I have built a big house from the surplus food I have harvested from the 'multiparty'. Of course I had to top up some money from my transport business. However, the finances from the food sales have assisted me a lot to build this house. I really appreciate. It would have been hard or it could take [a] longer time (maybe never) for me to build if it were not for the opportunity I got to cultivate in the estate land. (Interview with a peasant farmer, Chibwana Village, 18 February, 2018)

According to Maslow's hierarchy of needs, housing is one of the important basic needs people cannot live without. Improvement in livelihoods and wellbeing also entails having decent housing.

Increase in the number of working days

The occupation of estate land has helped in improving the livelihoods of the new occupants in numerous ways. Among the many benefits are increases in the number of working days among the people. In Thyolo and Mulanje, land for subsistence farming is very limited. In Chaona and Chibwana villages, many families have a small parcel of land (0.05 hectares) or none at all. Although tea is a labour intensive crop, not all villagers can be employed in the tea estates.

The occupation of estate lands for crop cultivation has increased the number of working days in the villages surround the estates in two ways: in the first place, the peasants who were once landless are now able to go to work every morning in their new parcels of land on the estate, thereby earning a living and supporting their families and other dependents.

The other way in which occupied land has increased the number of working days among the people is that it is easy to buy food crops

7 In many Malawian rural areas, one is regarded as building a good house if it is roofed with corrugated iron sheets.

within the villages. At Chaona village, the peasants lamented that before occupying the estates, the people used to go to distant villages to buy food for their families. Many things have changed now. Instead of visiting far away villages to get food, food insecure families are able to buy cheaper maize and vegetables from the peasants who have land on the estate. Their working days have increased in the sense that, instead of travelling to distant areas to access food, they are able to buy food within the shortest time and distance. The rest of the time can be spent concentrating on other non-farm activities. For the women, they can spend the rest of the time in collecting firewood, small-scale businesses, taking care of children and other household chores. One woman from Chibwana agrees:

> *Things were hard. We had to work piece jobs. Early in the morning we had to wake up and stand on the road to buy maize from traders coming from other villages. If it's not a market day that they will not pass, we had to follow them in their villages, very far, to buy. But now many people do harvest maize, potatoes, sugarcanes, cassava and many other crops including vegetables. You do not have to travel that far to access these food supplements. All are available in this village or the nearby villages. Those estate lands that have water, nearby people have sugarcane. It's all good. Thanks to the estate land.*
> (Interview with a female head of household, Chibwana village, Thyolo, 3 March 2018)

As can be seen from the narratives of the peasants, both those who have encroached and those who haven't, the benefits in terms of the number of working days are too numerous to mention. This is a group of people in rural areas in southern Malawi whose livelihoods would have been under threat if they had not been able to access the estate land in Thyolo and Mulanje to cultivate crops.

Social differentiation in newly occupied land

We were interested to examine how social differentiation in the form of gender, age, income status, education and social networks affected access to land and its related resources in the Thyolo case (Matipate). The agrarian structure of Thyolo area is composed of vast capitalist tea estate enterprises on one side and small-scale farmers on the other side. However, we should not assume that the small-scale farmers are a homogenous group. During the study, we found that there existed

Table 11.3 Selected 'peasant capitalist' cases from Chibwana and Chaona, Thyolo

Pseudonym	Age	Current production capacity	Cultivated hectares (2018)	Cultivated hectares (2020)	Other income activities (order of importance)
Tana	57	7t maize vegetables sugarcane	5[a]	4	Transport (motorcycle); livestock
Chakwana	65	5t maize vegetables	4	3	Transport; monthly pension benefits
Chitsulo	73	7.5t maize	5	4	Groceries; agro-dealing
Mweene	45	6t maize vegetables	5	4	Beer smuggling[e] from Mozambique
Khoviwa	63	8t maize vegetables	4	2[c]	Transport, retired public servant
Tikhala	66	4t maize vegetables	2.5	2.5	Transport[b]
Mmamera	65	5t maize vegetables	4	4	Transport
Mukhito	49	5.5t maize vegetables[f]	3	4[d]	Transport/ local politics

Source: Authors, 2018; 2020

Notes:

[a] These were estimates from the occupied land only. Some households had other parcels of land in the villages which were relatively smaller, ranging from 0.4 to 1 hectare, usually bought or inherited from their parents.

[b] Most of the transport businesses in the region use bicycles and motorcycles. Only one of the peasants had a truck, which was being hired out by others as a business.

[c] There were specific cases where, within the two year gap, the hectarage of some farmers decreased. This was chiefly due to scaling down production, or the estate farmers repossessed land.

[d] For those farmers who increased the amount of land, it was chiefly due to land transactions on the occupied land. As seen in the following analysis, land transactions were visible on the occupied land, though not sanctioned either by the communal chiefs or the state. The land does not legally belong to the peasants, hence making transfer of user rights from poor peasants to the peasant capitalist farmers a very unique transaction in this region. This portrays complicated, secretive, undocumented and personal arrangements among peasants.

[e] For some peasants, accumulation processes included illegal smuggling of goods from Mozambique to Malawi. Though they were uncomfortable about explaining the details, the said activities were lucrative in nature

[f] It was difficult to estimate the total annual produce per year of the farmers. This was because the occupants of land on riverbanks in the estate land grew vegetables all year round since they were able to irrigate their crops.

what Byres (2003, p. 20) would call 'peasant capitalism' in the occupied tea estates in Thyolo. Among the 110 households that were interviewed between January and September 2018, eight households from
the sample of households which occupied land showed characteristics
fitting the description of 'peasant capitalist' farmers. These eight households owned more land than the rest of the households and employed a
pool of labourers, though seasonal for majority of them. Table 11.3 is a
summary of the eight households (not using real names). In the period
January to April 2020, the researchers visited these households again to
collect more historical narratives from these prospective elite peasants.
Note that the amount of land they owned included fragmented parcels
spread across various parts of the idle land in the estates where land
occupation had occurred.

Inspired by Oya (2007), rural capitalism in Africa is can be
described using a number of themes. The first is the extent to which the
emergence of rural capitalists is part of a wide process of rural differentiation just like capitalism generally in Africa and elsewhere. Though
the peasants in Thyolo had the same chances of acquiring land, some
got much bigger parcels of land. This was done in two ways. The study
found that most of the rural capitalists in study villages in Thyolo had
financial capital to hire other labourers to clear more land during the
occupation period. As such, they have bigger parcels of land than the
rest. Additionally, with the existence of capital, they were able to hire
more labour to harvest more than the rest of the peasants, differenti-
ating themselves socially and economically. With improved transport
on the estates, the emerging capitalists were able to access markets in
the accumulation process. One would therefore argue that 'rural capitalism' was manifested in the occupied lands belonging to the white
colonial farmers.

Central to rural capitalism in the occupied land in Thyolo
is the complementarity of income generating activities among
the rural capitalist. The study discovered that all the eight 'successful' farmers in Thyolo had other income generating activities apart from crops and livestock production in the occupied
land. Though some ways of accumulating capital were illegal
but lucrative (such beer smuggling between Malawi and Mozambique), the peasants were able to explain the livelihood trajectories in
their accumulation processes. Oya (2007) terms the complementarity of
income generating activities in the accumulation process 'straddling'.

Apart from cultivating larger parcels of occupied land in the estates than the rest of the peasants, the rural capitalists had multiple sources of income, and some reported that the other activities generated more income than the farming in the occupied land. As in Thyolo, Khoviwa (not their real name) combined farming with pension funds and a transport business, both in the villages as well as outside the villages and the *Matipate* (occupied white owned estate land). Khoviwa's case is described in Box 11.1.

Box 11.1: Khoviwa's case

Khoviwa, born in 1957, is a successful farmer in Chibwana village, Thyolo district. He has been able to occupy six hectares of land from the white owned estate land. He used part of the capital accumulated from his government job to hire more labour to help him clear more land in the estates, about four hectares. The rest, one hectare, was given to him (leased) from another occupant who left the village. Khoviwa claims he pays rent to the said villager. Bearing in mind how critical land is in the region (average land ownership is 0.4h per household), Khoviwa boasts abundant land. He grows maize, groundnuts, sugarcane, vegetables and millet. He also has three cows. His access to capital came into being when he was a civil servant in Malawi government. He retired early to concentrate on his businesses. In his transport business, he has five motorcycles, which he hires out, making a considerable income of US$8,000 per year. He also sells surplus crops and gets income every month from his pension benefits. His previous diploma-level government job, businesses and pension benefits catapult him to become a rural capitalist and entrepreneur through multiple income generating activities.

Another theme that kept coming out from selected rural capitalist farmers was land acquisition. They owned more land than the rest, and hence the land acquisition mechanisms remained a crucial theme in this study. As explained earlier, these emerging capitalist farmers, with more connections to the market, obtained the land in two main ways: employing more labour during the occupations on the estates, and 'leasing' nearby parcels of land from other peasants who could opt for getting some cash in exchange for their parcels. One wonders therefore how one would lease land that they have just occupied on the estate land. In the legal sense, the land does not belong to the peasants. One of the households that had leased their parcel of land out to a rural capitalist farmer had this to say to explain the mystery:

During the occupations, we cleared about two hectares of land.
With shortages of farm inputs we could not afford to cultivate
in all of the parcels. As such, our neighbour, asked to 'buy'
the land from us. He paid us MWK500,000.[8] We took the offer.
We needed the money. We will clear another [piece of] land
for ourselves. The land is not ours anyway; it belongs to the
estates. (Interview with peasant farmer Chaona Village, 24
September 2018)

We can see 'land transactions' and 'land leasing' in areas that have
been occupied, not originally belonging to the peasants. To recap, this
is land that has been occupied which originally legally belonged to the
minority white farmers. The motivation for 'leasing' could be proximity to the village in which the 'rural capitalists' were residing. Crucial
to the emergence of rural entrepreneurship in the occupied land is the
intensive growing of vegetables, notably tomatoes. We can see that,
apart from occupying the white farmers' land, they also enjoy the road
infrastructure that was constructed for the purposes of plantation agriculture. In any agricultural enterprise, road networks play a pivotal role
in making agricultural marketing smooth. Vegetables, which fetch high
prices on the market, are highly perishable. Rapid access to markets
is possible when there is necessary infrastructure such as good transport networks. We argue therefore that the presence of a good transport
infrastructure in the villages surrounding the tea estates contributed
greatly to the emergence of 'peasant capitalism'.

It is important to note that many of the emerging rural capitalist
farmers had invested their proceeds in transport business (see Table
11.3). Many of the emerging successful farmers had bought motorcycles for transport businesses. One could argue that the proliferation of
the business in the area is because of the freedom of entry and exit
in the business. With proximity to Mozambique, where many of the
motorcycles were bought, it was easy for the farmers to invest in the
business.

If we go back to the Lenin-Chayanov debate, you would see that
it did not anticipate capitalism developing through political processes
such as land occupations, as this would hinder accumulation by the
dominant groups, in this case the large-scale tea enterprises in rural
Malawi. In a normal capitalist development process, there would be
processes of proletarianization, with peasants relying solely on selling

---

8 At the time of the study, MWK500,000 was equivalent to approximately US$715.

their labour in the large tea estates enterprises or any other capitalist enterprises. This is not the case in Thyolo where this study was done. Out of the 110 households that were interviewed in the study, only nine households representing 8.2 per cent, reported that their household members were employed in the estates as casual labourers. Moreover, these households doubled as both peasants and proletariats. With land occupations in the tea estates, peasants differentiated socially into rich peasants who relied on hired labour and producing solely for the markets, middle peasants who occupied land in th e estates but only for subsistence, and poor peasants who did not own land or occupy land from the estates. The emergence of new 'rural capitalists' negates a chunk of scholarly articles about rural Malawi that categorize the countryside as comprised of large-scale capitalist estate farmers on one side and the peasantry on the other. These studies obscure the fact that the rural peasants are a highly differentiated social group. We can see that rural Malawi is 'an army of peasants'[9] and that the peasant path that has been taken by the Thyolo peasants is leading to a 'new round of social differentiation' (Jordan 2017, p. 5). This new round is emerging from the peasantry, not the tea estates as traditionally or linearly argued. Hence, this finding subscribes to Lenin's notion and philosophy that those peasants in the occupied lands of Thyolo are 'aspirant capitalists' (see Hendricks 2014, p. 286).

The role of land occupations in land reform from below

We have seen in the previous sections that peasants in Thyolo, Malawi, have to make a tough choice: encroach on to tea estate land that has stayed idle for decades, or starve. Hundreds have chosen the former. With many state policies failing to decisively solve the land inequalities in the region, the peasants have sought solace in the land occupations for social reproduction purposes. The Community Based Rural Land Development Program (CBRLDP), which was a Malawian government land reform initiative to relocate 15,000 households from Mulanje and Thyolo to low-density districts, failed as a reform initiative. Despite the government's and the World Bank's position that the project was a success, scholars found that the people who were relocated from the densely populated districts of Thyolo and Mulanje to other districts to ease land tensions returned to their original districts. We therefore agree that the land occupations in Thyolo are one of the ways in which the

9 Rephrased from Karl Marx (1976); see also Jacobs (2017, p. 4)

peasants are quenching their quest to achieve land reforms from below. However, the scale at which this is done is low. Our study did not have the exact statistics of all the peasants encroaching on idle estate land, the amount of land being encroached, or the total number of peasants experiencing land poverty. However, our observations reveal that the majority of the peasants in Thyolo and Mulanje still remain excluded from the tea economy and the land resources.

Conclusions

From the study conducted in Thyolo villages, we learned that the households that occupied land on the tea estates owned by the white farmers were relatively better off than their counterparts who did not occupy any land from the estates. Examining the livelihood benefits which accrued from the land occupation processes has illustrated this. We can see the emergence of 'rural capitalism' in the occupied lands, which paints a picture that, with access to land in the area, peasants can use available resources for accumulation purposes. Though we agree that land occupations in Thyolo have the potential to achieve 'land reforms from below', the extent to which this is done is limited. The majority in the area remain land-poor. We argue that the peasants might not fully achieve land reform on their own without support from the state o r local land movements. There is still a need for state interventions in the plight of peasants in the region. We suggest that the state resettle the peasants to other districts that have land. This option means going back to the CBRLDP to address its challenges. The second option is redistribution of the idle estate land to the peasants. Another option is for the state to make deliberate efforts and create mechanisms to absorb the 'sea of peasants' in rural Malawi by engaging them in meaningful wage labour. A further option could be the state discussing with the white farmers and acting as a guarantor, so that the peasants can lease idle land from the white farmers. Finally, the stakeholders involved in land issues, such as the white farmers, the state and the peasants, can reach a compromise, where efficient technologies can be applied so that the estates can use less land, and the rest, in addition to the idle land, is redistributed to the land-starved peasants.

References

Bebbington, A. (1999) 'Capitals and capabilities: A framework for analyzing peasant viability, rural livelihoods and poverty', *World Development* 27 (12),

Bernstein, H (2009) 'V.I. Lenin and A.V. Chayanov: Looking back, looking forward', *Journal of Peasant Studies* 36 (1): pp. 55-81

Byres, T. J. (1986) 'The agrarian question and differentiation of the peasantry', in Rahman, A. (ed) *Peasants and classes: a study in differentiation in Bangladesh*, London, Zed Books

Byres, T.J. (2003) 'Paths of Capitalist Agrarian Transition in the Past and in the Contemporary World', in Ramachandran, V.K. and Swaminathan, M. (eds) *Agrarian Studies: Essays on Agrarian Relations in Less Developed Countries*, New Delhi, Tulika Books

Chinigo, D (2017) 'Contested extractivism' in Engels B and Dietz K (eds) *Contested Extractivism, Society and the State*, London, Palgrave Macmillan.

Chinigo, D. (2016a) 'Re-peasantization and land reclamation movements in Malawi' *African Affairs, 115*(458)

Chinigo, D. (2016b) 'Rural Radicalism and the Historical Land Conflict in the Malawian Tea Economy', *Journal of Southern African Studies, 42*(2)

Chirwa EW (2008) *Land Tenure, Farm Investments and Food Production in Malawi*, Discussion Paper No. 18, IPPG Programme Office, IDPM, School of Environment & Development, University of Manchester

Chinsinga, B. (2011) 'The politics of land reforms in Malawi: the case of the Community Based Rural Land Development Programme (CBRLDP)', *Journal of International Development*, 23, 380–393.

Hendricks, F. (2014) 'Class and nation in the agrarian questions of the South: notes in response to Moyo, Jha and Yearos'. *Agrarian South: Journal of Political Economy* 3 (2)

Hyden, G. (1980) *Beyond Ujamaa in Tanzania: underdevelopment and an uncaptured peasantry*, London, Heinemann

Jacobs, R. (2017) 'An urban proletariat with peasant characteristics: land occupations and livestock raising in South Africa,' *Journal of Peasant Studies*, vol. 45, no. 5–6, pp. 884–903 https://doi.org/10.1080/03066150.2017.1312354

Juma, C. (2011) *The New Harvest: Agricultural Innovation in Africa*, Oxford University, New York.

Isaacman, A. (1990) 'Peasants and rural social protest in Africa', *African Studies Review* 33 (2)

Kanyongolo, F. E. (2005) 'Land occupations in Malawi: challenging the neoliberal legal order', in Moyo, S. and Yeros, P. (eds) *Reclaiming the Land: The Resurgence of Rural Movements in Africa, Asia and Latin America*, London, Zed Publishers

Lenin, V.I. (1967) 'The development of capitalism in Russia. The process of the formation of a home market for large-scale industry', *Collected Works*, vol. 3, Moscow, Progress Publishers

Li, X., Qi, G., Tang, L., Zhao, L., Jin, L., Guo, Z., and Wu, J. (2012) *Agricultural Development in China and Africa: A Comparative Analysis*, Oxfordshire, Routledge. Taylor and Francis

Machira, S. (2009) 'Pilot-testing a land redistribution program in Malawi', *Agricultural*, 367.

Mangulama, J (2015). 'The Role of Bicycle Taxi Businesses in Rural Livelihoods: The Case of Lolo and Kanthawire Villages in Thyolo, Malawi.' Masters Thesis. China Agricultural University.

Marx, K. (1976) *Capital: A Critique of Political Economy Volume 1*, London, Penguin Books.

Moyo, S. (2007) 'Land in the Political Economy of African Development: Alternative Strategies for Reform', *Journal of Africa Development*, Vol. XXXII, No. 4, 2007

Mueller, B. T. (2011) 'The agrarian question in Tanzania: using new evidence to reconcile an old debate', *Review of African Political Economy*, 38 (127)

Mwiinga, B (2014) 'The Role of Agricultural Extension Services in Improving Agricultural Production of Small-Scale Farmers in Zambia. A case of Kanakantapa, Village', Masters Thesis, China Agricultural University

National Statistical Office (2018) *Malawi Population and Housing Census*. Zomba, Malawi

Oya C (2007) 'Stories of Rural Accumulation in Africa: Trajectories and Transitions among Rural Capitalists in Senegal', *Journal of Agrarian Change*, Vol. 7 No. 4

Peters, P. E. (2002) 'Bewitching land: The role of land disputes in converting kin to strangers and in class formation in Malawi', *Journal of Southern African Studies* 28 (1)

Waters, T. (2007) *The persistence of subsistence agriculture: life beneath the level of the marketplace*, Plymouth, Lexington

Afterword

Masego Madzwamuse

An ode to the book and the contributors

This is not the first time that the account of land displacement in Southern Africa has been documented. What is different in this volume is the voices that come through. The African scholar activist's stance that this book takes is an important one for Africans shaping their own narrative, providing a historical account and the context for contemporary conditions under which rural communities are dispossessed of their rights. It is an important contribution to challenging orthodoxies on the continent's land question and shining the spotlight on peasants as active agents and not bystanders in land struggles.

The book is a powerful account of both historical and contemporary conditions under which communities are dispossessed of their lands. It provides a comprehensive account of rural struggles and the nexus between the state and civil society as well as, in some cases, the ever-present role of corporate and private capital. By opening up the debate on neoliberalism in this space, this book debunks several myths about land reform in Africa and, most importantly, exposes the complexities that continue to be brought about by the duality of our legal systems. A dominant narrative that often emerges is one that immediately reduces rural struggles to tenure security purely on legalistic terms, ignoring common property rights that govern access to land and resources in southern Africa's rural landscapes.

The wide notion of formalization of customary land tenure systems which seems to underpin land policy reform on the continent is informed by a particular worldview that draws inspiration from private property tenure systems associated with the western notion of property rights. Liz Alden Wily (2011) makes a very important point about common property rights representing more than 70 per cent of the continent. And she concludes that it is only logical that reform discourse appreciates this tenure-holding as it provides an opportunity for the majority to claim their rights. An inclusive discourse on land should not be about titling, but should rather open up the debate to look at what holds back agricultural production on the continent, particularly the lack of infrastructure, and other conditions that are essential for small and medium-scale agriculture to flourish.

Odote (2021) posits that there needs to be a reconceptualization of how to strengthen community land rights and secure tenure beyond the doctrine of obtaining titling. This requires recognition of the unique nature of communal land rights with its nested and layered approach to rights and looking into how to best capture this in policy and legislative proposals. Thus there needs to be a rethinking. And this rethinking should not only lie with academia, it also has to be a rethinking of mobilizing socialists' struggles around land in southern Africa (Odote, 2021).

By highlighting the hypocrisy of state agents in southern Africa and their departure from the liberation struggle's promises, this book brings to the fore the aborted agenda of land redistribution in southern Africa's post-colonial policies.

Timothy Wise (2019) also made this important point in his recent book; *Eating Tomorrow: Agribusiness, Family Farmers, and the Battle for the Future of Food*. This book also reiterates the research by Moyo and Amanor (2008), where he poses the question that if states in southern Africa understand that agricultural production can be turned around by accelerating investment in infrastructure and tenure security, why are they not making these investments available for peasant farmers who are already involved in the bulk of agricultural production?

As such, the rural struggles as demonstrated in Mazwi and Mberi's chapter in this book are not just confined to land. These struggles are also very much about access to infrastructure and the right to participate in the market economy. The mobilization process needs to be intersectional in its approach and unpack the nuances within the land struggles – it is very much about the purposes for which rural communities fight for their land, the kind of land and what else is required to make it productive. It is not just about the ability to feed families but also to enable smallholder farmers to benefit from a market-based economy. We cannot get away from these questions for those who choose to engage with the market-based economy. These are fair questions to ask and worth surfacing.

Glimmers of hope

This publication comes at a time when the world is reeling from the worst pandemic in recent history and dealing with an ever-worsening climate crisis. SADC and various United Nations (UN) agencies estimate in the first half of 2020 was that about 45 million people of the region's 345 million population were at risk of hunger due to the impacts of climate and the Covid-19 pandemic (Kachingwe 2020). While these major problems unfold, some developments have taken place on the land question in our region. Under pressure from traditional donors and International financial institutions, Zimbabwe has quietly offered compensation to former large-scale farmers, mostly white, for the land they lost during the Fast Track Land Reform Program, seemingly rolling back a bold, albeit controversial, land reform policy (Murisa 2019). In neighbouring Botswana, women are celebrating a victory in the changes presented by the amendment of the Botswana Land Policy to allow married women to own land.

The new law is an amendment of the Botswana Land Policy of 2015 and other land policies that predate it, namely the Tribal Land Act of 1968, the Tribal Grazing Land Policy of 1970 and the 1993 Amendment of the TLA. This development is a momentous occasion that comes 54 years after independence and exposes the sharp contradictions that many states display between their public posture on women's rights and the track record displayed by the policy trajectory. Botswana is often touted as a shining example of a developmental state with a good track record in governance, and yet patriarchy continued to hold back the other half of its population (Kalabamu 2006).

In the above development, much coverage has focused on President Masisi's role in changing the policy. A less-told story is how this change in policy is a victory of long struggles by women's rights activists in Botswana and the many years of investment by Women and Law in Southern Africa, Emang Basadi in its glory days and by individual women's rights activists. The erasure and invisibilisation of women's rights movements in the long-standing struggle for land are reflected in this book as well. This is by virtue of a gender-blind analysis that is carried through this volume, where but one chapter touches on the question of women's land rights. By not paying attention to the struggles of women within the land rights movements we are missing out on the nuance of nested struggles[1].

Although most African and Asian farmers are women, only 15 per cent of global farmland is owned by women. According to Zenda (2021), land in the global South is considered the most fundamen-

---

1 **Editor's note**: Masego Madzwamuse presents a very pertinent criticism. We believe that the documentary film combined with this volume indeed does justice to the struggles of women in Mozambique, Zambia and Eswatini. Nevertheless, and being this a long running research academic project, women agrarian movements, gender analysis and aspects around social reproduction should and will deserve more dedication.

tal resource for women's living conditions, economic empowerment, and, to some extent, their struggle for equity and equality. Although a majority of women in southern Africa depend on land for their livelihoods, their land rights are still largely withheld. A question arises for me on the theoretical intersections of the struggles for land that are driven by social movements and the place of feminist thought.

Sarah Largardien Abdullah's chapter, which reviews the film *Land Struggles and Repression in Zambia, Mozambique and Eswatini*, is refreshing, as it begins to touch on the place of women in the struggle for land in southern Africa. This is an important contribution given the significant role women have played in peasant movements, challenging patriarchy and orthodoxies, and emphasising women's role in agricultural production. One wishes this gender lens could have been carried through the various chapters.

That a documentary accompanies the book, *We Rise for our Land; Land struggles and repression in Zambia, Eswahini and Mozambique,* is a powerful way in which different forms of knowledge are combined. This book does an excellent job of highlighting the insights of scholar-practitioners, but the documentary itself allows the rural folks to speak of their struggles in unintercepted ways. The peasants whose struggles are documented in this book have their own stories. A complimentary discourse of this nature and a complimentary packaging is forward-looking as it captures different forms of knowing.

However, Abdullah in her chapter posits that the dearth of civic and popular education in Zambia, Eswatini, and Mozambique, including about the law of the land, has resulted in people losing their land. This is a curious conclusion, given the number of long-standing civil society organizations that work on raising awareness on land rights and legal empowerment for rural communities, particularly in Zambia and Mozambique. Organizations such as the Zambia Land Alliance, Zambia Legal Aid Clinic for Women, and the Mozambique Bar Association have over the years done significant work on civic education for land rights. The conclusion Abdullah reaches points to the lack of connectedness of NGO efforts and the work that is done by social movements. It raises questions about the extent to which different practitioners, academics, scholars, and civil society agents themselves are connected.

As such, the alliances that we need to see emerging are not necessarily just alliances of social movements and social movements connecting their struggles. They also need to be alliances that are driven by civil society organizations connecting better. And perhaps further research in this area could look at how this can be done more effectively. Under what conditions does collaboration work and solidarity around different actors emerge? How might political settlements happen between the state and the peasantry (rural land movements)? According to Levy (2021), development and social thriving depend on a society's ability to address collective action problems and its ability to cooperate. Further citing the work of William Fergusson, Levy (2021) notes that 'dramatic change often requires coordinated and often near-simultaneous action, re-evaluative learning, and reconfiguration across large groups…yet once change gathers momentum it crosses a critical mass threshold, shifts can facilitate dramatic change'.

And then, unfortunately, the Africa land Policy Initiative has taken the route of improving land administration, not systematically undoing the injustices of the past and looking at how historical redress can be approached. One is constantly taken back to the contradictions of the role that the state plays, particularly states that are run by former liberation movements, and this complicates the question of how social justice can gain traction in these contexts – the challenge being how to get former liberation movements to go back to the noble effort of pushing for the economic freedom of their people, especially where land is concerned. This battle of ideology is a fascinating and complex one that makes the work of social movements complex in our times.

In cases where dual legal systems exist, communities are left at the mercy of the courts, as we see with the cases in Zambia. The problem, however, is that what is taking place in Zambia is not confined there. We see it repeated in many parts of the continent, and Africa and its land tenure have never fully resolved the question of how to deal with common property laws and with customer lending systems similar to what we see in the economy. There is duality, where African tenure is highly informalized and left without the protection of the modern law system or the state's recognition. The increased interest in rural lands for agricultural investment is leaving communities highly exposed to losing their resources before the courts, as the case in Zambia demonstrates.

It is the interest of capital that often triumphs backed by modern law; citizens are essentially left to the relatively archaic governance systems. In most cases, capital's interests are prioritized while communities are confined to unproductive land that is far from water sources and therefore unsuitable for agricultural production. Local communities face pressure from the extractive sector, including agribusiness. The DRC chapter is very refreshing in its analysis of the reality that the legal system is not always just and has, in most cases, simply worked to protect the interests of the elite.

The land question really is a site of struggles for justice on the legal empowerment front. It is a push back against the continued informalization and sometimes criminalization of African lives which continues unabated. And as such, it points to the limitations of legal empowerment approaches that tinker on the periphery of land reform. A lot of work still needs to be done towards true empowerment. What does justice look like in this context? How do we account for overlapping rights as well as respect the property rights of women? This question becomes more urgent in the context of climate change, where southern Africa is one of the regions that is most vulnerable. This reality is only going to get worse in the future and therefore the question requires a level of urgency.

The fundamental struggle is very much about access to productive land that can support peasants' livelihoods and build resilience to climate change. And it is building up because of the pressure that climate change is going to put on the land question. But it's also the pressure of the economic collapse that is emerging, and the question of economic recovery. This will call for some of the previously unresolved questions to form the centre stage of policy advocacy. But it also points to the importance of connecting movements and connecting struggles. Linking the land struggles to the climate justice agenda is a powerful way to confront the colonial legacy of peasants' displacement in southern Africa and the struggle drivers of their vulnerability to climate change.

References:

Kachingwe, N. (2020) 'Policy Brief: *Chakula ni uhai* / Food is Life: Accelerating the goal of food security for all in SADC by 2025, Post Covid-19', Johannesburg, Southern Africa Trust

Kalabamu, F. (2006) 'Patriarchy and Women's Land Rights in Botswana', *Land Use Policy* 23, pp. 237-246

Levy, B. (2021) 'Collective Action, Meet political Settlements', *Working with the Grain,* https://workingwiththegrain.com/2021/01/27/collective-action-meet-political-settlements/. Accessed 17 April 2021.

Moyo, S. and Amanor, K.S. (eds.) (2008) *Land and Sustainable Development in Africa,* London, Zed Books

Murisa, T. (2019) *To Compensate or Not To? Revisiting the debate on compensation for former large-scale farmers in Zimbabwe,* Harare, SIVIO Institute, https://www.sivioinstitute.org/wp-content/uploads/2019/05/To-Compensate-or-Not-To.pdf. Accessed 17 April 2021

Odote, C. 2021. 'The Place of Communal Land Rights in Africa's Land Reform Discourse', *Afronomics Law,* https://www.afronomicslaw.org/category/analysis/place-communal-land-rights-africas-land-reform-discourse. Accessed 17 April 2021

Wily, L.A. (2011) '"The law is to blame": the vulnerable status of common property rights in sub-Saharan Africa', *Development and Change,* 42(3), pp. 679-871

Wise, T.A. (2019) *Eating Tomorrow: Agribusiness, Family Farmers, and the Battle for the Future of Food,* New York City, New Press

Zenda, C. (2021) 'Botswana Abolishes Law Excluding Married Women From Land Ownership', *Fair Planet,* 5 January, https://www.fairplanet.org/story/botswana-abolishes-law-excluding-married-women-from-land-ownership/. Accessed 17 April 2021

INDEX

www.ingramcontent.com/pod-product-compliance
Lightning Source LLC
Chambersburg PA
CBHW052126270326
41930CB00012B/2771